THE INTELLECTUAL DESIGN OF JOHN DRYDEN'S HEROIC PLAYS

THE INTELLECTUAL DESIGN OF

JOHN DRYDEN'S HEROIC PLAYS

by Anne T. Barbeau

New Haven and London, Yale University Press

Published with assistance from the foundation
established in memory of Philip Hamilton McMillan
of the Class of 1894, Yale College.

Library of Congress catalog card number: 71–81412

Designed by John O. C. McCrillis,
set in Baskerville type,
and printed in the United States of America by
The Carl Purington Rollins Printing-Office of
the Yale University Press, New Haven, Connecticut.
Distributed in Great Britain, Europe, Asia, and
Africa by Yale University Press Ltd., London; in
Canada by McGill-Queen's University Press, Montreal; and
in Latin America by Centro Interamericano de Libros
Académicos, Mexico City.

To my parents

Acknowledgments

The original idea for this study arose during the course of my studies under David M. Vieth, who has graciously continued to give me advice and encouragement during the past years. The idea was developed into my dissertation, "John Dryden's Scheme of Values," with the guidance and helpful criticism of David L. Stevenson, at the City University of New York. I am indebted to Helaine Newstead, Margaret L. Wiley, and Samuel I. Mintz for reading the early version and contributing generously to its further development. I am particularly grateful for the extensive and penetrating commentary provided me by Eugene M. Waith; his direction enabled me to give the book its final form. I also acknowledge my appreciation to Wayland W. Schmitt of Yale University Press for his kind help during these many months. I give thanks to Gale Griffin for her editorial advice and assistance. Finally, I want to express my deepest gratitude to my friend Camille E. LeBlanc for her invaluable encouragement from the onset of this work.

Contents

Introduction

A more elusive and complex figure than Dryden in English literature is difficult to find. He so completely avoids extreme opinions for the sake of a middle-of-the-road attitude concerning political and ethical obligations that one might be at a loss to identify his views. The rarity, too, with which he drops his public mask is disconcerting to the twentieth-century reader, who expects the writer to reveal his soul as in the intimacy of friendship. Again, Dryden's idea of history or the historical process as a major source for verifying moral philosophy, his suggestion that what can withstand the test of historical circumstance is valid, might present some difficulty to today's reader, for whom such a clear, objective norm, however appealing to the intellect, has often less value than private conscience.

If Dryden is elusive in such a late work as *The Hind and the Panther,* in which he devotes a few lines to his private conversion and hundreds to the historical reasons for the validity of the teachings of the Roman Catholic Church, he is even more so in his early dramatic and nondramatic poetry. Perhaps for this reason these works have been neglected or treated superficially. T. S. Eliot, in his *Homage to John Dryden,* suggests that Dryden's plays have not been read carefully: "His gravest defects are supposed to be displayed in his dramas, but if these were more read they might be more praised." Dryden, he continues, was not trying to compete with Elizabethan or French drama, but "was pursuing a direction of his own." In the following analysis of the heroic plays, I hope to show what this "direction" is, and also to demonstrate that it is one similar to that followed in his early narrative poems *Astraea Redux* and *Annus Mirabilis.*

The heroic plays are essentially plays of ideas, and the early narrative poems, statements about the nature of the historical process. Characters in these works are without nuances or ambiguity but are simply the best or most efficient means of expressing certain concepts. Sensuous experience, on these terms, would hardly be relevant to the works. Eliot, in the *Homage*, writes of Dryden's words that they "state immensely, but their suggestiveness is almost nothing." This lack of suggestiveness is evident in the realm of private, sensuous experience, but Eliot's analysis does not hold true in the intellectual sphere. Dryden's design and language are replete with explicit and implicit allusions to biblical, historical, and mythological events, so that his works are exciting and intellectually suggestive beyond most of their counterparts in English literature.

In the following study, an analysis of Dryden's plays as plays of ideas is followed by a chapter on his political theory. A reading of the five heroic plays succeeds this chapter, and the emphasis is placed on Dryden's ethics, of which his politics are a part. The fourth chapter, an evaluation of Dryden's ideas on dramatic theory, should reveal whether he is indeed, to use Eliot's phrase, "pursuing a direction of his own." Finally, in the fifth chapter, the early narrative poems are compared to the heroic plays in order to underline their common scheme of values.

1

Dryden's Plays of Ideas

Samuel Johnson's accurate judgment of Dryden is that the latter's "favourite exercise" consists in ratiocination and that, as a result, he is deficient in portraying natural passion and sensibility.[1] This estimate would have had a pejorative connotation for a reader of the late eighteenth century, when sentimental drama had sufficiently displaced, in the public esteem, that theater of ideas which had reached its apogee in the dramatic works of Dryden, Etherege, and Congreve. Nowadays, however, it would simply put Dryden in league with George Bernard Shaw, whose lack of natural passion does not prevent him from winning favor in the twentieth-century theater. Sir Walter Scott shares Johnson's view of Dryden as one who cares little for private passions such as love, declaring that he has little understanding of a "mere moral and sentimental passion" and so rightly confines "his observation to the more energetic feelings of pride, anger, ambition, and other high-toned passions."[2] Modern critics, on the other hand, have overemphasized the importance of love in Dryden's plays, have, in fact, reduced the heroic plays to a mere conflict of love and honor without realizing that Dryden's interest lay in the "more energetic feelings." Although lovers and intrigues of love can be perceived at the plot level, Dryden's heroic plays

1. "John Dryden," in *Lives of the English Poets, 1* (London, 1946), 256.
2. *The Life of John Dryden*, ed. Bernard Kreissman (Lincoln, Neb., 1963), p. 408. Sir Walter Scott may have been influenced by Samuel Johnson, who says of Dryden: "Dryden's was not one of the *gentle bosoms:* Love as it subsists in itself, with no tendency but to the person loved, and wishing only for correspondent kindness, such love as shuts out all other interest, the Love of the Golden Age, was too soft and subtle to put his faculties in motion" (p. 255).

are essentially concerned with man's proper role in the state. Read correctly, they reveal the same kind of interest in political and social questions one finds in *Astraea Redux, Annus Mirabilis,* and *Absalom and Achitophel.* The passions of anger, pride, and ambition, those "energetic feelings" mentioned by Scott, are chiefly important to Dryden in their public consequences, that is, insofar as they are related to the life of the state.

Classified as plays of ideas, Dryden's heroic plays might find a more significant place in the history of English drama than has hitherto been accorded them. Most of the critics who have been overly severe in their evaluations have used Shakespeare's dramatic technique as the norm. But Dryden "is not Shakespeare *manqué,*" as Robert Etheridge Moore remarks; he has created "something uniquely his own."[3] Margaret Sherwood notes that these plays "are so different in *motif,* language, and construction from ordinary drama that a standard of judgment is hard to form for them."[4] Dryden's characters are ideas of human nature; each one is a rational construct, a walking set of attitudes. Clearly, Dryden does not attempt to create the kind of multifaceted and subtly shaded individual Shakespeare creates; he is primarily concerned with the public manifestation and consequences of certain strong passions. Thus, when so eminent a critic as Allardyce Nicoll assails heroic drama for a "falsification of all psychology"[5] and Bonamy Dobrée speaks of its "exaggerated fancy in the realm of certain emotions,"[6] they are failing to come to grips with what is at the core of Dryden's heroic drama.

3. *Henry Purcell and the Restoration Theatre* (Cambridge, Mass., 1961), p. 10.

4. *Dryden's Dramatic Theory and Practice* (New York, 1966; first published, 1898), p. 59.

5. *A History of English Drama 1660–1900* (Cambridge, 1961), *1,* 129.

6. Introduction, *Five Heroic Plays* (London, 1960), p. vii. Dobrée also remarks on the unreality of emotions in heroic plays in *Restoration Tragedy 1660–1720* (Oxford, 1929), pp. 13, 91.

Beneath the surface of a conventional plot, a love story which purposely does not involve his audience emotionally, Dryden sets to work to dramatize sets of highly complex opinions concerning the obligations of man within his society. All of the characters are designed to exemplify various attitudes concerning the obligations of a son to his parents, of a subject to his sovereign, and of a man to his own conscience. What George Bernard Shaw writes about the characters in his own plays of ideas also applies to those in Dryden's: "stage characters must be endowed by the author with a conscious self-knowledge and power of expression, and, as you observe . . . a freedom from inhibitions, which in real life would make them monsters of genius."[7] Whether he be a villain, a fool, or a hero, each character in Dryden's plays is endowed with logic, acumen, and the apt words with which to express his particular attitude toward man and the state.

Coupled with their power of self-expression, Dryden's characters also generally represent only fragments of a whole man, one fragment often being paired with its opposite. William Arrowsmith, in his analysis of "A Greek Theater of Ideas," finds that such fragmentation and pairing of major figures are signs of plays of ideas. Arrowsmith remarks about the characters in Euripides' drama that they "function like obsessional fragments of a whole human soul: Hippolytus as chastity, Phaedra as sexuality. The wholeness of the old hero is now represented divisively, diffused over several characters."[8] Similarly, in Dryden's heroic drama, the whole man has been fragmented into parts which embody conflicting principles. In *The Conquest,* for example, Ozmyn exemplifies "exact virtue," for he has an overriding concern for external law, custom,

7. "Mr. Shaw on Mr. Shaw," *New York Times* (June 12, 1927), reprinted in *Shaw on Theatre,* ed. E. J. West (New York, 1958), p. 185.

8. William Arrowsmith, "A Greek Theater of Ideas," in *Ideas in the Drama; Selected Papers from the English Institute* (New York, 1964), p. 15. Arrowsmith points out that in a theater of ideas "the emphasis will be upon ideas rather than character," so that a certain flatness in characterization is to be expected.

and tradition, while Almanzor, who scorns convention and follows his natural instinct to good, exemplifies impulsive virtue. A similar antithesis occurs in the characters of Boabdelin and Lyndaraxa, the former masking his tyranny with the name of civil law, the latter rationalizing her rebellion and treachery by calling such predatory behavior the law of nature.

The political ideas expounded in Dryden's heroic drama are not merely plaster decoration but an integral part of the design. They are "elements in a complex chemical combination and transformation," to use John Gassner's phrase about plays of ideas.[9] Each character, representing but a fraction of the whole man, sees a different aspect of man's obligations within the state. Some of the characters in each play believe they must pursue the dictates of conscience—that part of the natural law which, Dryden suggests, is inscribed in the minds of men—rather than externally imposed laws. A tension is created between these characters and those who would uphold external laws at the expense of conscience. As Dryden sees it, there are two general kinds of external law—parental and civil. Parental law is often referred to as part of the natural law and is therefore distinct from civil law. These two forms of external law frequently come together in the heroic plays because the same character is monarch and parent. Thus the heroic plays are designed to give the reader or spectator an insight into a wide range of the conflicting obligations within society that man as a moral-political creature must resolve.

Dryden's heroic plays are in fact part of the great surge of interest in political philosophy which prevailed in England from the reign of Charles I through that of Queen Anne. In spite of a superficial resemblance to Caroline Platonic drama or to Jacobean romantic drama, in spite of plot lines borrowed from French romances, these plays have a unique political and ethical orientation. Although critics have often regarded them as tales of "a Land of No-where" suited for a "debilitated"

9. Ibid., Foreword, p. viii.

age,[10] a correct reading will place the plays for a twentieth-century reader as a dramatic rendering of, and within, the English Restoration *Weltanschauung*.

Dryden creates an action of epic scope in which to present many conflicting views of man within the state. He treats the rise and fall of kingdoms and the expansion of Christianity by conquest or by martyrdom. History, he suggests, has a predetermined direction: kingdoms have a youth, maturity, and decay, and heathen religions must, in the course of nature, be supplanted by that religion which the heavens favor. Those characters who are intemperate tend to arrogate a larger share of freedom than fate intended; they seek their private ends of ambition and revenge, oblivious of the large, predetermined context in which they move. In spite of their plots and machinations, these overreachers are swept off the scene by the end of each heroic play, while the normative characters, who have been painfully aware of the limitations on their freedom of action, are amply rewarded for their restraint and patience. Dryden thus constructs an action which is instructive in the traditional, Horatian sense. All the characters who have spurned external and internal laws meet disaster, so that what appears to be the working of fate during the course of the plays is finally revealed to be that of divine justice. No one speech, therefore, or single character's remarks can be said to represent Dryden's point of view. The entire action must be considered if one is to arrive at his underlying principles.

In general, the most useful analyses of Dryden's heroic plays have been those in literary history, concerned with his sources.[11] Critics have largely neglected the works as exciting

10. Allardyce Nicoll, *A History of English Drama, 1,* 88.

11. Scott is the chief critic who has argued for a French source; he has a modern representative of his viewpoint in L. N. Chase. Those who argue for an English source include C. G. Child, J. W. Tupper, F. E. Schelling, Kathleen Lynch, and Alfred Harbage. Others mention a variety of sources; these critics include Saintsbury, Allardyce Nicoll, W. S. Clark, and Arthur C. Kirsch. Reuben A. Brower and A. E. Parsons argue convincingly for some classical sources. It

in themselves. Recent views of the plays have all too expectedly
stressed the element of love, which is surely only at the surface
of the heroic plays and, like the heroic couplet itself, merely
the framework within which Dryden creates his "patterns" of
political humanity. Among those critics who have given dis-
proportionate emphasis to the motif of love, Thomas H. Fujimura argues (oddly, I think) that love in Dryden's heroic plays
is a "force divorced from morality" and that honor, too, is
simply a passion.[12] Fujimura concludes that the heroic play is
"essentially, a naturalistic, and, in part, a romantic revolt
against Christian humanism; and thus it is in harmony with
Restoration comedy, which is a naturalistic and realistic flaunt-
ing of the same Christian humanism."[13] Against Fujimura's
notion that Dryden's characters are governed merely by passion, Jean Gagen writes that there is a "real, though romantic-
ally exaggerated, ethical content" in the love and honor of the
normative characters.[14] Scott C. Osborn distinguishes the "re-
fined love" from the "terrestial passion."[15] From an ethical
standpoint, probably the most useful analyses of the heroic
plays have been written by John A. Winterbottom and Eugene
M. Waith.[16] Both scholars, however, are too preoccupied with
the development of the hero to provide a complete study of
the basic ethical and political problems.

The unique quality of Dryden as dramatist, I contend, seems
to be his ratiocinative, dispassionate manner of depicting various political relationships within society. Perhaps he is not en-

---

is probable that Dryden borrowed from French and English and ancient and
modern sources to create his heroic plays. It is what he has accomplished with
the help of these borrowings that deserves greater study.

12. "The Appeal of Dryden's Heroic Plays," *PMLA, 75* (1960), 40.

13. Ibid., p. 45.

14. "Love and Honor in Dryden's Heroic Plays," *PMLA, 77* (1962), 209.

15. "Heroical Love in Dryden's Heroic Drama," *PMLA, 77* (1958), 481.

16. John Winterbottom, "The Development of the Hero in Dryden's
Tragedies," *JEGP, 52* (1953), 161–73; Eugene M. Waith, *The Herculean Hero
in Marlowe, Chapman, Shakespeare and Dryden* (New York, 1962).

tirely alone as a dramatist of ideas in England, for J. B. Priestley, in *The Art of the Dramatist,* writes of George Bernard Shaw: "Out of his own passion for ideas, his intellectual delight in discussion, the masterly debating style he forged for himself, a brisk good-humour that came naturally to him (partly because he was less emotionally committed than most writers) . . . he created a new type of drama."[17] Dryden, like Shaw, attempts to transport his reader or viewer to an intellectual Olympus from which the general tendencies and follies of mankind can be viewed.

Society, in Dryden's view, contains many misguided individuals but few evil men. One finds no villains like Iago or Goneril in these plays; the tyrants, traitors, and rebels are all acting from a conviction of the rightness of their action; they may have begun with an erroneous premise (for instance, that chance rules all events or that power is divine), but then deduced their thoughts and actions accurately from that premise. By means of such characters, Dryden invites his audience to a tolerant appraisal of their fellowman; he suggests that incorrect thinking, not wicked hearts, brings about rebellions or tyrannies. Underlying Dryden's dramatic technique is the optimistic idea that if men can be made to reason correctly their wills or desires will follow suit.

In order to depict what he must have considered certain universal tendencies in human nature, Dryden creates a wide range of characters in each play who can be understood only through their interrelationships with each other. To isolate the hero Almanzor from other characters in *The Conquest,* as many critics have done, is to misunderstand Dryden's dramatic technique. Taken as a group, these characters supplement one another; their points of view are the various pieces of a jigsaw puzzle, the fragments of a whole man. Each of the characters has the façade of a hero and champions his own set of values with brilliant rhetoric. Dryden thus maintains a re-

17. J. B. Priestley, *The Art of the Dramatist* (London, 1957), p. 49.

markable objectivity in the expository part of his plays, and what has been said of Congreve's plays could be said of these —that it is difficult at the surface to separate the True-Wits from Witwouds. Not only does an elegant mode of speech blur the essential differences between true heroes and would-be heroes—the virtuous characters and the lawbreakers—but their sincerity of purpose, their sense of philosophical conviction, seems to keep them undifferentiated in the scenes of argumentation.

Dryden's would-be heroes, however, are distinguished from his true heroes by the design of the plays. The former exist to be crushed by the tide of events; their views are not valid enough to withstand the test of circumstance. Like Witwouds, they are betrayed by their own impotence; they cannot adapt themselves to the larger pattern of historical change. Dryden regards history in a curiously religious manner. In *Annus Mirabilis* and *Astraea Redux,* as well as in the heroic plays, he suggests that history, since the start of the Christian era, has been moving forward in an ever-increasing implementation of the Redemption in the secular sphere. The return of Astraea to the world is imminent, he implies, and men can therefore look ahead to the establishment of a utopian society in which commerce, science, and the arts will flourish.

The measuring rod for any point of view, then, is not whether it can be sustained by argument, but whether it is viable when it is up against the onward course of history. The Witwouds argue successfully at times, but they do not act with equal success. When the rewards and punishments have been distributed at the end of a heroic play, there is no Lear-like vision of an unjust, iron fate. This is one respect in which Dryden's serious drama differs from that of Shakespeare. Far from being in conflict with divine justice, history, for Dryden, is the temporal expression of that justice. Hence, patient virtue is eventually rewarded, but impatient virtue forfeits its recompense. Characters like Abdelmelech, Valeria, and Melesinda are in haste to commit suicide because they believe the course of events is irrevocably opposed to their idea of justice.

Dryden's method of playwriting was admirably suited to the mood of the post-war period of the Restoration. Weary of vituperative, partisan pamphlets, Dryden's audience welcomed his lucid, low-keyed, dispassionate disquisitions on man as a moral and political creature. Bonamy Dobrée writes that Restoration tragedy is "primarily a courtly art . . . to act before fashionable audiences, and not meant for the groundlings of the Phoenix or the Globe."[18] Dryden's plays of ideas would probably have found a more sympathetic response from such a courtly audience than from Elizabethan groundlings, for these would hardly have been content to remain the detached spectators that his plays require. In addition to being addressed to an audience capable of a certain ironic detachment, Dryden's heroic plays are also directed to the intelligent reader. What he says in the remarks prefixed to *The Spanish Fryar* (1681) can be applied to his heroic drama: his ambition, he writes, is "to be read," because the "hidden beauties of a play," the "silent graces," such as "clearness of conception" and "purity of phrase," must "of necessity escape our transient view upon the theatre." John Butt, in *The Augustan Age,* makes an accurate judgment when he concludes that Dryden approached drama as a "man of letters," and not wholly as a dramatist.[19]

Dryden's fashionable audience would have been familiar with the scientific ideas of the day and, therefore, prepared for the quasi-geometrical design of Dryden's plays. The spacing and interrelating of the fourteen or so characters in each play appears mechanical in that it is more clear-cut and intelligible than one might expect after a reading of Shakespeare or Fletcher. But this very aspect of Dryden's plays would fit neatly into the mid-seventeenth-century intellectual climate, since "with the advent of Galilean physics and the Keplerian

18. *Restoration Tragedy,* p. 94.
19. (London, 1965), p. 16.

astronomy, it began to appear at least possible that all parts of
the universe were mechanically interrelated."[20] Kepler, in particular, thought that the basic arrangement of the world could
be abstracted and expressed in geometric and mathematical
terms. In England not all scientists stressed experimentation
of the Baconian kind; Harvey himself discovered that blood
circulates by an application of Galileo's principle of measurement.[21] Dryden's plays of ideas would therefore have appeared
part and parcel of the mechanistic philosophy rapidly gaining
ground in the seventeenth century. Cecil Deane, indeed, has
noted that Dryden's method of characterization, his "absurdly
symmetrical arrangement of conflicting loves and hates," re-
flects a debt to Descartes' mechanistic views.[22]

With such an eclectic thinker as Dryden, however, it is just
as possible to find traces of Baconian thought and Royal Society methodology in the heroic plays as it is to find traces of
Descartes. In the debates, for instance, Dryden gives each side
of a question a fair hearing, as though he were conducting an
experiment. In *Tyrannic Love* Maximin, the usurper and
tyrant, is given equal time with the captive Christian queen.
After maintaining such objectivity in the expository part of
the plays, Dryden allows each point of view to be set in motion
and to result in specific political actions. To use Bacon's words,
he is conducting "experiments of *light*" in the first instance

20. Charles Singer, "The Insurgent Century," in *A Short History of Scientific
Ideas to 1900* (Oxford, 1960), p. 256.

21. Ibid., p. 275.

22. Cecil V. Deane, *Dramatic Theory and the Rhymed Heroic Play* (London,
1931), pp. 29, 35. Deane writes that the "very formula, *Cogito, ergo sum,* facili-
tates the idea that in order that a character may exist it is enough that he
should reason" (p. 29). Moreover, since Cartesianism is an attempt to explain
reality in terms of geometry and mechanics, Deane argues, then the "absurdly
symmetrical arrangement of conflicting loves and hates" in the heroic plays
may be a "reflection" of Cartesianism. In spite of this similarity between Dryden
and Descartes, Deane concludes that nothing in the poet's work indicates that
he was a follower of Hobbes or Descartes.

and "experiments of *fruit*" in the second.[23] If he were merely interested in the analysis of divergent points of view, he would not be so careful to put them all into action and to give them varying degrees of success. Like Bacon, he makes utility one of the tests of truth. He wishes to discover what set of attitudes will most benefit the individual and society.

Dryden, then, arranges historical circumstances in his plays to indicate which side of the argument he favors. As a dramatist, he acts the part of god, judging secretly and giving rewards or punishments according to merit. In this respect, his dramatic technique resembles that of Orrery, his kinsman and fellow heroic dramatist.[24] He describes the heroic play as an epitome of the ways of providence in a letter about Orrery's dramaturgy:

Here is no chance which you have not foreseen; all your heroes are more than your subjects, they are your creatures. And though they seem to move freely in all the sallies of their passions, yet you make destinies for them which they cannot shun. They are moved (if I may dare to say so) like the rational creatures of the Almighty Poet, who walk at liberty, in their own opinion, because their fetters are invisible; when indeed the prison of their will is the more sure for being large; and instead of an absolute

23. "But then only will there be good ground of hope for the futher advance of knowledge when there shall be received and gathered together into natural history a variety of experiments which are of no use in themselves but simply serve to discover causes and axioms, which I call *Experimenta lucifera*, experiments of *light*, to distinguish them from those which I call *fructifera*, experiments of fruit." Francis Bacon, *The New Organon and Related Writings*, ed. Fulton H. Anderson (New York, 1960), Aphorism 99, Book 1, p. 96.

24. W. S. Clark, "Dryden's Relations with Howard and Orrery," *MLN*, 42 (1927), 16–20. Clark explains that Orrery "had married Margaret Howard, daughter of Theophilus Howard, Earl of Suffolk, who was brother to Thomas Howard, Earl of Berkshire. Thus, Dryden's patron, Sir Robert Howard, and Orrery were first cousins. Dryden himself in 1663 became of kin to these heroic dramatists by his marriage to Lady Elizabeth Howard.

power over their actions, they have only a wretched desire
of doing that which they cannot choose but do.[25]

What Dryden is describing in this passage is a tension which
creates much of the excitement in heroic drama, a tension
between the apparent spontaneity of action on the part of
rebels and overreachers and their actual enslavement to sub-
rational impulses. Those who argue that they "walk at liberty"
in these plays have cast aside all laws as mere fetters on their
individual choice; yet far from enhancing that area of choice,
they have entered into the sphere of necessity, because the
appetites which they serve are moved according to a fixed
natural law. An intellectual acceptance of law is therefore in-
dispensable, in these plays, to any exercise of choice.

According to Louis Bredvold, Hobbes had given a new importance to the ancient problem of free will and necessity,[26]
It is likely, therefore, that Dryden's audiences would have
found relevant his frequent allusions to destiny, heaven, fortune and fate. The area of individual freedom, for Dryden,
lies in the acquisition of patience, that is, a childlike trust in
the justice of historical events and a determination to hold on
to life as long as it is possible to do so virtuously. There is no
freedom to shape historical events because these have already
been determined by supernal forces at the start of each play.
Often, therefore, the characters are unwitting pawns in the
elaborate, historical chess game.

An example of this tension between the poet's sovereign
control and the character's apparent free will can be found in
The Indian Emperour: Odmar thinks he has freed himself

25. "To Roger, Earl of Orrery;" in *Of Dramatic Poesy and Other Critical
Essays, 1,* ed. George Watson (London, 1962), 4; hereafter cited as Watson.

26. Louis I. Bredvold, "Dryden, Hobbes, and the Royal Society," *MP,* 25
(1928), 432. Bredvold goes on to say that Dryden "must have been interested
in necessitarianism, speculated on its implications, and enjoyed testing out its
argumentative strength in verse." Bredvold takes Dryden's philosophical interests more seriously than Samuel Johnson, who remarks that he sees no
reason at all for Dryden's continual references to fate and necessity, *1,* 256.

from all obligations to his country and family by a simple act of will but, in fact, has become the blind instrument in the Spanish conquest of the New World. In *The Conquest,* too, Lyndaraxa's seemingly free actions result in the Christian takeover of Granada; and Placidius' unreasoning spirit of vengeance at the end of *Tyrannic Love* has the unintended effect of saving the Christian empress. Dryden does not always favor the Christians; those in *The Indian Emperour* who think they have freed themselves from their obligations to conscience by their service to the Pope and Spanish king and are persecuting Indians for the sake of gold may themselves be punished shortly. Cortez prophesies that such gold will "fatally" be brought to Spain. The Spaniards have been instrumental in bringing Christianity to the New World, as the Earth Spirit attests, but those who have behaved unlawfully have brought a curse upon their country.

What Dryden seems to believe is that those who think they are free either from external laws or from the bondage of conscience are actually imprisoned by their own insatiable will. This will is pushed here and there by passions aroused by the workings of fate, with the result that it becomes the means of their own undoing and the instrument for the restoration of the virtuous characters to their former happiness. The illusion of liberty which accompanies the turning away from all law is balanced, in the heroic plays, by the illusion of bondage which accompanies obedience to law. Zempoalla, in a moment of rage, asks the physically chained but spiritually free Montezuma if she is "captive to a slave." In spite of her proclaimed freedom from all obligations, she is bound by her own passions to pursue a fatal course.

In his view of man's obligations within society, Dryden appears to resemble in part such conservatives as Thomas Hobbes and Sir Robert Filmer. Like them, he believes that subjects are bound to obey even a usurper and tyrant, provided such a ruler has established a certain order in the state. On the other hand, he differs from them in his insistence that the laws which are imposed by the state should not be rated higher than conscience, that is, the private moral impulse of each subject. If the rights of private conscience are not respected by the ruler, then the subject must offer resistance of a nonviolent kind, even though such resistance may lead to punishment.

The "patterns of exact virtue" in *The Conquest* and in other heroic plays are those who are obedient to externally imposed laws; Ozmyn, Acacis, Guyomar, Saint Catharine, and Aureng-Zebe appear, at first, to conform perfectly to the requirements of parental and civil law. All of these characters, however, end by disregarding external law to act according to the dictates of their conscience. Ozmyn and Benzayda, in *The Conquest,* disregard parental law and leave Granada in the midst of a Christian siege, when Ozmyn is supposed to be defending his country and fulfilling his civil obligations; yet Dryden can still call this pair "patterns of exact virtues" in his preface to the play because their disobedience is of a passive, nonviolent kind and necessary to their fulfilling private obligations toward each other.

A similar disobedience on the part of a strictly virtuous character occurs in each heroic play: Acacis, in *The Indian Queen,* disobeys his mother, Queen Zempoalla, in order to protect his friends. Guyomar, in *The Indian Emperour,* also disobeys his parent and monarch when he refuses to let Montezuma kill Cortez. Saint Catharine disregards her mother's pleas as well as those of Empress Berenice and refuses to seek an escape from martyrdom. Similarly, Aureng-Zebe refuses to let the Emperor, his father, cow him into obediently giving up Indamora. Each of these characters, at the start of the play, seems precise in his obedience to external laws, but is later put in a position where he must resist the explicit command of a recognized authority in order to follow his own moral impulse. Such disobedience is not destructive of the political order and therefore acceptable. They are all ready to accept banishment, imprisonment, or death as the penalty for resistance. In his portrayal of these characters, Dryden seems to go far beyond Filmer and Hobbes in allowing the subject to choose the dictates of conscience over the commands of a monarch and parent.

Dryden is closer to Hobbes and Filmer, however, in his condemnation of armed rebellion even for matters of conscience. Although a subject has been unjustly treated, he should not have recourse to arms, but should be satisfied with passive resistance or exile. Montezuma, Porphyrius, and Almanzor are characters guided by their own impulses to good, and they use force to overthrow an unjust, established ruler. Dryden compares these characters to storms and tempests, suggesting that their doings are great natural disasters which befall the state. By the middle of the heroic play, this type of character learns to bend his will to an external authority, and his chains and imprisonment are symbolic of the social and political bonds he now accepts. The clearest censure of armed rebellion occurs in *Tyrannic Love,* where Berenice more than once warns Porphyrius about the guilt he will incur by turning on his benefactor Maximin, even though the latter is a tyrant, usurper, and murderer.

The heroic plays usually have a pair of male characters who express Dryden's concept of the norm, for that norm is a duality to him, a composite of internal moral impulse and external moral obligation to civil and parental law. Some critics have suggested that Dryden creates "dualities" and "syllogisms" for the sole purpose of appearing to be clever. But his dualities and syllogisms are at the very heart of his plays; he presents neatly logical points of view on man's obligations within society, much as a scientist would present mathematical formulae, and then lets the sweep of historical events show their strength or weakness. The syllogism which underlies his heroic drama is that if a man begins by reasoning from false premises, his actions will soon be correspondingly unsound and dangerous to the society in which he lives. There is, then, a simple organization behind the plays: the poet first gives an exposition of the various points of view in ratiocinative discourse, then allows the representatives of those points of view to go into action. Dryden himself defends this kind of organization in his lines to Orrery, whose heroic drama he praises because a number of characters are made to move "in those narrow channels which are proper to each of them" and because the scenes of "argumentation and discourse" are logically, causally connected to "the doing or not doing some considerable action."[27]

The pair of male heroes, whether it be Montezuma and Acacis in *The Indian Queen* or Almanzor and Ozmyn in *The Conquest*, represents the double norm of internal and external law. In the course of each play the heroes come closer together: Almanzor and Montezuma, the fierce upholders of their own moral impulse and scorners of civil law, learn to accept civil authority (and parental law in Almanzor's case), while Ozmyn and Acacis learn to resist some external laws for the sake of conscience. Guyomar, who saves the life of his father in preference to that of his mistress early in the play, thus giving clear proof of Aeneas-like piety, later resists the commands of his father and monarch in order to save the life of Cortez, his erstwhile benefactor.

Dryden's dramatic method appears to be to start out with two heroes that together form one hero: each one has one-half of that which is essential to the hero. Eugene M. Waith has suggested that Almanzor's spark of energy, his reliance on individual moral impulse, is a sign of wit. One might agree but add that Ozmyn's reliance on external sources of law is equally a sign of judgment. Oxmyn's correctness of behavior should not be confused with the dullness and servility of Abdalla. As *The Conquest* progresses through its ten acts, Almanzor acquires judgment, accepts the norms which society imposes from with-

27. Watson, *1*, 2, 9.

out, and Ozmyn acquires wit by learning to make his own
rules. The contrast between the two is crystallized in the opening bullfight, where Almanzor breaks every rule of the game
while Ozmyn follows these rules all too precisely. The norm of
Dryden's heroic drama, therefore, is a healthy balance of wit
and judgment, a via media which is reached by the pair of
heroes in each of the plays. A vigorous moral impulse from
within the individual is essential, as well as recognition of the
validity of external forms of law; between the nonconformists
who rely on internal law and the political conservatives of the
time who demand strict conformity to externally constituted
laws, a middle way can be located. Dryden seems to be searching for a resolution of the political and philosophical con-
flicts which abounded in his era; in his search for a means of
reconciling extremists of the right and left wings lies the fas-
cination of the heroic plays for us.

In his notion of a play, as we should expect, Dryden departs
sharply from Aristotle and the tradition of mimesis. Whereas
Aristotle emphasizes the action or plot of a play, Dryden insists
on an intellectual variety among his characters and calls his
play an "image of human nature" rather that the imitation of
an action. By "image" he means pattern or rational construct;
his images are related to objective, extra-mental reality in
essence, but not necessarily in appearance. Poetry must "*be*
ethical,*" he asserts, but need not be closely mimetic: it need
only "resemble natural truth."[28]

The poetic reality which Dryden envisions is more an
analogy to than an imitation of the world about us. In order
to express the essence of human nature, it may be necessary
to distort psychology, to stretch probabilities somewhat, just
as El Greco or a modern expressionist painter may distort
anatomy to capture what is under the surface. Thus, the character of Maximin, the impious atheist who persecutes Saint
Catharine, may seem exaggerated if he is measured by a na-

28. "A Defence of *An Essay*," Watson, *1*, 120.

turalistic norm of human behavior; but if he is studied as a model of the lawbreaker, a pattern of the rebel turned tyrant, then he appears well constructed, consistent, even highly captivating. Dryden thinks of the dramatist as a builder or an architect; he need not be afire with inspiration, but should, rather, deliberately examine the "images of nature" within his mind, selecting those which best suit his idea. Since he thinks the artist is an artificer, not an instrument moved by divine impulse, he can argue that intellectually perceived characters are "natural" and that a formal, architecturally balanced design in a play is "natural." He can even insist, from his point of view, that the unities are "natural" and that rhyme —in particular the intricately wrought heroic couplet—is "natural" in dramatic discourse. The heroic plays thus project a world that is appealing to the reasoning faculty—a foreshortened world where providence, under the guise of fortune, judges the good and the bad without delay.

Dryden's formally constructed microcosm in the heroic drama is one in which ethical alternatives are clear and unmistakable. Basic to each of these plays is a group of sharply distinct characters, nearly all of whom are in love and are forced to choose among a wide variety of ethical possibilities. The characters explain and sometimes rationalize their choices, always with verve and brilliance. The external and public consequences of their attitudes—the rebellions, usurpations, or assassinations—give one indication of how virtuous they are, and the judgment of providence, acting through historical events, gives another.

Dryden's serious drama, as he himself points out in his critical writings, is first and foremost a "design" which is then covered with "ornament," that is, with a beautiful surface— heroic conventions, well-turned couplets, and suggestions of contemporary aristocratic manners that make the plays "resemble natural truth." The surface of the heroic drama has often been confused with the design by critics accustomed to dealing with Shakespearean drama; this surface is often a disguise rather than an indication of what the play is really about. Dryden frequently states, as this study will show, that the design of a play is the work of judgment, while it is in the ornamentation that the poet gives his fancy free rein.

In an age of masks, wigs, and exaggerated personal ornament, it is not difficult to imagine that a play's surface could be at odds with its content, even in counterpoint with it, nor is it difficult to see that a heavy sincerity of surface would be out of keeping for a Restoration man of wit (one need only try to think of Dorimant or Horner with a solemn face). R. E. Moore, who calls Dryden's plays "baroque," finds a tension between the "fetters" of the heroic couplet and the "fierce passions of the characters" and between a sense of "sovereign control" and a vision of "tumultuous action."[29] Dryden's biographer Sir Walter Scott hints at a similar tension at the very core of the heroic plays: he reminds us that the poet regarded his plays as "good sense, that looked like nonsense."[30] Many critics who have been severe in their judgment, I think, have stopped at the fanciful surface and not penetrated to the moral design. They have accepted the conventional remarks about love and honor as the total play.

Although the heroic plays are often considered as wholly separate from Dryden's nondramatic poetry, a comparison of the schemes of values found in these works with those found in *Astraea Redux, Annus Mirabilis, MacFlecknoe,* and other works indicates that there is a remarkable consistency in Dryden's thought which has not been previously stressed. A superficial difference between his dramatic and nondramatic works of the first dozen years or so of his career as a poet is that the dramatic works seem to deal with an imaginary space and time, and the nondramatic with contemporary events and characters. This difference, however, is not so great as one might sup-

29. P. 20.
30. Pp. 163–64.

pose. In the poems Dryden transforms contemporary characters into heroes or would-be heroes who might well have
appeared in the plays; Charles in *Astraea Redux,* for instance,
bears a remarkable resemblance to all the suffering heroes of
the plays, from Montezuma to Aureng-Zebe, and the tyrannical
Dutch in *Annus Mirabilis* are given much the same character
as the tyrants of heroic drama. Conversely, the plays are filled
with usurpations, rebellions, and restorations which are clearly
analogies to the contemporary political scene. All these works
have a common scheme of values; when individual ambition
or revenge has superseded adherence to external laws to bring
about anarchy, then the direction men must choose is a return
toward a rule of law within a freely accepted civil order.

The rebels in *Astraea Redux,* the Dutch in *Annus Mirabilis,*
the lawless poets in *MacFlecknoe,* and the usurper Maximin
in *Tyrannic Love* are all cast in a similar mold. They become
a law unto themselves and are, in the end, foiled by their own
"impious wit," all their machinations proving fruitless. The
Dutch ships are too large and their fleet is too crowded; they
perish in their pride and ostentation. For all his self-proclaimed
inspiration, Shadwell is relegated to the realm of Non-sense
and to Acrostic Land. Similarly, in spite of his determination
to achieve control over the minds of his subjects, Maximin is
protected by the Christian Empress whom he persecutes and
is assassinated by his slavish follower Placidius. Dryden's Witwouds thus bring about their own destruction, but the True-
Wits act with patience and moderation, placing the common
good above their private interests and submitting to punishment even when they have not deserved it. Eugene M. Waith
points out that the "bracketing of dullness with malice, lust,
and self-interest is revealing. *Per contra,* the witty man is generous and devoted to the public interest."[31] The implication
here is that to scorn virtue by disobeying the laws of conscience or of the state is equivalent to abnegating reason. The

31. p. 164.

Witwouds may appear as brilliant as the True-Wits in the discussions, but their actions show that there has indeed occurred a loss of perspicacity.

Dryden's heroic plays suggest that there is an abstract plan behind the workings of history, that of Israel coming out of Egypt and moving toward a Promised Land. Overreachers and rebels sink into oblivion, impatient men of virtue despair and fall by the wayside, but patient men see the deliverance. In these plays Dryden takes a momentous historical event and describes a full arc from anarchy, rebellion, and injustice to a restoration of justice and order. Within this scheme he takes into consideration both private and public moral obligations, dealing on the one hand with the bond between family members and between lovers and, on the other, with that between monarch and subject, between rival political factions, and between warring nations. The attitude toward history which underlies these plays is optimistic in the same way in which Dante's work is a "Comedy": Dryden chooses to believe that history is not in the hands of men but is the working out of a preordained plan which will providentially bring about the instauration of peace and justice on earth. In *Astraea Redux* and *Annus Mirabilis,* he is even more explicit about this historical spiraling toward a new Golden Age, toward "times whiter Series" and the "Spicy shore."

2

Dryden's Conservatism

The political and ethical views which form the foundation of Dryden's heroic plays can best be understood by a comparison with views articulated by such contemporary conservatives as Thomas Hobbes and Sir Robert Filmer. The familiar remark of Aubrey, in the *Brief Lives,* that Dryden admires Hobbes and "oftentimes makes use of his doctrine in his plays "corroborates what many other students of heroic drama have suspected, namely that Hobbes' influence on the dramatist must have been extensive.[1] Dryden's acquaintance with Filmer's political philosophy is well attested in his panegyric on the coronation of Charles II, in which he epitomizes Filmer's position in the *Patriarcha:*

> When Empire first from families did spring,
> Then every Father govern'd as a King;
> But you that are a Soveraign Prince, allay
> Imperial pow'r with your paternal sway.[2]

According to Alan Roper, author of *Dryden's Poetic Kingdoms,* Dryden "found the idea of the king as *pater patriae* a poetic coin of wide currency, both as an apt expression of certain political attitudes and emotions and in its specifically patriarchalist associations."[3] The passages of political philosophy in the heroic plays, far from being mere "strained po-

1. Ed. Andrew Clark (Oxford, 1898), *1,* 372.

2. *To His Sacred Majesty, A Panegyrick on His Coronation,* in *The Works of John Dryden, 1,* ed. Edward Niles Hooker and H. T. Swedenberg, Jr. (Berkeley and Los Angeles, 1961), ll. 93–96, p. 35; hereafter cited *Works,* California edition.

3. (London, 1965), p. 74

litical declamation" as Louis I. Bredvold would have it,[4] are
responses to vital currents of political thought in the contemporary scene. The tyrants and rebels of Dryden's plays
seem to take Hobbes' ideas and adapt or distort them to their
own uses; on the other hand, some of the more dutiful characters, who regard obedience to one's king as a moral obligation, appear to take Filmer's view of man and the state.

Thomas Hobbes

A comparison of Dryden and Hobbes will reveal that, although they may differ in their notions of what man is, what
sort of laws bind him, and what the rights and obligations of
a sovereign are, the very manner in which they differ indicates
their relationship. What testifies to the influence of Hobbes
upon Dryden and his contemporaries, as Samuel I. Mintz
points out, is that even his critics had "to employ his own
method of rational argument" in answering him.[5] Most of the
debates which occur in the heroic plays are clashes between
various points of view concerning man and the state, one of
which can be identified loosely as Hobbesian.

It is possible that Dryden's emphasis on what is logical and
intelligible, his creating of characters from the patterns of
human nature within his own mind, and his multiplying of
scenes of argumentation were due, in part at least, to Hobbes'
influence. As Professor Mintz remarks, Hobbes thought that to
"discover order in the universe one must look into one's own
mind; to create order one must reason correctly about the con-
structions of the mind, and about the sense-experiences which
gave rise to them."[6] Dryden, as well as Hobbes, sometimes
equates reasoning and ratiocination, so that logical expression
and knowledge become one. To reason, Hobbes suggests, one
must first impose apt names; secondly, one must proceed to

4. *The Intellectual Milieu of John Dryden* (Ann Arbor, Mich., 1962), p. 136.
5. *The Hunting of Leviathan* (Cambridge, 1962), p. viii.
6. Ibid., p. 25.

connect the names and make assertions; "and so to syllogisms."[7] The ratiocinative bent which Samuel Johnson and
other critics have found in Dryden may, therefore, be part of
his heritage from Hobbes.

One clear thematic link between Hobbes and Dryden is the
question of the pursuit of power. Hobbes regards as "a generall
inclination of all mankind, a perpetuall and restlesse desire of
Power after power, that ceaseth onely in Death."[8] A number
of characters in Dryden's heroic plays also take that view of
mankind. These characters may be rebels and usurpers or tyrannical hereditary rulers, but all agree that power is synony-
mous with divinity, that it is the summum bonum; moreover,
they seem unable to find a middle ground between absolute,
arbitrary power in the sovereign and lawless dissension or
anarchy in the state.

The problems posed by the pursuit of power on the part of
several characters in Dryden's heroic drama far outweigh those
created by sentimental love. Sometimes Hobbes' ideas are distorted when they appear in these plays, but they are, on the
whole, still recognizable. Hobbes, for example, believes that a
man's price is "not absolute; but a thing dependant on the need
and judgment of another." This "price" constitutes, for
Hobbes, the *"value,* or WORTH of a man."[9] Elsewhere,
Hobbes writes in a similar vein that what distinguishes one
man from another is not "wit, or riches, or blood, or some other
natural quality," but his standing in the eyes of the sovereign
authority—hence, his price.[10] The motif of price and "worth"
is a prominent one in heroic drama. Dryden seems to agree in
large part with Hobbes' idea of worth, for he suggests that, in
addition to self-esteem, one ought to seek for legitimate prizes
such as fame and the sovereign's appreciation. He uses Hobbes

7. Thomas Hobbes, *Leviathan,* ed. Michael Oakeshott (Oxford, 1957), I.v.,
p. 29; hereafter cited as Hobbes.
8. Ibid., I. xi., p. 64.
9. Ibid., I. x., p. 57.
10. Ibid., II. xxvii., p. 193.

constructively just as Restoration clergymen did who incorpo-
rated "the materialist analysis of man within the traditional
Christian view."[11] For Dryden a man's value to the state is a
good part of his worth, but it does not obviate the inward and
more spiritual measurement of accomplishments. Thrones are
toppled when generals such as Montezuma and Almanzor are
denied what they think is a fair price for their services. They
must be educated to look beyond external rewards for their
services. Rebels and tyrants alike in the heroic plays think that
their entire worth lies in the possession of a crown; only the
adulation and submission of the crowd can give them a sense
of their own value. Lyndaraxa, for example, demands that her
Moors bow to her before she dies in order that she may "taste
an empire."

The norm of the heroic plays is clearly not a stoic renuncia-
tion of price. Although Almanzor is educated by Almahide to
a point where he can accept a "secret joy of mind" as payment
for his actions, he never stops complaining about the lack of
tangible reward. Aureng-Zebe, similarly, complains about the
injustice of his having no external value to the Emperor, in
spite of his loyal support during the rebellion:

> How vain is virtue, which directs our ways
> Through certain danger to uncertain praise!
> Barren, and airy name!

Dryden incorporates the Hobbesian approach to value or price
because it behooves our human nature to seek rewards. In
Religio Laici, he castigates the Stoics for seeking only virtue,
"A Thorny, or at best a barren Soil." When the pursuit of
prizes is possible without a breach of law, such a pursuit is not
only legitimate but desirable. In comparison to Milton, who
regards Fame as the "last infirmity of Noble mind," Dryden
seems quite pragmatic.

11. Bruce King, "Dryden, Tillotson, and *Tyrannic Love*," *RES,* n. s. *16* no. 64
(1965), p. 366.

To Hobbes, the state of nature which precedes the making
of a covenant is a state of predatory struggle for rewards.
Hobbes writes that in this state "every man has a right to every
thing" and is governed only "by his own reason."[12] Even after
the covenant has been drawn up, there is always the danger of
a return to the state of war if "Leviathan," the government,
does not keep tight hold of the reins. For Dryden, too, the state
of nature is in part a predatory struggle, and for this reason he
distrusts the mob, the lower echelon of society, and regards it
as a powder keg. If the government is disrupted and the civil
structure reduced to chaos, then the country might become the
scene of a predatory hunt for prizes. Hobbes and Dryden thus
share a vision of man as a fallen, imperfect creature, prone to
rebellion and tumult.

The reason for a virtual condition of war in Hobbes' state
of nature is that the law of nature is so easily misunderstood.
Each individual is free to interpret moral principles and need
account only to his own conscience. Hobbes writes: "The unwritten law of nature, though it be easy to such, as without
partiality and passion, make use of their natural reason, and
therefore leaves the violators thereof without excuse; yet con-
sidering there be very few, perhaps none, that in some cases
are not blinded by self-love, or some other passion; it is now
become of all laws the most obscure, and has consequently
the greatest need of able interpreters."[13] When the sovereign
promulgates laws to his subjects, then the unwritten natural
law can be clearly apprehended and the state of war termi-
nated.

Dryden's idea of the state of nature, however, adds another
dimension to that of Hobbes. In *Astraea Redux, Annus Mira-*

12. Hobbes, I. xiv., p. 85. But Howard Warrender points out that "the State
of Nature is not by any means a condition in which there are no obligations;
still less is it a state where there are no moral principles" (*The Political
Philosophy of Hobbes; His Theory of Obligation* [Oxford, 1957], p. 102).
13. Hobbes, II. xxvi., p. 180.

bilis, and a later poem, "To My Honour'd Kinsman," Dryden speaks of a Golden Age in which men lived in peace and ease; the state of nature is one of indolent happiness. In a number of allusions to the Fall of Adam and Eve, Dryden suggests that the world of the hunter, of the predatory struggle for prizes which Hobbes envisages, is a consequence of sin. But even postlapsarian man, in Dryden's view, is not without a spark of good; government is not the main force that keeps him from preying on his neighbors. Even when social order is disrupted in the heroic plays and existence appears to be a struggle for prizes, certain men like Acacis in *The Indian Queen,* Ozmyn in *The Conquest,* and Guyomar in *The Indian Emperour* prefer to be victims of another's rapacity rather than behave like hunters themselves. Since their society is in a state of chaos, they are bound by internal moral impulses, by conscience rather than social compact; for this reason they may be called "patterns of exact virtues."[14]

Nor are all the hunters who participate in the predatory struggle for prizes as base as Lyndaraxa or Nourmahal, who, with their counterparts in other heroic plays, care only for possessions and power. The heroes Montezuma, Cortez, Porphyrius, and Almanzor, on the other hand, care chiefly for the glory which accompanies admirable deeds, and they refuse to act basely even for the sake of a crown. Whereas Hobbes argues that the "desire of power, of riches, of knowledge, and of honour" may all "be reduced to the first, that is, desire of power,"[15] Dryden distinguishes the desire for power from the love of honor. Lyndaraxa, for example, disrupts the political structure and civil order of Granada for the sake of her ambition; Almanzor, on the other hand, topples Boabdelin and later Abdalla from the throne of Granada because both these rulers refuse him the right to give freedom to his prisoners: Boabdelin will not let him liberate the Duke of Arcos, and

14. "Of Heroic Plays," Watson, *1,* 165.
15. Hobbes, I. viii., p. 46.

Abdalla will not allow Almahide to gain her liberty. Thus, Almanzor disrupts the political order in retaliation for an injustice which has been done to him; his rights have been invaded, and he is fighting in defense of them. Instead of seeking power over others, the heroes Almanzor, Montezuma, Cortez, and Porphyrius are always seeking to excel in generosity; they are essentially apart from the social hierarchy and consider themselves free agents within nature. Almanzor explains this aspect of the hero:

> But know, that I alone am king of me.
> I am as free as nature first made man,
> Ere the base laws of servitude began,
> When wild in woods the noble savage ran.[16]

Such an unsocial being as Almanzor would therefore care more about protecting his liberties than pursuing power, even though he attempts to win Almahide as the prize of his endeavors, thereby joining the hunters in their struggle.

Of all the laws which bind men—civil, natural, and religious—Hobbes makes civil law the most important. Private citizens, according to him, ought not to try to interpret the law of nature; even moral philosophers are always contradicting each other in explaining that law; therefore, natural law cannot be binding unless promulgated by the sovereign: "For though it be naturally reasonable; yet it is by the sovereign power that it is law."[17] It is manifest, Hobbes explains, that "the measure of good and evil actions, is the civil law"; consequently, the exercise of private reason on matters of law should be restricted to those areas untouched by civil law.[18] The use of private judgment to measure good and evil, in fact, can be seditious and presumptuous and can lead to the

---

16. *The Conquest of Granada*, Pt. 1, I. i., p. 25, in *John Dryden (Three Plays)*, edited by George Saintsbury (New York, n.d.).

17. Hobbes, II. xxvi., p. 180.

18. Ibid., II. xxix., p. 211.

weakening of the commonwealth.[19] Hobbes' emphasis on positive law comes under attack in the heroic plays. Dryden shows the limitations of this attitude by presenting a series of rulers who argue that civil law, as they interpret it, is above every other consideration. Such rulers meet with servile obedience from the worst of their courtiers, such as Traxalla in *The Indian Queen* and Placidius in *Tyrannic Love,* but these fawning servants eventually turn against their masters. At the same time the tyrants meet with resistance from the best of their courtiers, such as Montezuma and Almanzor, those who would have been most loyal if treated well. Dryden may be reacting against Hobbes in suggesting that a monarch who sets civil authority above natural law and liberties brings rebellion into his state.

An example of slavish obedience to civil law is the governor Arimant in *Aureng-Zebe,* for he follows Hobbes' rule that a public minister fall back on the "dictates of reason" only when "written instructions" fail.[20] Arimant realizes in Act I that the Emperor's command to imprison Indamora is unreasonable, yet he tells Prince Aureng-Zebe: "you know the hard command,/I must obey." He justifies his action in the manner of the defendants in the Nuremberg trials: "My duty must excuse me, sir, from blame." He even calls the Emperor's command "absolute."[21] When Arimant acts more justly toward Indamora in subsequent scenes, it is because her beauty has enslaved him just as the Emperor's power had done: "Madam, you have a strange ascendant gained;/You use me like a courser, spurred and reined."[22] Arimant is nevertheless so ennobled by his humble service to the virtuous Indamora that by the end of Act IV he no longer behaves like a slavish minister; in spite of his old age he goes to battle to die with glory. Thus, his perfunctory obedience to civil law has been trans-

---

19. Ibid.
20. Ibid., II. xxvi., p. 177.
21. *Aureng-Zebe,* in *John Dryden,* ed. Saintsbury, I. i., p. 288.
22. Ibid., II. i., p. 292.

formed to a more valuable and passionate type of service once
he has balanced civil with natural moral obligations.

In the development of Arimant, Dryden shows that a minister is a better servant to his prince when he does not follow
commands slavishly. Conversely, in the deterioration of Placidius in *Tyrannic Love,* Dryden reveals that a servile courtier
usually seeks private gain rather than his prince's welfare.
Placidius is more cunning and unscrupulous than Arimant.
He encourages Maximin's adulterous passion for Saint Catharine by arguing with her on behalf of Maximin and by attempting to send her a seductive dream through necromancy.
Although Placidius is in love with Maximin's daughter
Valeria, he is not ennobled by this affection; he is of a mercenary disposition, and his love takes on the aspect of bargain-
ing. He asks Valeria's love as the "price" and "ransom" for the
life of Porphyrius, whom he knows full well she loves. He seals
the bargain by disregarding the Emperor's orders and freeing
Porphyrius: "I, whom deep arts of state could ne'er beguile,/
Have sold myself to ruin for a smile."[23] When he is cheated
of his prize by Valeria's suicide, Placidius assassinates Maximin
in a blind rage. Rather than let Maximin fall by the hand of
the noble, passionate Porphyrius, Dryden lets him be mur-
dered by this fawning courtier, to illustrate that the most
dangerous man in the Emperor's court is he that serves without a thought of justice.

Perhaps the clearest statement of Dryden's point of view on
the kind of obedience due a monarch can be found in *Aureng-
Zebe.* When the Emperor, a Hobbesian type, tries to inspire a
slavish and fearful obedience in his only virtuous son Aureng-
Zebe, the latter explains that honor, not fear, is the proper
bond between sovereign and subject. The Emperor demands
that Aureng-Zebe give up Indamora, arguing: "Give willingly
what I can take by force;/And know, obedience is your safest

---

23. *Tyrannic Love,* in *The Works of John Dryden,* ed. Sir Walter Scott and
George Saintsbury (Edinburgh, 1882–93), V. i., p. 448.

course." His son replies: "I'm taught, by honour's precepts, to obey:/Fear to obedience is a slavish way." Dryden thus implies that a subject ought to obey willingly and not out of fear of punishment. He seems here to disagree with Hobbes, who explains that in a "COMMONWEALTH *by Acquisition,*" where a sovereign takes the realm by force, men are bound by covenant on the basis of fear of death or bonds.[24] Thus, Hobbes indicates that fear as well as willingness to serve can be a ground for the social covenant.

The almost obsessive love of order and peace without dissent which characterizes conservatives like Hobbes and Filmer and those of subsequent centuries cannot be found in Dryden. Bernard Schilling, in *Dryden and the Conservative Myth,* exaggerates Dryden's political views by suggesting that he favors suppression of individual energy for the sake of civil order. Dryden would indeed suppress that individual energy which leads to a struggle for power and gain, but not that which strives for the protection of liberties. In one of his last works, "To My Honour'd Kinsman," he states his position clearly in describing as patriots those who "in Peace, assert the Peoples Right;/With noble Stubbornness resisting Might."[25] Mere civil order is not to be preferred to the basic rights of an Englishman.

In matters of religious worship, Hobbes would give the private citizen no freedom, or, at best, a vague residual freedom to consult his own conscience. Neither does he give the clergy a voice independent of civil authority in determining the beliefs of the people, for fear there would be two kingdoms, *"temporal,* and *ghostly."* Having shown nature's law to be subject to interpretation by the sovereign, Hobbes adds that "there is no reason men should be the less obliged by it [law], when it is propounded in the name of God."[26]

24. *Aureng-Zebe,* ed. Saintsbury, II. i., p. 302; Hobbes, II. xx., p. 129.
25. *The Poems and Fables of John Dryden,* ed. James Kinsley (London, 1962), ll. 184–85, p. 610.
26. Hobbes, II. xxvi., p. 188; II. xxix., p. 215.

Besides interpreting divine law, the sovereign prescribes the form of worship which all citizens must follow. "But seeing a commonwealth is but one person," Hobbes reasons, "it ought also to exhibit to God but one worship . . . the property whereof, is to be uniform."[27] If the sovereign should be an enemy of Christianity, then the citizen may follow the new faith externally but keep his own belief inwardly: "nor is it he that in this case denieth Christ before men, but his governor, and the law of his country." "Profession with the tongue," he explains, "is but an external thing." Hobbes, in effect, reduces Christianity to two main tenets, *"faith in Christ, and obedience to laws"*: the former is a silent, inward acquiescence to Christian teachings, the latter an external submission to the state's commands, even when this necessitates the worship of idols.[28]

Dryden frequently places Hobbesian religious opinions in the mouths of impious characters in the heroic plays. One particularly striking example is Maximin, who rails at the gods with increasing bitterness throughout *Tyrannic Love,* yet who persecutes everyone professing a religion different from his own. When Apollonius is converted, Maximin protests that no citizen should dare to adopt a faith other than the ruler's.[29] In the same scene, however, Maximin shows that it is not so much impiety that he fears as rebellion; he thinks that if the people begin by changing faiths, they may end by making "new kings." He reasons that "factious teachers" will make the people so bold in their new opinions that they will cast off all duty to the state. As an answer to this Hobbesian point of view, Dryden has Porphyrius give a memorable speech on freedom of conscience to Maximin:

> Faith is a force from which there's no defence;
> Because the reason it does first convince:

27. Ibid., II. xxxi., p. 240.
28. Ibid., III. xlii., p. 327; III. xliii., p. 385.
29. *Tyrannic Love.*, ed. Scott-Saintsbury, II. iii., p. 405.

And reason conscience into fetters brings;
And conscience is without the power of kings.[30]

Porphyrius agrees with the Emperor that a difference of religion in a country might be a weapon in a rebel's hand, but he distinguishes between limiting the political power of a minority religious group and impeding their religious worship. Citizens of a faith other than the ruler's should be content with practising their religion and should not ask for civil power: "Those who ask civil power and conscience too,/Their monarch to his own destruction woo." This attitude on the part of Porphyrius need not reflect Dryden's own view. On the basis of the debates in *The Indian Emperour* about religion and the state, it is clear that Dryden would favor freedom of worship for all citizens and would even be willing to give members of other religions some share of power.

The Spaniards in *The Indian Emperour* are, like Maximin, spokesmen for a point of view that might, in a general way, be called Hobbesian. They confuse political and religious issues; all except Cortez seem to think that a military conquest of Mexico will result in Christianizing the area. Montezuma, who explains that religion is spread by persuasion rather than force, finds religion's "extent must be in men, not lands."[31] When Pizarro and the Spanish priest put the Emperor on the rack and try to convert him by means of torture, Montezuma protests that he is being persecuted for the sake of what he, with his natural reason unaided by faith, "cannot come to know."[32]

Cortez represents the Christian norm in this play, for he seems to uphold freedom of conscience in condemning the persecutors of Montezuma. His indignation and sorrow on discovering Montezuma on the rack suggest that he prefers

30. Ibid., IV. i., p. 441.

31. *The Indian Emperour,* in *Works,* California edition, *9,* ed. John Loftis and Vinton A. Dearing (1966), I. ii. 298, p. 42.

32. Ibid., V. ii. 60, p. 100.

persuasion to force in matters of belief. Moreover, at the end of the play Cortez is willing to share the rule of Mexico with Guyomar without consideration of his religion. Cortez does not think that differences of belief will lead to civil strife.

Hobbes' insistence that a single, public, uniform worship prevail in the state is also echoed by the Zegry faction in *The Conquest of Granada*. Ironically, this very faction is the cause of Moorish Granada's downfall. The Zegrys' hatred of the Abencerrages, a group of Moors more kindly toward Christians, brings strife and dissension within the state. According to one Zegry, the Abencerrages have Christian blood and some Christian practices and are therefore to be held inferior to other Muslims in the state: "Their mongrel race is mixed with Christian breed;/Hence 'tis that they those dogs in prisons feed." In their passion for the external institution of Islam, they have forgotten the meaning of their religion; Abdelmelech, one of the Abencerrages, points out: "Our holy prophet wills, that charity/Should even to birds and beasts extended be."[33] Like Maximin in *Tyrannic Love* and some of the Spaniards in *The Indian Emperour*, the Zegrys pursue power avidly while pretending to follow the established religion with more purity than others.

Hobbes, then, would bind the subject immediately by civil law; only after the explicit law of the sovereign has been obeyed may the subject apply natural law or Christian revelation to those areas of his life untouched by civil law. Dryden, on the contrary, makes all laws—civil, natural, and religious—immediately binding. If all three realms of law are not reconcilable—if to obey a civil command means to commit a moral offense—then the virtuous individual must prefer external bonds to the shaking off of inward fetters: for "reason conscience into fetters brings."

Hobbes reduces religion to an argument ad hominem: he makes Moses and a few other great prophets the sole recipients

33. *The Conquest*, ed. Saintsbury, Pt. I, I. i., p. 24.

of God's revelation and insists that the rest of humanity can
only believe their report.[34] And yet, religion, he states, is not
so much "a submission of the intellectual faculty" to another
man's opinion, as the "will to obedience, where obedience is
due."[35] Even if one believes that Moses was inspired by God,
still it is by the authority of the sovereign that his words are
law. Dryden seems to react against Hobbes' stress on authority
in the heroic plays. In *Tyrannic Love,* for instance, where
Maximin represents the Hobbesian view on religion, Saint
Catharine converts droves of philosophers offstage and the
Stoic Apollonius onstage by rational argument, not by authority or miracles. In *The Indian Emperour,* too, the Christian priest who tries to convert Montezuma by a mere appeal
to authority, insisting that the Indian abandon his "carnal
reason" for an "unerring head" (the Pope), fails miserably.
While Dryden would share Hobbes' distaste for private inspiration, he would make the individual's reason the final
determinant of religious belief.

Hobbes would resolve the conflict between Church and
State by letting the latter swallow up the former: "But the
church, if it be one person, is the same thing with a commonwealth of Christians."[36] The civil authority stands in the same
relationship to the citizen as Moses stood to the ancient Hebrews.[37] Dryden, on the one hand, shares Hobbes' fear of a
politically powerful clergy; on the other, he is nowhere near
such Erastianism as Hobbes displays. Montezuma and Cortez,
the spokesmen for natural reason and Christianity respectively,
in *The Indian Emperour,* agree in condemning those avari-

34. Hobbes, II. xxvi., p. 188; III. xxxiii., pp. 254–55.
35. Ibid., III. xxxii., p. 243.
36. Ibid., III. xxxiii., p. 255.
37. Ibid., II. xxvi., p. 188. What Hobbes writes about Scripture need not be
taken very seriously, according to Howard Warrender: "a great deal of Hobbes'
argument tends to show that Scripture has little bearing upon Salvation. Hence
the declaration of what Scriptures are to be taken by the citizen as authentic
is a matter which can safely be left in the hands of the sovereign" (p. 336).

cious and power-hungry clergymen represented by the "Christian Priest." Montezuma speaks early in the play of "ghostly kings" that "would parcel out my power," and Cortez censures these "enemies of crowns" who "saucily teach monarchs to obey,/And the wide world in narrow cloisters sway."[38] Most of those remarks which critics have called anticlerical in Dryden's works are actually directed specifically at such politically-minded clergymen. In *Don Sebastian* and *The Spanish Fryar* as well, these "ghostly kings" are censured. Even in *The Hind and the Panther*, Dryden, a new convert, is not very gentle in his treatment of the Roman Catholic priest who was advisor to James II; he describes him as a Martyn, "A church-begot, and church-believing bird," one who has assumed such importance that he "from a Priest became a Prince." The condemnation of the Martyn is placed in the mouth of the Anglican Panther, and so the Roman-Catholic Hind, in a rebuttal, points out that "No church reform'd can boast a blameless line;/Such *Martyns* build in yours, and more than mine." The wise ruler, at the end of this poem decides to establish freedom of religion but to withdraw none of the Anglican Church's privileges except the "Licence to oppress":

> He therefore makes all Birds of ev'ry Sect
> Free of his Farm, with promise to respect
> Their sev'ral Kinds alike, and equally protect.[39]

Dryden's norm, then, is a moderate sort of separation of Church and State, with clergymen freely exercising their spiritual leadership by means of argument and example.

Although a number of critics have noted that Dryden echoes some of Hobbes' ideas in his plays, they have often taken absolute positions, arguing either that Dryden followed Hobbes

---

38. *The Indian Emperour, Works*, California edition, *9*, I. ii., 315–20, p. 43; V. ii. 125–30, p. 102.

39. *The Hind and the Panther*, ed. Kinsley, Pt. III, ll. 1244–46.

or that he condemned him outright by placing his doctrine in the mouth of "villains."[40] What is fairly certain is that Dryden admired Hobbes enough to consider his philosophy an important basis of argumentation in his plays. Without referring to Hobbes by name, he places recognizably Hobbesian ideas in the mouths of his characters, chiefly tyrants and rebels. These are not simply "villains" but brilliant politicians and lawbreakers who justify their behavior by a complicated *Weltanschauung*. The lawbreakers in Dryden's plays are never quite foiled in argumentation; it is history or the onward rush of events that reveals their weakness and sweeps them off the scene. The Hobbesian doctrine, consequently, can be argued in rational discourse, Dryden suggests, but it simply will not work in the actual world, in the historical setting, because it is too far from the via media. The Hobbesian rulers bring about dissension in the state by their tyrannical behavior, and the rebels destroy themselves along with their ruler, leaving room at the top for more moderate leaders.

Dryden, however, agrees with Hobbes' view of man in the state to this extent: he shows that when the political structure or civil order of the state is disrupted, a lawless state of nature ensues, a predatory struggle for prizes prevails. Virtuous men, therefore, will only passively resist the unjust acts of a tyrant to avoid bringing chaos into the state, and will not seek to gain

40. These critics include Louis Teeter, "The Dramatic Use of Hobbes' Political Ideas," *ELH*, 3 (1936), 140–69; M. E. Hartsock, "Dryden's Plays: A Study in Ideas," in *Seventeenth Century Studies*, ed. R. Shafer (Princeton, 1938); Thomas H. Fujimura, "The Appeal of Dryden's Heroic Plays," *PMLA*, 75 (1960), 37–45; John A. Winterbottom, "The Place of Hobbesian Ideas in Dryden's Tragedies," *JEGP*, 57 (1958), 665–83. M. E. Hartsock and T. H. Fujimura stress Dryden's acceptance of Hobbesian notions while the others emphasize the differences between Hobbes and the poet. It seems more likely that Dryden regarded Hobbes' materialistic conception of man and the state as accurate but incomplete; instead of reacting to the *Leviathan*, he seems to want to incorporate it into a larger, Christian view of life. Bruce King affirms that "Restoration divines saw Christianity as an improvement upon pagan philosophy, not a rejection of it" (p. 336).

power by the destruction of the civil order; if Almanzor and Montezuma are temporarily guilty of rebellion, it is because they are defending their liberties rather than seeking the crown, and yet, even on these terms, their armed rebellion is not condoned.

Sir Robert Filmer

Sir Robert Filmer, among Dryden's contemporaries perhaps the leading exponent of the divine right theory, provides another measuring rod by which to analyze Dryden's conservatism. Although Filmer was an author of considerable standing in the Restoration, he has since fallen into obscurity, possibly because of Locke's ridicule of his ideas in the first *Treatise on Government,* a veritable *MacFlecknoe* of political philosophy. The scholarship of Peter Laslett has given Filmer's reputation a new luster, so that it is now possible to consider him with Hobbes as one of the foremost political conservatives of the age.

In practical application Filmer's political views are similar to those of Hobbes. Like Hobbes he tends to emphasize external sources of law rather than internal. In *The Anarchy of a Limited Mixed Monarchy* (1648), he argues that a king ought to be absolute and arbitrary, "for to make a law according to law, is *contradictio in adjecto,*" as the sovereign power lies in the very ability to make laws.[41] In essence, however, Filmer is a different kind of conservative than Hobbes. First, he makes obedience to civil law a matter of moral obligation rather than of practical necessity; and second, he bases his theory of absolute monarchy on historical precedent rather than on a social contract. He acknowledges the theoretical gulf between himself and Hobbes in a critique of the *Leviathan:* "It may seem

41. Sir Robert Filmer, *Patriarcha and other Political Works of Sir Robert Filmer,* ed. Peter Laslett (Oxford, 1949), p. 277; hereafter called Filmer.

strange I should praise his building, and yet mislike his foundation."[42]

Filmer's conservatism is traditionalist; he argues chiefly from time-hallowed precedents, mostly biblical, to support his view of a direct chain of command between God and king. His approach stands, therefore, in sharp contrast to that of Hobbes or of the rationalist who writes without special consideration for revealed truths. Filmer's justification for absolute monarchy can be summed up in this way: whether a king be a lawful, hereditary ruler, a usurper, or a conqueror, once he has acquired dominion he represents the paternal and kingly authority of God on earth; the king's commands are therefore binding in conscience unless they conflict with an explicit divine law, in which case the subject ought to accept punishment rather than violate either the divine law or the civil law.

Filmer's insistence that both the hereditary king and the usurper can represent the paternal authority of God may well have influenced Dryden's political thought. Certainly, Dryden's support of Cromwell as a divine instrument in restoring England's peace is not so hard to reconcile with his view of Charles as a king sent by providence to open up a new millennium if we consider that, according to Filmer, both Cromwell and Charles may have had divine sanction:

> many times by the act either of a usurper himself, or those that set him up, the true heir of a crown is dispossessed, God using the ministry of the wickedest men for the removing and setting up of Kings: in such cases the subjects' obedience to the fatherly power must go along and wait upon God's providence, who only hath right to give and take away kingdoms.[43]

42. Filmer, *Observations Concerning the Originall of Government* (1652), p. 239.
43. Filmer, *Anarchy*, p. 284.

This passive view of history as expressive of the will of God resembles that which underlies the heroic plays of Dryden. The heroes and heroines are always waiting for deliverance from tyranny by means of the just and divinely ordained sequence of historical events. In *Astraea Redux,* too, General Monck does not attempt to replace Charles on his throne by open force; he makes use, rather, of "wise delay."[44] Cromwell, in the *Heroique Stanzas,* does not seize power during the Civil War, for he "fought to end our fighting"; instead, the rule of England is conferred upon him by heaven: "And yet *Dominion* was not his Designe,/We owe that blessing not to him but Heaven."

Because the overthrow of a hereditary king only occurs, in Filmer's view, "by the permission of God," the subject has no right to rebel and withhold his obedience from the usurper: "The first usurper hath the best title, being, as was said, in possession by the permission of God; and where a usurper hath continued so long, that the knowledge of the right heir be lost by all the subjects, in such a case a usurper in possession is to be taken and reputed by such subjects for the true heir, and is to be obeyed by them as their Father."[45] Locke's reductio ad absurdum of Filmer's *Patriarcha* ought not to blind us to the fact that primogeniture is not the only basis for belief in a king's divine right. Although God may designate some kings through an unbroken descent of heirs, Filmer reasons, yet he may sometimes raise a usurper and his posterity to a crown. The subject can never have "an infallible certitude, but only a moral knowledge" of who the rightful king is, such moral knowledge being grounded on "peaceable possession" of the crown.[46] Thus, the subject, for ethical and religious rea-

44. *Works,* California edition, *1*, ll. 151–52, p. 26.

45. Filmer, *Observations upon Aristotles Politiques Touching Forms of Government Together with Directions for Obedience to Governours in dangerous and doubtfull times* (1652), p. 232.

46. Ibid.

sons, should not disrupt the status quo, even if he doubts his king's hereditary right to the crown.

Where Hobbes would argue that a usurper or conqueror must be obeyed because the people he governs have entered, for reasons of practical necessity, into a contract with each other, Filmer contends that heaven has placed this usurper on the throne and that the subjects are bound by their sense of duty, of moral obligation, to obey him. Dryden would concede, as is clear from the heroic plays, that a subject ought to obey the reigning monarch, no matter how he came to the crown. He points out, however, that this obedience can be based on gratitude for benefits conferred. In *Tyrannic Love,* Berenice thinks that Porphyrius is "bound in trust" to the usurper Maximin because he received both his office and his arms from him:

> 'Tis virtue not to be obliged at all;
> Or to conspire our benefactor's fall.[47]

Similarly in the *Heroique Stanzas,* Dryden evinced his gratitude and that of the English people for the benefits conferred by Cromwell: "Peace was the Prize of all his toyles and care." Domestic peace and foreign conquests ("He made us *Freemen* of the *Continent"*) were gifts that England took from the hand of Cromwell and that necessarily bound England to him.

The chief tie between king and subject, in Dryden's view, is a natural and moral one, that of gratitude. In the *Leviathan,* Hobbes indeed mentions gratitude as the fourth of the natural laws, but he does not give it the emphasis that Dryden does. The latter's view that a subject binds himself by accepting benefits from his ruler is demonstrated in *The Conquest of Granada.* The Moorish king Boabdelin has accepted financial and military benefits from Ferdinand, benefits which were conferred upon him as a vassal. Yet he refuses to consider himself bound to the Christian king. The argument between the Duke

47. *Tyrannic Love,* ed. Scott-Saintsbury, II. i., p. 399.

of Arcos and Boabdelin in Act I centers on this problem. Ferdinand had conquered Boabdelin in battle and had made him his vassal; even if this oath of vassalage, made under duress, cannot be considered valid, still Boabdelin's subsequent acceptance of benefits conferred by Ferdinand on the assumption that it was valid made the oath binding:

> *Boabdelin.* The force used on me made that
>   contract void.
> *Duke of Arcos.* Why have you then its benefits enjoyed?
> By it you had not only freedom then,
> But, since, had aid of money and of men;
> And, when Granada for your uncle held,
> You were by us restored, and he expelled.[48]

Boabdelin owes allegiance to Ferdinand for much the same reason that Porphyrius owes obedience to Maximin in *Tyrannic Love,* and England owes its loyalty to Cromwell in *Heroique Stanzas.*

In his *Panegyrick* on the coronation of Charles II, Dryden echoes Filmer's *Patriarcha* by tracing the origin of the monarchy to the patriarchs of ancient times, saying of Charles that, by his mild, forgiving temper, he brings together "Imperial pow'r" and "paternal sway."[49] This view of Charles as father of his people is carried further in *Annus Mirabilis,* when Charles is represented distributing bread to the citizens of fire-ravaged London:

> The Father of the people open'd wide
>   His stores, and all the poor with plenty fed:
> Thus God's Anointed God's own place suppli'd,
>   And fill'd the empty with his daily bread.[50]

Here Dryden's idea of a king as one who takes God's place in

48. *The Conquest,* ed. Saintsbury, Pt. I, I. i., p. 28.
49. *To His Sacred Majesty, A Panegyrick on His Coronation,* in *Works,* California edition, *1,* l. 96, p. 35.
50. *Works,* California edition, *1,* st. 286, ll. 1141–44, p. 102.

conferring benefits on his people finds expression. Like Filmer, Dryden considers the subject's obligation to be moral and natural, a return of gratitude such as a child would give to its parent.

In the heroic plays, moreover, the king-subject relationship often overlaps that of parent-child, so that the king's "paternal sway" is a constant issue. Rebellion is doubly heinous when it is a familial as well as a political transgression. Aureng-Zebe best sums up Dryden's view of rebellion when he rejects Solyman's offer of "twenty thousand hands" to redress the wrongs done to him by his father and emperor:

> I own no wrongs: some grievance I confess;
> But kings, like gods, at their own time redress.
> Yet some becoming boldness I may use;
> I've well deserved, nor will he now refuse.[51]

The "becoming boldness" which Aureng-Zebe permits himself is a humble petition that the Emperor give him his due, "as your general, and your son." When the Emperor rejects this petition and pursues Aureng-Zebe's ruin, Dianet, another courtier, offers troops which would rise to rebellion under Aureng-Zebe's leadership. The Prince foregoes this second chance at rebellion, saying that he "neither would usurp, nor tamely die."[52]

Although Dryden condemns rebellion as strongly as Hobbes and Filmer, he seems to have reacted against these two conservatives on the issue of a limited monarchy. Hobbes claims that "to divide the power of a commonwealth" is "to dissolve it," and explains that if the king's power is limited, then it "is not superior to him, or them that have the power to limit it," hence the sovereignty lies in the assembly that limits him.[53] In the *Anarchy,* Filmer asserts likewise that when "the law

---

51. *Aureng-Zebe,* ed. Saintsbury, II. i., p. 290.
52. Ibid., p. 303.
53. Hobbes, II. xxix., p. 213; I. xix., p. 126.

must rule and govern the monarch, and not the monarch the law, he hath at the most but a gubernative or executive power."[54] Such gubernative power, Filmer argues, would undermine the entire theory of divine right, which is based on the king's personal responsibility to God: "It is not the law that is the *minister of God,* or that *carries the sword,* but the ruler or magistrate."[55]

Hobbes' argument that whoever has the right to limit the monarch has, in fact, the sovereign power seems ratiocinative in comparison to Filmer's argument from tradition and from fear of chaos. Whereas Hobbes can envision a shift of sovereign power, Filmer can only contemplate its disintegration:

> So in all popularities, where a general council, or great assembly of the people meet, they find it impossible to dispatch any great action, either with expedition or secrecy, if a public free debate be admitted; and therefore are constrained to epitomize and sub-epitomize themselves so long, till at last they crumble away into the atoms of monarchy, which is the next degree to anarchy; for anarchy is nothing else but a broken monarchy, where every man is his own monarch, or governor.[56]

Since the monarch is God's representative, in Filmer's view, his power cannot be subdivided without being cancelled.

Like Hobbes and Filmer, Dryden sees a lawless state of nature lying just below the surface of society and, like them also, he sees the majority of men as basically untractable, always on the brink of rebellion. On the other hand, he considers absolute monarchy somewhat dangerous too, suggesting throughout his heroic drama that it is the excess of power in a monarch and the abuse of that power which lead to dissension in the state.

54. Filmer, *Anarchy,* p. 282.
55. Filmer, ch. xxiii, p. 101.
56. Filmer, *Observations upon Aristotles Politiques,* pp. 223–24.

The question of whether or not a monarchy should be limited is posed frequently in the heroic plays. Boabdelin in *The Conquest* and Maximin in *Tyrannic Love* make similar complaints about the balance of power; they bemoan the fact that their respective parliaments will not grant them monies readily and wish to deprive the country of a victory abroad just to limit the monarch's power at home. This situation is, of course, somewhat reminiscent of the complaints of Charles I against Parliament in connection with his Scottish Wars.

Boabdelin reasons that since the senate's "thrift has ruined [him] in war" he ought to have arbitrary rule:

> Power has no balance, one side still weighs down,
> And either hoists the commonwealth or crown;
> And those, who think to set the scale more right,
> By various turnings but disturb the weight.[57]

Boabdelin has acted arbitrarily in dismissing Almanzor after the latter had led the army in a major battle; the resulting popular upheaval and eventual recall of Almanzor illustrate the impractical nature of such arbitrary rule. Boabdelin loses face when he is forced to bow to the mob's will: "In tumults people reign," he wails, "and kings obey."[58] From having wielded power in excess, Boabdelin is reduced to acknowledging his impotence.

Like Boabdelin, Maximin finds his senate reluctant to finance a war, the success of which might make him "absolute." These legislators, the Emperor laments, are interested only in securing "propriety and peace," that is, they think more of the economic standing of their country than of its power and glory abroad. Maximin concludes that there is no middle ground between a government by the people and a monarchy; like Filmer, he says that either the senate is "a name" or else the monarch is a mere "pageant prince." For Maximin, as well as

57. *The Conquest*, ed. Saintsbury, Pt. II, I. ii., p. 90.
58. Ibid., p. 91.

for Hobbes and Filmer, a division of power is impossible. The
question of expediency is a major one for Maximin; just as
Filmer thought that a popular assembly could not "dispatch
any great action, either with expedition or secrecy," so Maximin thinks that "Two equal powers two different ways will
draw,/While each may check, and give the other law."[59] Dryden's play *Tyrannic Love* shows, on the contrary, that it is
Maximin's arbitrary rule that is inexpedient and ineffective.
His tyranny alienates all his well-wishers, drives his only child
to suicide, and brings about his assassination by Placidius.

Dryden shows a direct correlation, then, between a king's
lack of regard for the rights of his subjects and the political
anarchy and rebellion which conservatives deplore. He suggests that it is the responsibility of the king to rule by law
rather than by arbitrary command. He seems, however, to
leave the power to check and punish the despotic king in the
hands of God rather than in the hands of the subjects; in this
he resembles Filmer. In *Annus Mirabilis,* the King's prayer
during the fire of London expresses Dryden's view of heavenly
intervention in history:

> O pass not, Lord, an absolute decree,
>   Or bind thy sentence unconditional:
> But in thy sentence our remorce foresee,
>   And, in that foresight, this thy doom recall.
>
> Thy threatenings, Lord, as thine, thou maist revoke:
>   But, if immutable and fix'd they stand,
> Continue still thy self to give the stroke,
>   And let not foreign foes oppress thy Land.[60]

In the heroic plays, heaven punishes the tyrant through the
power-seekers, those who rebel against him for their own private gain but who in fact gain nothing. Filmer may well have

59. *Tyrannic Love,* eds. Scott-Saintsbury, I. i., p. 386.
60. *Works,* California edition, *1,* sts. 269–70, ll. 1073–80, p. 100.

been the authority for this view of heaven's role in history, for he asserts that God makes use of lawless men to remove bad kings: "Yet the ministry of men who execute God's judgments without commission is sinful and damnable. God doth but use and turn men's unrighteous acts to the performance of His righteous decrees."[61]

The only monarchs who are normative in the heroic plays are Ferdinand and Isabella in *The Conquest,* and it is instructive that they refer to good government as "freedom." Ferdinand wants to free Granada from the "long yoke of Moorish tyrants," and Isabella wants that country to "shake off its double bands:/At once to freedom and true faith restored."[62] Nor do they simply invade Granada; rather they send the Duke of Arcos to plead Ferdinand's "just and rightful claim" on the basis of a contract between himself and Boabdelin. That the Moorish king has broken faith with Ferdinand is probably evinced by the actual turn of events; Ferdinand does not even need to conquer Granada, for it disintegrates from within and is finally betrayed by some of its own inhabitants. The lesson for monarchs, therefore, appears to be that if they will have a long and profitable reign they had better govern under law and not infringe on the rights of their subjects. In his poem "To by Honour'd Kinsman," Dryden describes the Prince and Parliament as the "Barriers of the State on either Hand:/May neither overflow, for then they drown the Land."[63] Nothing in the heroic plays contradicts this later statement which clearly supports a limited monarchy.

Although at the surface Dryden, the political theorist, seems to resemble Hobbes when he places dispassionate, ratiocinative arguments in the mouths of his characters, he is essentially closer to Filmer. Recognizably Hobbesian views are uttered by tyrants and rebels in these plays, but the design of each supports

61. Filmer, ch. vi, p. 62.
62. *The Conquest,* ed. Saintsbury, Pt. II, I. i., p. 85.
63. *The Poems and Fables,* ed. Kinsley, ll. 176–77, p. 610.

Filmer's idea of history. What Dryden uses as a measuring rod of right government is historical precedent, not rationalistic argument. He takes a particular segment of history and makes it an example of a universal law. Each heroic play treats of the internal dissension and the abuse of power that precede the fall of a mighty nation. The scenes of argumentation reveal political and moral views that subsequently result in actions affecting the public welfare, so they are instructive not merely as debates but as sources of the following acts of rebellion or usurpation.

In his narrative poems, Dryden often takes an event that is still newsworthy and raises it to a universal plane by a series of allusions to historical precedents. For example, he speaks in the same breadth of Typhoeus, Otho, David, and Adam in *Astraea Redux*, a poem concerning Charles II. Dryden tends to spatialize time, to blur the difference between one century and another and to emphasize the similarity between cycles of change. He contrives a web of historical allusions to take the gloss off the new occurrence by placing it on a par with more remote events, thus providing the reader with something of the perspective he needs in order to view the contemporary scene calmly. Similarly, in the heroic plays, Dryden takes moments of great historical change which suggest parallels with the contemporary scene. Characters in Roman, Aztec and Moorish courts display much the same political views as those which prevail in Restoration England. *Aureng-Zebe* alone is set in the seventeenth century, but the story occurs in India and thus has the same advantage of distance in terms of space which the historical events of the other plays possess in terms of time. *Aureng-Zebe* is particularly relevant to the reign of the aging, childless Charles II since it deals with the disharmony created within the Indian state over the problem of succession.

Whereas Filmer argues from historical precedent by citing chiefly biblical sources, Dryden regards all of recorded history as being to some extent authoritative. Hence, in his early narrative poems, *Annus Mirabilis* and *Astraea Redux*, he draws from classical history, mythology, Christian European history, and contemporary history, while reserving a considerable space for biblical sources; two of the climaxes in *Annus Mirabilis* are extended allusions to Scripture; the first is the comparison of the war to Creation in stanza 140 to suggest that this struggle is necessary in the making of a better world, and the second is the comparison of London, reborn after the fire and welcoming merchants from abroad, to the Messiah receiving gifts from the Magi. Such allusions, which underlie most of Dryden's mature poetry as well as his early poems, suggest that Dryden sought the measuring rod of truth not in his own mind but in a synthesis of man's recorded historical experience.

Although Dryden resembles Filmer in arguing from historical precedents rather than from abstract propositions, they differ in their attitudes toward the contemporary scene. Filmer resembles the boy who held his finger in the dyke, so clearly does he see his country on the verge of anarchy; Dryden, on the other hand, is the soul of optimism whenever he looks at the scene about him in these early years. The reason for his hopefulness, in part, is that at this time he looks forward to a new golden age. In his early poetry, Dryden suggests that history is moving in a linear way from the Fall to the Redemption, and from there to a millennium which is about to begin: "And now times whiter Series is begun/Which in soft Centuries shall smoothly run."[64] He does not see his own day as a chaotic one, and he interprets England's new economic position in Europe as a key to a new world, a new brotherhood, where commerce will be a means of supplying all with necessities rather than the means of enriching a few. The curious mixture of the pragmatic and the ideal in these early works is epitomized in his apostrophe to the Royal Society in *Annus Mirabilis;* Dryden admires these learned men not only for penetrating to the

64. *Astraea Redux, Works,* California edition, *1,* ll. 292–93, p. 30.

"Law,/And rule of being in your Makers mind," but also for
drawing from it ideas "To fit the levell'd use of humane kind."

DRYDEN AND THE RIGHTS OF CONSCIENCE

Dryden's conservatism can be clearly distinguished from
that of Hobbes and Filmer in the matter of the rights of conscience. Dryden considers the inner convictions of a subject
beyond the reach of civil power, and particular scenes from
The Indian Emperour and *Tyrannic Love* have been cited
above as illustrating his distaste for forcible conversions and
persecutions. In *The Hind and the Panther*, Dryden makes a
plea for freedom of conscience which is substantially like his
earlier stance in the heroic plays. He argues that the "laws of
nations and of nature too" require that the mind of a subject,
as opposed to his actions, should be beyond the reach of the
state:

> Of all the tyrannies on humane kind
> The worst is that which persecutes the mind.
> Let us but weigh at what offence we strike,
> 'Tis but because we cannot think alike.[65]

In "To my Honour'd Kinsman," Dryden gives as an example
of a patriot the grandsire of his kinsman, who refused to lend
Charles I money "against his Laws" and was committed to a
dungeon for retaining his "Birthright Liberty."[66]

Even if Dryden frequently champions the rights of conscience, he stops far short of Milton in suggesting remedies for
an invasion of these rights by a tyrant. Armed resistance is out
of the question. Montezuma, in *The Indian Queen*, leads a
rebellion in defense of his rights: "Yet I attempted not to
climb your throne/And raise myself, but level you and me."[67]

65. *The Hind and the Panther*, Pt. I, ll. 239–44.
66. *The Poems and Fables*, ed. Kinsley, ll. 191–93, p. 610.
67. *The Indian Queen*, in *Works*, California edition, *8*, ed. John Harrington
Smith, Dougald MacMillan, and Vinton A. Dearing, (1962), II. i., ll. 35–36,
p. 194.

He overthrows one tyrant, the king of the Incas, but only gives more power to another and worse tyrant. Likewise, Almanzor overthrows Boabdelin because this king treats him unjustly, but the successor to Boabdelin behaves even more unjustly, so that the first king is brought back to the throne. It is ironic that Almanzor has been toppling thrones in order to preserve his honor and sense of dignity, yet he is regarded with contempt by the cynical Zegry leaders in Granada:

> *Abdalla.* Would he [Almanzor] were ours!—
> I'll try to gild the injustice of his cause,
> And court his valour with a vast applause.

> *Zulema.* The bold are but the instruments o' the wise;
> They undertake the dangers we advise:
> And, while our fabric with their pains we raise,
> We take the profit, and pay them with praise.[68]

Dryden thus demonstrates repeatedly that an armed uprising against a monarch for the sake of basic liberties is inexpedient; such a use of force results in a change of tyrants but not in reform. Rebellion in the hands of Almanzor or Montezuma is a great natural disaster. It is significant that these turbulent characters are often compared to such cataclysms in nature as tempests and storms at sea.

The alternative to armed rebellion is passive resistance, which Dryden approves in supporting the rights of conscience against the king. Several of the characters who are normative in the heroic plays choose prison or exile rather than obey a law which is contrary to the dictates of their conscience. Benzayda, in *The Conquest of Granada,* cannot carry out her father's order to kill Ozmyn as a "just revenge" for her brother's death:

> When parents their commands unjustly lay,
> Children are privileged to disobey;

68. *The Conquest,* ed. Saintsbury, Pt. I, II. i., pp. 36–37.

> Yet from that breach of duty I am clear,
> Since I submit the penalty to bear
> To die, or kill you, is the alternative;
> Rather than take your life, I will not live.[69]

Each heroic play contains a similar variation on the theme of passive resistance. Porphyrius, Guyomar, Aureng-Zebe, all normative characters in their respective plays, refuse to comply with a civil or parental authority; all of them, moreover, are willing to submit to imprisonment or death, or else to go into exile for the sake of their private sense of right.

Dryden's antipathy to the use of force against established authority is undoubtedly part of the general reaction to the Civil War but it is also connected to his strong historical bent. The institution of monarchy is sacrosanct simply because it has proved workable in history. Whatever has become customary over the centuries must be natural to man, whereas the innovation of the present decade may be a fashion to be cast off in the next. In *Religio Laici* he extends this attitude into the realm of theology and warns the doubtful Christian not to create public discord in airing his theories:

> In doubtfull questions 'tis the safest way
> To learn what unsuspected Ancients say:
> For 'tis not likely *we* should higher Soar
> In search of Heav'n, than *all the Church before:*
> Nor can we be deceiv'd, unless we see
> The *Scripture,* and the *Fathers disagree.*[70]

What Dryden champions is a negative sort of freedom of conscience: he exhorts the individual to follow his inner light but not to impose it upon the external order of things. The private and public spheres, he thinks, ought to be kept separate for the sake of both individual happiness and public harmony.

69. *The Conquest of Granada,* ed. Saintsbury, Pt. I, IV. ii., p. 62.
70. *Religio Laici,* in *The Poems and Fables,* ll. 435–40, p. 293.

3

A Reading of the Heroic Plays

Critics often regard Dryden, John A. Winterbottom remarks, "not as an independent thinker but as a mirror of his time."[1] One detects a vague dislike among some of these critics for the man Dryden, whose reserve and aloofness seem to have made him enemies in every age, but especially in his own. As he himself notes, "More libels have been written against me than almost any man now living; and I had reason on my side to have defended my own innocence. . . . [But I] have suffered in silence, and possessed my soul in quiet."[2] One wonders if this proud reticence on the part of Dryden, his unwillingness to reveal his private thoughts or feelings, may not have alienated those who, in the eighteenth or nineteenth centuries, might have judged him with more kindliness. Fellow artists, however, have been more generous in their evaluations of Dryden, the man and the writer—Congreve, Pope, Samuel Johnson, and Sir Walter Scott being the most eminent of these.

Sir Walter Scott argues that not only did Dryden maintain a "decided and acknowledged superiority over all the poets of his age," but that he "alternately influenced and stooped to the national taste of the day."[3] Dryden's values, then, were not

---

1. "The Place of Hobbesian Ideas," p. 665.

2. *A Discourse Concerning the Original and Progress of Satire* (1693), Watson, 2, 126. Bernard N. Schilling, in *Dryden and the Conservative Myth* (New Haven, 1961), notes that Dryden had a "certain reserve and modesty that disdained to come out of itself just to satisfy others." He points out that it is "easy to misunderstand and so dislike a man who does not explain himself, who except as a professional writer kept to himself, minded his own affairs and seemed self-sufficient" (pp. 83–84).

3. *The Life,* p. 1.

only shaped by the Restoration, but they helped to shape that era. His five heroic plays cover approximately ten of the formative years of his genius, and a close look at these works will reveal, to use Scott's expression, Dryden's "better judgment" at work improving "that of his readers."[4]

Those critics who emphasize the surface of the heroic plays at the expense of the design, or the wit at the expense of the judgment, have assumed that Dryden meant to amuse rather than improve his public. D. W. Jefferson, for example, asserts that Dryden uses the "heroic melodrama as a playground for his powers of wit and rhetoric," and so he concludes that the plays have little moral substance.[5] Such an opinion cannot be held if the design of the plays is duly examined. There is clearly a connection between the scenes of argumentation in which he exposes the several sides of political and philosophical issues and the action in Dryden's heroic drama. The usurpations, assassinations, rebellions and suicides are not the result of momentary impulses but are the logical outcome of attitudes concerning man's responsibility within the state set forth in previous scenes of discourse. It is in the acting out of the Hobbesian and other views that moral judgment on the part of the author is demonstrated. The characters who are extreme—those who break all laws, those who break positive civil law for the sake of natural rights, or those who break natural law for the sake of civil order—tend to rely on physical might and to exaggerate their capacity to control events and other men. Eventually, as a result of their excessive ac-

4. Ibid., p. 2.

5. "The Significance of Dryden's Heroic Plays," *Proceedings of the Leeds Philosophical and Literary Society*, 5 (1940), 125, 137; reprinted in *Restoration Drama: Modern Essays in Criticism*, ed. John Loftis (Oxford, 1966), pp. 161–79. At the other extreme, Bruce King, in "Dryden, Tillotson, and *Tyrannic Love*," regards Dryden's heroic drama as entirely homiletic. Dryden's plays, he argues, are "most intelligible as illustrations of how man lives by his passions when not under the spiritual influence of Christianity," and Dryden's characters are "examples of fallen mankind, living by desire and appetite" (p. 375). But Dryden is surely more concerned with political than with theological issues in his drama.

tivity, they create a trap in which they will be caught. The normative characters, on the other hand, practice spiritual rather than physical fortitude. They win out because of their quiescence and endurance.

It is the contention of this study, despite Moody Prior's argument to the contrary in *The Language of Tragedy*,[6] that a gradual deepening of thought occurs between *The Indian Queen* and *Aureng-Zebe*. Toward the end of his career as a heroic dramatist, Dryden is far more interested in private moral problems and seems to skirt the broader political and historical issues. *Aureng-Zebe* has therefore a homiletic quality in comparison with *The Indian Emperour,* which is a play about intolerance, political expansionism, and the decay of an empire.

A recent critic has remarked that *The Indian Emperour* concerns "idealized primitives" who come face to face with "Spanish atrocity." He assumes that Dryden is simply following the well-worn tradition of the noble savage in dramatizing the ideas of *Les Canibales*.[7] In fact, there is a careful balance between lawless Indians and lawless Christians, for Dryden wants to show that human nature is much the same everywhere. The unscrupulous Indians include the Taxallans, Orbellan, Almeria, and Odmar, while their Spanish counterparts include Pizarro, Vasquez, and the Priest. The play cannot be reduced to a mere statement of primitivism. The Indian empire is on the brink of decline, and it takes only a handful of Christians to topple it. If Dryden had wanted to show the nobility of the Indians, he would hardly have made them bring about their own ruin. First, the base Taxallans help the handful of Spaniards attack Montezuma and, later, Odmar frees the Spanish prisoners and betrays his people. If the design of the play is correctly observed, Dryden may be said to attack the

---

6. *The Language of Tragedy* (New York, 1947), p. 174.

7. John Loftis, Commentary to *The Indian Emperour,* in *Works,* California edition, *9,* p. 315.

whole notion of primitivism in this play, and to show a complex mixture of good and bad in every culture.

The exciting and somewhat baffling complexity of *The Indian Emperour* stands in sharp contrast to the simplicity of *Aureng-Zebe*. In the latter play the virtuous central character is tested three times: first, he must overcome the natural impulse to succor Indamora when she is imprisoned at the command of his father, the Emperor; secondly, he must give up his worldly ambitions when his father asks him to choose between the throne and Indamora, threatening disgrace if he chooses his betrothed; finally, he must willingly face death when Nourmahal, his stepmother, asks him to choose between death and incest. Aureng-Zebe's choices move from the natural plane to an almost supernatural one. When Nourmahal comes before him with her offer of incestuous love, she is closer to absolute evil than any previous character in the heroic plays. The reformation of Arimant and of Morat also lends a somewhat homiletic aspect to this play. *Aureng-Zebe* reveals Dryden's deepening concern with basic moral choices as opposed to larger historical issues.

The theme of the geographical expansion of Christianity constitutes the larger pattern of the middle three heroic plays. In *The Indian Emperour* we witness the collapse of an Indian empire which is torn by dissension and betrayed from within. In *Tyrannic Love* we see the deterioration of heathen Rome in the persons of Maximin and Placidius, who destroy each other and make way for the Christians. In *The Conquest of Granada* we observe the fall of the Moorish empire which is also (like the Mexican kingdom) delivered to the Christians by native traitors. Christianity, then, is shown to expand not simply by conquest or by force of civil authority; its enemies seem rather to bring about their own defeat. The victory belongs to the force that shapes history rather than to the strength of Christians; as the earth-spirit tells Montezuma: "A God more strong, who all our Gods commands,/Drives us to exile from our native lands."

Christianity is brought face to face with another religion as a result of New World explorations in *The Indian Emperour,* of Maximin's persecution of what he considers a dangerous minority in *Tyrannic Love,* and of the drive for the reunification of Spain in *The Conquest.* The divergent religions are thus brought together in a political situation, so that the relationship between religion and the state, as well as that between private conscience and civil law, can be examined. Several debates between Montezuma and the Spaniards, Porphyrius and the Emperor Maximin, the Zegrys and the Abenccrrages concern religious freedom. Montezuma argues in favor of such freedom in the first play and is supported by Cortez. These two achieve a moment of brotherhood in Act V, when Cortez learns that the Indian King is being tormented for his religious beliefs and, having freed him from the rack, kneels to beg his forgiveness for Spanish crimes. Montezuma in turn asks forgiveness of Cortez for having ill repaid a personal debt of gratitude to the Spanish leader:

> You have forgot that I your Death design'd
> To satisfie the Proud *Almeria's* mind:
> You, who preserv'd my Life, I doom'd to Dye.[8]

In *Tyrannic Love* the theme of freedom of conscience presents a different aspect. This time it is not a heathen religion that ought to be tolerated by Christians, but the Christian religion that requires such freedom. Porphyrius tries to make Maximin understand the necessity with which conscience binds a man. Later, when Catharine has chosen to be a martyr, a new aspect of conscience is brought forward; Catharine resists the logic and practical arguments of Berenice and the authority of her mother Felicia because she feels bound in conscience to be a martyr.

In *The Conquest* the problem of intolerance recurs between the factions of the Zegrys and Abencerrages. The latter faction is partly Christian in blood and in behavior, though loyal to

8. Ibid., V. ii., ll. 141–43, p. 103.

the Muslim king. We learn in the first act that because of their "mongrel race," the Abencerrages are particularly hated by the Zegrys. The highly intolerant Zegrys are, ironically, those who betray Granada and fight on the Christian side for hope of reward. Ozmyn, the Abencerrage warrior, gives one of the most striking examples of tolerance in all the heroic plays when he accompanies his prospective father-in-law in battle, insisting that he will hold a shield before the old Zegry and help save his life even though he disapproves of his fighting on the Christian side. Ozmyn's speech on this occasion is one of Dryden's most moving pleas for liberty of conscience:

> Goodness and virtue all your actions guide;
> You only err in choosing of your side.
> That party I, with honour, cannot take;
> But can much less the care of you forsake:
> I must not draw my sword against my prince,
> But yet may hold a shield in your defence.[9]

The entire Abencerrage faction represents, in a sense, an appeal for toleration, since they are partly Christian and therefore not quite of the prince's religion, yet they are politically loyal to the end.

In the second part of *The Conquest* as well as in *Aureng-Zebe,* Dryden appears to be more interested in the private, moral dilemmas of the individual than in the public or political dilemmas. The reconciliation of Ozmyn and Benzayda with their two fathers and the temptation to adultery faced by Almanzor and Almahide are situations which are of a private, moral nature, and not essential to the larger political-philosophical design of the play. In *Aureng-Zebe,* for the first time, Dryden does not present us with two great warring camps—Incas against Aztecs, Christians against Non-Christians, Abencerrages against Zegrys. The rebellion and strife occur within the family of the Emperor of India. Family rela-

9. *The Conquest,* ed. Saintsbury, Pt. II, II. i., p. 100.

tionships rather than public or political allegiances bind most of the characters, so that the focus of the play is on the immediate moral choices of the characters rather than on the historical and social consequences of those choices. These characters are therefore more rounded than their predecessors, as a close reading of the works will demonstrate. The design of *Aureng-Zebe*, however, still resembles those of the earlier heroic plays because it shows a society moving from a state of lawless nature to a rule of law. When the play opens all the sons of the Emperor are vying for the succession to the crown except Prince Aureng-Zebe, who refrains from violence even though he knows that Indian law commands his death should Darah, his elder brother, mount the throne. Aureng-Zebe inherits the crown of India at the end of the play because of his enduring loyalty; like Job he appears to have been put to the test by providence and found worthy of greater rewards than he would otherwise have gained.

In all of Dryden's heroic plays, the central agent seems to be fate, providence or heaven, to which nearly all the characters refer in their conversation. But what indicates the importance of an unseen, shaping force behind the events of these plays is the fact that none of the heroes accomplish much that is productive. We are faced with the novel situation of having heroes who, as J. W. Tupper notes (with evident annoyance), appear "to do much, but who, when the work of bringing about a happy issue is analyzed, [do] not accomplish much."[10] The would-be heroes, on the other hand, seek their selfish goals with violence and cunning, and yet act in the end against their own interests, even to the point of ensuring the success of

10. "The Relation of the Heroic Play to the Romances of Beaumont and Fletcher," *PMLA, 20* (1905), 605. Michael W. Alssid also notes that the hero is peculiarly inactive in heroic drama. He remarks, concerning *Aureng-Zebe*, that "Morat serves, paradoxically, as an agent of destiny whose evil powers have greater power to prevent the evil machinations of the Emperor than all of Aureng-Zebe's fruitless displays of virtue" ("The Design of Dryden's *Aureng-Zebe*," *JEGP, 64* [1965], 465).

the quiescent characters. Dryden creates one paradox after another: his heroes are close to victory when they are willingly imprisoned or bound in chains for the sake of conscience, whereas the would-be heroes are closest to their undoing when they have shaken off all laws as shackles and seem to be acting with the freedom of gods.

Eugene M. Waith has suggested in his instructive study, *The Herculean Hero,* that Dryden's Almanzor and other heroes who act impulsively belong to the Herculean tradition. He points out that the traditional portrayal of Hercules in drama makes him an exemplar of spiritual endurance as well as of physical fortitude.[11] In Dryden's version of the Herculean hero, it is precisely the suffering Hercules who is emphasized; the heroes Almanzor, Montezuma, and Morat seem less than admirable when they are acting tempestuously and shaking kingdoms by their physical valor, but when they undergo tests of spiritual endurance they emerge as men of "infinite heroic potential."[12] By means of this paradox, Dryden implies that a great part of virtue lies in realizing the limits of free will and in resigning to providence the task of establishing a just order.

Dryden's heroic plays, in the final analysis, are not simply melodramatic plots yoked with scenes of witty argumentation, but plays of ideas in which discourse and action stand in an almost mathematical relationship It may be that the design is too exact, but it is surely not wanting. Those critics who have failed to see any underlying structure in these works have usually stressed the love story out of all proportion to its significance. Love in heroic drama is not, as Lewis N. Chase supposes, a passion that "nullifies all other ideas in the lover, and makes him its absolute slave,"[13] but is, rather, the occasion

---

11. Waith, *The Herculean Hero,* pp. 14–15.

12. Ibid.

13. Lewis Nathaniel Chase, *The English Heroic Play* (New York, 1965; first published, 1903), p. 117.

whereby a slavish or noble disposition will reveal itself. Love does not change the characters but is the catalyst which brings their essential natures to the surface. Placidius, in *Tyrannic Love,* describes this effect of love:

> Love various minds does variously inspire:
> He stirs, in gentle natures, gentle fire,
> Like that of incense on the altars laid;
> But raging flames tempestuous souls invade;
> A fire, which every windy passion blows;
> With pride it mounts, and with revenge it glows.[14]

Although Abdalla and Abdelmelech are inspired with love for the same woman in *The Conquest,* their passion is manifested in entirely different ways: Abdalla serves his mistress without regard for right and wrong and even usurps his brother's throne for her, whereas Abdelmelech will not let his love blind him to familial and civil obligations.

Love is only one of several passions that force the characters to unmask their true natures. Ambition, revenge, envy, and pride are just as important in bringing about choices with grave political consequences. Those characters who bring the passion of love under the surveillance of reason in the heroic plays are able to control the impulse to revenge or ambition. The dramatist does not so much distinguish between noble and terrestrial love, or between love and honor, as between heroes and would-be heroes. Heroes are capable of meeting their obligations toward their king, their friends and their consciences, but the latter throw their obligations to the wind and follow the path of self-gratification, first feeding their pride with schemes of rebellion and usurpation but soon satisfying their baser and more urgent instincts. In pursuing the objects of their lust, the would-be heroes abandon the prudence and cunning that characterized their more ambitious moments, and so they bring themselves to harm.

14. *Tyrannic Love,* ed. Scott-Saintsbury, II., ii., p. 407.

The Indian Queen

Dryden wrote *The Indian Queen* in collaboration with Sir Robert Howard, and it is still a matter of controversy whether it can, with certainty, be called the first of his heroic plays. The California edition of Dryden gives an adequate summary of the external evidence relevant to this problem.[15] More significant, perhaps, is the fact that a number of themes and characters which are developed in this first play reappear in the next four works in slightly different guises. Dryden's five heroic plays may, to a casual observer, appear to be pretty much alike, and in formal procedure they are: each has a strict geometrical design—a politically and historically significant action along with a range of characters, each the exponent of a single political attitude.[16] It is in subject matter that the plays differ.

In *The Indian Queen* Zempoalla and Traxalla are at one extreme, having rebelled and together usurped a throne; at another extreme is the Inca, a loose conception of a Hobbesian ruler who thinks that his arbitrary will is law for his subjects.[17] These extreme characters regard power as quasi-divine; they make it the chief goal of their lives, and in this respect are more like each other than they are like the moderate or normative characters, whose goals are justice and

15. Notes to *The Indian Queen*, in *Works*, California edition, *8*, 283. Concerning the authorship of this play, Robert Etheridge Moore writes that "It is this denser texture that leads one to believe that *The Indian Queen*, though first published under Howard's name alone, had been rather fully reshaped by the greater poet" *(Henry Purcell*, p. 158).

16. Chase observes correctly that each character in these plays has a tendency "to become the exponent and champion of a single phase, a single idea" (p. 103).

17. Mintz gives the following aperçu of Hobbesian types in heroic drama: "In the heroic drama of the period the Hobbist was presented as a rebel, usurper, tyrant, or Machiavellian, and he expressed, either by word or deed, a point of view loosely adopted from the *Leviathan,* and largely distorted. Tyrants justified their conduct by claiming the prerogatives of a 'mortal god', Hobbes' absolute sovereign" *(The Hunting,* p. 137).

liberty. Montezuma, the impulsive hero, and Acacis, the man of precise virtue, are representative of two norms; even though Montezuma rebels against the Inca, it is not power he seeks but justice, and though Acacis respects positive commands from his monarch, he prefers to die rather than see the unjust execution of his friends.

Zempoalla is a usurper who has rejected natural and human laws for the sake of power, having deposed the lawful king, her brother, because she "scorn'd to pay/Natures mean debts, but threw those bonds away" (I.ii. 34–35).[18] Her duty to her brother would fall under natural law and her duty to her king under human or civil law, but she regards all such obligations as "bonds." She needs complete freedom of action to impose some order on an irrational universe. The gods, in her view, are not just but merely whimsical:

> —yet it does move
> My Rage and Grief, to see those Powers above
> Punish such men, as, if they be Divine,
> They know will most Adore, and least Repine.
>
> (I.ii. 4–7)

In a world governed, as she sees it, by chance, man must "by great deeds force Fate to change her mind" (I.ii. 24). Such is the advice she gives to Traxalla, the suitor who helped her usurp the Mexican throne. She argues, in Hobbesian fashion, that power is the basis of divinity and of justice:

> *Trax.* Princes are sacred.
> *Zemp.* True, whilst they are free;
> But power once lost, farewell their sanctity:
> 'Tis power to which the Gods their worship
>   owe,
> Which, uncontroul'd, makes all things just
>   below.
>
> (III.i. 157–60)

18. *Works,* California edition, *8,* 191.

In the *Leviathan*, similarly, Hobbes asserts that God reigns because of his *"irresistible power"* and is worshipped because he can reward or punish.[19] Zempoalla has become a rebel and a usurper because of her conviction that such pursuit of power brings man closer to his summum bonum.

Throughout the play her claim of power and freedom from laws is ironically undercut. In the first part she declares that she must wait for her subjects' opinion of Traxalla to change before she can marry him (I.ii. 40–45); she is thus bound to follow the public's fancy rather than her own, just as the tyrant Boabdelin in *The Conquest* must bend to the public will and recall Almanzor. She has dismissed honor as a mere "itch" (III.i. 96) and thinks she has escaped the bonds of duty, when she has actually become enslaved to immediate, practical considerations. She fears to lose her throne and for this reason sentences her royal prisoners to death: "Prudence permits not pity shou'd be shown/To those that rais'd the War to shake my Throne" (III.i. 88–89). In spite of this prudence and self-interest, Zempoalla brings on her own downfall through her passion for Montezuma. Zempoalla twice saves Montezuma from death, thereby unwittingly protecting the rightful heir to the Mexican throne. Her passion underlines the fact that she is enslaved to her own self, rather than free from all laws. When Montezuma stands before her in chains, she cries: "But is he bound ye Gods, or am I free?" (III.i. 36). Later, when Montezuma (again in chains) refuses her proffered love, she exclaims: "Slave—Slave—Am I then Captive to a slave!" (IV.i. 96).

In spite of her contempt for law, Zempoalla wears the mask of religion for a large part of the play, just as Maximin, the counterpart of Zempoalla in *Tyrannic Love,* covers his actual scorn of the gods with a show of supporting the established Roman religion. She vows to the "Great God of Vengeance" at the start of the play that she will offer up all that she wins

19. Hobbes, II. xxxi., p. 234.

as sacrifice or else die: "Make me thy off'ring if I break my Vow" (I.ii. 83). Thus, she builds a superstructure of right and wrong over her original crime against her brother and king. As the play progresses, Zempoalla deceives herself into thinking that her actions are pious; she reminds others of her "sacred" and "solemn vow" (II.ii. 23) and of her "Piety" (IV.i. 79). Her mask of piety, however, does not prevent her from revealing some contempt for divine beings. She thinks of the gods as servants who need only be paid for services rendered:

> That Prince, upon whose ruines I must rise,
> Shall be the Gods, but more my sacrifice:
> They with my slaves in Triumph shall be tyed,
> While my devotion justifies my pride;
> Those Deities in whom I place my trust,
> Shall see when they are kinde, that I am just.
>
> (II.ii.32–37)

The words "devotion" and "just" have a mercenary connotation in this speech; she is saying, in effect, that she will pay the gods a certain quantity of blood for merchandise received. During Zempoalla's visit to the conjuror, she grows so impatient at the spirits' delay that she insolently threatens to end their "Flame and Sacrifice" if they do not attend her bidding (III.ii.72–73). When they refuse to forecast her fate, she calls them tyrants and slaves in the same breath—tyrants because they "refuse to free/The Soul you gave from its perplexity," and slaves because they are bound "by harsh decrees;/And those, not you, are now the Deities" (III.ii.109–14). She then declares she will burn down the altars if the gods do not make Montezuma love her. At this point Zempoalla reveals that her "Piety" consists in making arrangements with supernatural slaves to provide for her own comfort.

Zempoalla is deceived in her notion of courage as well as of piety. When she commits suicide in the last act, she is convinced that she performs a courageous deed; ironically, only her passion for power drives her to such a desperate act. All the characters in the play have been reconciled to her, and even Montezuma says: "Live Zempoalla—free from dangers live" (V.i. 262). But the Indian Queen thinks that "All that cou'd render life desir'd is gone" and is "pleas'd to see" that her fate is left in her own hands. Her suicide is a last assertion of power:

> But I will help the Gods;
> The greatest proof of courage we can give,
> Is then to dye when we have power to live.
>
> (V.i. 295–97)

Significantly, her life was the forfeiture promised if she failed to keep her bargain with the "Great God of Vengeance." What she thinks of as a free act of courage is in fact a necessary consequence of her commitment to the pursuit of power. Although she wears a heroic mask to the end, she is actually a hero manqué: her lawless behavior has caused disorder in her family and state and has swept her off the historical scene into oblivion.

Zempoalla is the original for a series of power seekers in Dryden's heroic plays, including Maximin in *Tyrannic Love,* Lyndaraxa in *The Conquest of Granada,* and Nourmahal in *Aureng-Zebe.* If these characters are examined in sequence, it is clear that Dryden gives more and more psychological motivation for the acts of villainy that they commit. Zempoalla usurps the throne for an almost theoretical admiration for power. Her choice appears intellectual in nature. Maximin is similarly intellectual in his ambition to attain a godlike power over human wills; he is a more rounded character than Zempoalla, however, for he is an expansionist military leader, and, like Tamburlaine, a man of low origin inspired by imperial dreams. Lyndaraxa, the comparable power seeker in *The Conquest,* seems to be even more realized as a character. She acts partly out of a womanish jealousy of Almahide, to whom everyone pays court as to the future queen of Granada. Lyndaraxa's exercise of "maistrie" over her lovers Abdalla and Abdelmelech, her siren-like temptation of Almanzor, and her insistence that she taste a moment of majesty as she lies dying, all these different facets of her vanity make her credible as a power seeker, one who would break every law to achieve eminence. Nourmahal is again a better-developed character and a woman of far more intense emotions than her predecessors. Eugene Waith calls her "a grander and more terrible Lyndaraxa."[20] A vindictive, shrewish woman who in her prime has married an old man, she is unjust toward Aureng-Zebe because she wants to gain the throne for her own son Morat. She veils her ambition with "clamorous virtue" in Act II, nagging her husband about his love for Indamora and his impotence. Later, like Phaedra, she falls in love with her step-son and, ironically, the loudly virtuous shrew turns into a siren, tempting Aureng-Zebe to incestuous lust.

Like Zempoalla, the Inca prizes power too highly. He is, however, at the opposite extreme from the Indian Queen because he is a duly constituted monarch, not a usurper, and whereas she is unrestrained and would break any law to achieve her goals of power and revenge, he seeks to maintain his power simply by the exercise of arbitrary will. The Inca's dullness is thus opposed to the excessive wit of Zempoalla, just as later the dullness of Boabdelin and of the Emperor in *Aureng-Zebe* will be opposed to the uninhibited wit of Lyndaraxa and of Nourmahal, respectively.

The Inca follows the pattern of a Hobbesian monarch in that he substitutes his civil authority for moral or natural law. Although he is bound both by gratitude and by his pledged word to his mercenary general Montezuma, who had won the battle against Zempoalla, the Inca thinks he can wipe away these obligations by a simple arbitrary statement. When Montezuma asks for the hand of his daughter, the Inca refuses

20. P. 177.

him because of his unknown lineage; besides failing to keep his pledge, he behaves ungratefully by calling Montezuma's heroic deeds during the battle mere "feeble aid." Ironically, the Inca thinks of his own mind as "large" and "unconfined" early in the play (I.i.3–6), yet he despairs after his defeat by Montezuma (now in league with Zempoalla): "Death's easier than the changes I have seen,/I wou'd not live to trust the world again" (V.i.158–59). Dryden suggests through the character of the Inca that whoever thinks to find an exclusive basis for right action in the arbitrary will of the sovereign may crumble at a time of political upheaval.

The Inca is the first in a series of arbitrary rulers that includes Boabdelin in *The Conquest* and the Emperor in *Aureng-Zebe*. As Dryden develops his conception of the dull tyrant, he places more emphasis on sensuality; the tyrant would curb the pleasures of others, but cannot deny his own flesh. Boabdelin, for example, in the first part of *The Conquest,* thinks only of his forthcoming marriage with Almahide when he ought to be concerned about the Christian siege; and in the second part he gives himself up to jealousy and impotent rages even though his kingdom is visibly disintegrating. The dull tyrant in *Aureng-Zebe* is a full-blown Epicurean who thinks of his ease when the kingdom is in a state of rebellion. He gives the following advice to his son Morat:

> Believe me, son, and needless trouble spare;
> 'Tis a base world, and is not worth our care:
> The vulgar, a scarce animated clod,
> Ne'er pleased with aught above them, prince or God.
> Were I a god, the drunken globe should roll,
> The little emmets with the human soul
> Care for themselves, while at my ease I sat,
> And second causes did the work of fate;
> Or, if I would take care, that care should be
> For wit that scorned the world, and lived like me.[21]

21. *Aureng-Zebe*, ed. Saintsbury, III.i., p. 309.

The Emperor corresponds to the Inca of *The Indian Queen* in the same way Nourmahal does to Zempoalla. He is a character who has been so carefully developed that he appears drawn from life though he is as much a part of an abstract design as the Inca. In his last heroic play Dryden seems to achieve his goal of a careful balance between the appearance of "natural truth" and the reality of "ethical" ideas.[22]

Traxalla, another extreme character in *The Indian Queen,* is the first of a series of rebels who betray their monarchs for the sake of a woman. Traxalla helped Zempoalla usurp her brother's throne; his love for her is merely a changeable passion, for he falls in love with Orazia during the course of the play and is willing to break trust with Zempoalla in turn. His twisted notion of "justice" parallels the Indian Queen's false notion of "piety." He demands "justice" of Zempoalla for his services during the usurpation; she rewards him by allowing Montezuma to kill him (V.i.66–67, 208–10). Characters who correspond to the treacherous Traxalla in later plays are Odmar in *The Indian Emperour,* who betrays his own people to the Christians for the sake of Alibech and, when she rejects him, tries to rape her, and Abdalla in *The Conquest,* who usurps his brother's throne and eventually fights in the Christian camp against his brother for the sake of Lyndaraxa. Placidius, in *Tyrannic Love,* is comparable to these traitors, because he betrays and eventually assassinates Maximin for the love of Valeria. Although Arimant, in *Aureng-Zebe,* is distantly related to these weak and disloyal men, he is treated with much subtlety and he emerges as a sympathetic character. Originally a tool of the tyrannical Emperor, he begins to disregard his master's orders when he falls in love with Indamora. He does not, however, use violence against the king or join the rebellious troups; he merely circumvents certain unjust commands. With the exception of Arimant, all these men betray their trust and disrupt civil order because of an irresponsible

22. "A Defence of *An Essay,*" Watson, *1,* 120.

and emasculating passion: if they seek power it is only as a means of satisfying this passion.

Whereas Zempoalla, the Inca, and Traxalla represent extreme positions in the ethical continuum that Dryden seems to have posited, Montezuma, Acacis and Orazia take center or normative positions. These characters have an overriding concern for justice rather than for power. Acacis is, to a large extent, the antithesis to Zempoalla; like his mother he makes a vow to the gods, binding himself to commit suicide if she persists in her injustice. In contrast to her scorn of all law, he exhibits a scrupulous respect for both the laws of the state and the commands of conscience. Montezuma says of him at the start that his "Vertue is calm" (II.i.103). Acacis, however, alters during the play from a cold follower of duty to a passionate lover and friend. When the dictates of his mother and queen come into conflict with those of conscience, Acacis does not resort to violence but vows instead to commit suicide if the dilemma cannot be resolved (III.i.105–06).

After he has lost a duel with Montezuma, his rival for Orazia's love, Acacis nearly commits suicide. He is prevented from doing so by Orazia. This incident, which precedes his actual suicide by one act, may indicate that Acacis is inclined to despair and lacks the patient trust in providence which Orazia evinces; he is rather too quick to part with his life. His voluntary immolation in Act V stands in sharp contrast to his mother's death. He makes it an act of protest against his friends' plight: "I had no power in this extremity/To save your life, and less to see you dye" (V.i.174–75). In the larger design of the play, this suicide appears futile and seems chiefly the result of Acacis' pessimism, since his friends are liberated shortly thereafter.

Acacis is therefore a tragic figure, a suffering and virtuous character. He carries the burden of representing unmerited human suffering in a heroic play that, on the whole, gives us a grand and optimistic view of history. Several of the succeeding heroic plays have comparable characters: Valeria in *Tyrannic Love*, Abdelmelech in *The Conquest,* and Melesinda in *Aureng-Zebe.* A visible change occurs, though, as we move from Acacis to Melesinda. Acacis represents precise virtue as well as tragic weakness and distrust of fate. Melesinda, on the other hand, is mostly weak and dependent; she is rejected by her husband Morat, yet she follows him around asking for pity and bewailing her doom. After his death she commits suicide to rejoin her love in another world, rejecting Indamora's practical objections. Like Melesinda, Abdelmelech exhibits a sense of doom along with a great degree of weakness in love. Although he does not go so far as to betray his king in the manner of his rival Abdalla, Abdelmelech is unable to shake off the "spell" of Lyndaraxa and finally commits suicide because he has loved "too well." Valeria is a pessimistic character in *Tyrannic Love,* but chiefly because she thinks she is doomed for her father's sins and because her love is unrequited. In each successive play, then, the character who kills himself out of despair is less and less a pattern of virtue and more an exemplar of tragic weakness. Such a character must resolve his problem immediately because he cannot patiently suffer in the hope that providence will bring about a change of events.

The character of Acacis is the fountainhead for two different streams of characters in Dryden's heroic drama. While his sense of doom gives rise to the group of characters just mentioned, his precise virtue develops into such patterns of virtuous behavior as Guyomar in *The Indian Emperour,* Catharine in *Tyrannic Love,* Ozmyn in *The Conquest,* and Aureng-Zebe in the play of that name. All these normative characters are needed as foils to the fiery, individualistic heroes—Montezuma, Cortez, Porphyrius, and Almanzor. The contrast between correct virtue and passionate virtue which occurs in every pair of heroes is a variation on the dichotomy between judgment and wit. Acacis and his precisely virtuous descendants in heroic drama are models of restraint and judgment, but Montezuma and his descendants are models of noble passion and wit. In the fully three-dimensional character Aureng-Zebe, the two come together to a large extent, though there is a continual struggle between his passionate and obedient sides:

> Strong virtue, like strong nature, struggles still;
> Exerts itself, and then throws off the ill.
> I to a son's and lover's praise aspire,
> And must fulfill the parts which both require.[23]

Montezuma and Acacis seem to exchange virtues during *The Indian Queen,* just as other pairs of heroes do in Dryden's later heroic plays. Acacis takes on some of Montezuma's fire while Montezuma improves in calm virtue. Eugene M. Waith asserts that Almanzor's and, by extension, Montezuma's "flame" is "analogous to the true spark of wit, which is opposed to dullness, the enemy of all that is great."[24] It would be going too far, however, to speak of Acacis and Ozmyn as representing dullness; they exemplify, to be sure, the somewhat laborious art, the exact judgment in matters of ethics that Ben Jonson and Horace exemplify in matters of literary creation, but they are a far cry from dullness. Just as Dryden always sets up dual norms in criticism, balancing the wit of Shakespeare and Homer against the more precise art of Jonson and Virgil, balancing Juvenal and Horace, Spenser and Milton, so he sets up a pair of male heroes to exemplify the two forces by which a man achieves greatness within society—an inner spark of good, of native nobility, and a respect for laws promulgated by kings and parents.

Montezuma, the passionate hero, is aptly portrayed by means of sea and tempest imagery in *The Indian Queen,* which suggests, as we have seen, that such a hero is a great natural force rather than a member of society. Thomas H. Fujimura explains that Montezuma has learned the noble passions of love

---

23. *Aureng-Zebe,* ed. Saintsbury, I.i., p. 289.
24. P. 164.

and honor apart from society,[25] and J. Winterbottom speaks of such a hero as a "social iconoclast" who must become the "embodiment of a social ideal."[26] Although Montezuma turns against the king he has served, he rebels because of the king's injustice rather than to gain power. He soon realizes that his actions have simply hoisted Zempoalla to a new position of power, and that she is a far worse tyrant than the Inca. By freeing himself from his obligations to the Inca (however unjust the latter has been), Montezuma has simply enslaved himself to the forces of revenge and endangered the life of his beloved Orazia. Zempoalla, seeing the enemy general arrive in her camp, exclaims: "Great God of Vengeance—/ I see thou dost begin to hear me now" (I.ii.81–82). Montezuma is, despite his individualism and apparent freedom, part of a scheme devised by higher powers.

When Montezuma realizes his mistake, he tells Orazia that he will "redeem" himself (II.i.49), as if his power in the universe were so great that he could topple a kingdom one day and restore it the next. When he is imprisoned and prevented from exercising his might against what he considers unjust, Montezuma imagines there is no more order in the universe. It is ironic that he resembles Zempoalla in the following passage, wondering as she does if the universe is governed by chance:

> Can there be Gods to see, and suffer this?
> Or does mankinde make his own fate or bliss;
> While every good and bad happens by chance,
> Not from their orders, but their ignorance?
> (II.iii.48–51)

In spite of this moment of despair, Montezuma learns, with Orazia's encouragement, to suffer patiently and await some deliverance by time. He begins to control his own passions

25. "The Appeal," p. 44.
26. "The Development," p. 161.

instead of the world outside him; he achieves mastery over those natural impulses which have led him to revenge as well as to courage. In chains, he exercises free choice, turning down the Queen's offers—as Aureng-Zebe does Nourmahal's— and choosing to return to prison when momentarily freed from bondage:

> No more, proud heart, thy useless courage boast!—
> Courage, thou curse of the unfortunate,
> That canst encounter, not resist, ill fate!—
> (IV.ii.86–88)

Montezuma learns, while he is in prison, the value of suffering in patience under tyranny rather than trying to set the kingdom to rights by rebellion. Dryden suggests here, as Sir Robert Filmer had done in his political writings, that the most virtuous ought to await deliverance at the hands of providence, for guilt is incurred in rebellion.

Almanzor, the central character of *The Conquest,* is a greatly enlarged Montezuma. Sir Walter Scott, noting the resemblance between these two characters, writes that "it must be allowed, there is a striking resemblance between these two outrageous heroes who carry conquest to any side they choose, and are restrained by no human consideration, excepting the tears or commands of their mistress."[27] Almanzor and Montezuma can hardly be called "outrageous heroes" if we consider that they are virtually in bondage for the greatest part of the plays; they contribute very little, as J. W. Tupper notes, to the outcome or denouement.[28] Montezuma is like Prometheus bound. Nor do these heroes obey the commands of their mistresses, but rather open their eyes to the nobler ideals which these put before them. When Almanzor tempts Almahide to adultery and reminds her of his past services, she teaches him

27. P. 70.
28. P. 605.

to seek a virtue above reward. His relationship to Almahide is not one of subservience like that of Abdalla to Lyndaraxa.

Other characters in Dryden's heroic drama related to Montezuma are Cortez in *The Indian Emperour* and Porphyrius in *Tyrannic Love*. Cortez is a man of great natural impulse who nearly gives up the war with the Indians for the sake of Cydaria, Montezuma's daughter; he is prevented from becoming a rebel by Orbellan's breaking of the truce and leading the Indians to attack. Like Montezuma in *The Indian Queen,* Cortez chafes at injustice, and he rails at the inquisitorial tactics of his Spanish colleagues in the last part of the play. Porphyrius, too, in *Tyrannic Love,* is that character of fire and tempestuous emotion who represents the individualistic half of the ideal hero (Catharine represents exact virtue). He is always ready to lead a rebellion against Maximin, it seems, on account of the latter's tyranny over Christians, and, in particular, over the Empress Berenice, a new convert. All these individualistic heroes spend the greatest part of the plays learning the value of restraint and moderation; they become more and more like the representatives of exact virtue.

Orazia represents a sensible, attainable virtue in *The Indian Queen,* and is the first of a line of sensible heroines—Cydaria in *The Indian Emperour,* Berenice in *Tyrannic Love,* Almahide in *The Conquest,* and Indamora in *Aureng-Zebe.* All these women have an unshakeable optimism and patience in misfortune, trusting that a better turn of events will come. Orazia stops her father and Acacis from going to "meet Death"; she seems willing to suffer death only when someone else inflicts it. She is loyal to her father and to Montezuma; she sacrifices neither filial piety nor her love but simply waits patiently until a reconciliation of the two individuals occurs. Her jealousy, which leads her to prefer Montezuma dead rather than unfaithful to her in life, is an indication of how she has not stifled passion for the sake of virtue.

Just as Orazia acknowledges her human frailty and continues to hope for change, however bleak her circumstances, so the heroines in Dryden's later heroic plays seem to follow a moderate path, accepting their human frailty rather than aiming for angelic heights. Kathleen Lynch points out that Dryden's heroes are "excellent Platonic philosophers on occasion," but often "chafe under the restraints of servitude"; she adds that his "heroines are better Platonists, yet they make concessions in love which will not bear the closest Platonic scrutiny."[29] The sensible, enterprising heroines of Dryden's plays are certainly far removed from the cold and unbending ladies of early sonneteers. Berenice and Almahide are both married, for example, yet they listen to the passionate declarations of their lovers and both confess their own love; they are compassionate mistresses—Almahide refuses Almanzor's advances gently, saying "think that I deny myself, not you," and Berenice reveals in an aside that "Love blinds my virtue:—If I longer stay/ It will grow dark, and I shall lose my way." Indamora, the wittiest of these heroines, even flirts with the husband of Melesinda in order to lengthen the life of Aureng-Zebe by a little span, and she is coy with her aged admirer Arimant in order to use him as a messenger. The change from Orazia to Indamora is again toward a rounded, three-dimensional character; Orazia is solemn compared to the ingenious Indamora.

The Indian Queen seems to contain most of the characters and themes that are developed more elaborately in the next four heroic plays. This play constitutes an important statement on the Restoration, in spite of the fact that Dryden employs heroic conventions at the surface. The basic problems which had affected England during the past twenty years are here: Zempoalla's usurpation, her war against her brother and king, would certainly remind Dryden's upper-class audiences of the recent Civil War. The Interregnum in Mexico during which Zempoalla reigned and the heir Montezuma was raised in

29. "Conventions of Platonic Drama in the Heroic Plays of Orrery and Dryden," *PMLA 44* (1929), 470.

the Peruvian court would bring to mind Cromwell's protectorate and Charles' stay in France. Finally, the Restoration of Charles II by peaceful rather than military means would seem echoed in Montezuma's bloodless Restoration in Act V. Moreover, Montezuma's granting amnesty and liberty to Zempoalla parallels Charles' Declaration at Breda in which he granted a large measure of liberty to the Puritans.

In addition to these overall historical parallels, one may find a resemblance between the various attitudes toward man and the state espoused by the characters in *The Indian Queen* and those held in England in the seventeenth century. Zempoalla represents Hobbes' idea of man in the state of nature, a power-hungry, leveling type of character who recognizes no authority over man except that deriving from power; her servant Traxalla would probably represent the worst of those who rebelled against Charles I, while her son Acacis would represent a younger generation that grew up during the Interregnum and therefore would be torn between its obligations to the new and to the old regime. The Inca, a dull tyrant who thinks his arbitrary command is the highest law, would be a Hobbesian king, the opposite extreme to Zempoalla. In the Inca, as in the later tyrants Boabdelin and the Emperor of *Aureng-Zebe,* one can recognize the worst traits of the first two Stuarts and also of Louis XIV; these kings are legally instituted yet they go too far and raise the ire of their noble courtiers by placing their arbitrary will above other laws (such as the laws of gratitude and of friendship, part of the natural law). Montezuma represents a mean between these extremes, reconciling natural and civil law; he rebels against the Inca because the latter had committed an injustice against him and had justified it on the ground that he, the king, is author of law; yet Montezuma comes to realize that he cannot serve moral or natural law entirely apart from civil law (his rebellion becomes a pursuit of *revenge* when he sides with Zempoalla). Montezuma's realization that he must shun violence and strive to reconcile his vision of natural law—his private moral impulse—with civil authority makes him the norm in *The Indian Queen*. His subsequent endurance in chains redeems him and makes him fit to mount the throne of Mexico.

In suggesting a few parallels between the events of Dryden's first heroic play and contemporary British history, I would not imply that Dryden is creating historical allegory. It would be futile to look for one-to-one relationships: Dryden, like Alexandre Dumas, is merely using history as a nail on which to hang his picture of life. It is a pattern of history, a process, a formula for change, that one finds in the heroic plays, not a specific historical situation. Dryden makes a universal statement about rebellions, usurpations, and restorations. By his very choice of the heroic mode, he has taken a detached stance, an eighth-sphere point of view on political situations.

Essentially, Dryden takes cognizance of two types of rebellion in the heroic plays, and these may reflect two aspects of the rebellion against Charles I in England. First, there is the rebellion of the hero—Montezuma, Almanzor, or Porphyrius—against the king because of certain injustices committed; although this kind of rebellion is usually abortive, the tyrant who commits injustices and raises the ire of his noble courtier is to blame as much as the courtier himself. A second type of rebellion is that of the power seeker—Zempoalla, Lyndaraxa, Maximin, and, to some extent, Morat—against the king; this rebel attacks the kingship, the legally constituted authority, rather than a particular unjust king, and the rebellion is followed by his usurpation and tyrannical rule. Eventually, the power seeker is consigned to oblivion; he suffers a violent death because he lived by the sword. In each play, writes Allardyce Nicoll, "it is only the evil and weaker characters" whom Dryden dispatches.[30] These heroic plays show that the tyranny of a king is a direct cause of anarchy in the state, and that rebellion on the part of either a well-meaning hero or a power seeker

30. *A History*, *1*, 111.

feeds the flames. Only the citizen who respects both the moral and the civil law can bring constructive, orderly change to the historical scene. Dryden's plays imply a definite direction to historical change; heavenly justice working in history seems to be guiding mankind toward a millennium, a just and redeemed world. What earlier Christian writers might have described as the progress of the striving individual soul, Dryden applies to the social sphere, charting the pilgrimage of mankind to the new Jerusalem.

The Indian Emperour

In *The Indian Emperour* Dryen deals with the Spanish Conquest of the New World—an extremely difficult subject which would seem impossible to reconcile with Dryden's optimistic, millennial view of history. He manages, however, to uncover some justice in this event by stressing the disintegration of the Indian society rather than the military strength and artful stratagems of the Spanish. He makes the Indians' defeat the result of their own actions: the Taxallan Indians ally themselves with the foreigners; the Indian Orbellan attacks the Spanish after Cortez has agreed to stop the war; Montezuma's desire for complete revenge makes him delay the execution of the Spanish officers who are his prisoners and makes him forget the prophecy about his one "day of power"; and finally, Odmar, Montezuma's son, frees the Spanish officers and helps them defeat his own countrymen. If the design of *The Indian Emperour* is seen this way, it becomes clear that Dryden is writing a play about the disintegration of the Mexican state rather than about the Spanish Conquest. Similarly *The Conquest of Granada* is a play about the internal dissensions within Granada that bring about its eventual betrayal and downfall, rather than one about Ferdinand's military conquest of Granada. Dryden suggests that providence, the shaping force in history, does not make use of armies or military strength as its primary instrument in creating a vast historical change;

rather it employs secret passions of revenge, ambition, and lust, and works through these to undermine a kingdom, paving the way for a simple takeover by an aggressor.

One indication of how complex this play really is can be found in the representations of virtue: Cortez, the Spanish leader, represents the kind of virtue that is natural and impulsive, while Guyomar, the Indian warrior, represents a virtue comprised of self-restraint and obedience to externally imposed laws. The two heroes tend to come together during the play, just as Acacis and Montezuma do in *The Indian Queen* and Ozmyn and Almanzor do in *The Conquest;* Guyomar becomes more passionate and Cortez more restrained. Dryden seems to foil our expectations purposely by showing his Indian hero, not as a noble savage, an impulsively moral primitive, but as a very civilized man who needs a bit more impulsiveness to be heroic, while showing the opposite in the Spanish hero. Thus the primitivistic clichés such as those found in Aphra Behn's *Oroonoko* are sharply undercut.[31] Only by isolating Montezuma and the evil Spaniards Pizarro and Vasquez from the rest of the characters is it possible to argue that Dryden is contrasting noble savagery with corrupt civilization. If one keeps the entire cast of characters in view, the Indians do not appear idealized.

In two cases the primitivist point of view is defeated during the course of the play. When Cortez arrives in Mexico he argues against Vasquez' notion that Indians are "untaught" and "salvage" and points out that "their Customs are by Nature wrought,/ But we, by Art, unteach what Nature taught" (I.i. 13–14). A short acquaintance with the Taxallan Indians, however, soon wrenches this cry from Cortez: "Where, banish'd Vertue, wilt thou shew thy face/ If treachery infects thy *Indian* race! (I.ll. 214–15). The treachery of these Indians is but a preface to the worse behavior of Orbellan and Odmar, not to mention Almeria. Cortez, who begins by thinking that all In-

31. Loftis, Commentary to *The Indian Emperour.*

dians are in a primitive, unfallen state, obedient to nature's law, is soon undeceived by some of them. A second reference to the primitivist point of view occurs during a discussion on love between Cortez and Cydaria. The Indian princess imagines that there is a difference in kind between Spanish lovers and Indian lovers: "Here Love is Nature, but with you 'tis Art" (II.iii. 68). Cortez soon enlightens her by telling her that love is as natural in Spain as in Mexico, but it is only "fetter'd up with customs more severe" in order to protect the women from fickle lovers. But even though Cydaria is spontaneous in declaring her love, not all Indians are so: Alibech refuses to declare her preference for Guyomar and tells him and Odmar that she will decide according to their services:

> For to my self I owe this due regard
> Not to make love my gift, but my reward,
> Time best will show whose services will last.
> (I.ii. 159–61)

She is as fettered by custom as any Spanish lady.

In the debates between Montezuma and the avaricious Spaniards Vasquez and Pizarro, a certain natural nobility is contrasted with hypocrisy. In the scene also, where Pizarro and a Christian priest torture Montezuma because he prefers "carnal reason" to the "Un-erring Head" of the Pope, Dryden indicates to what depth of sophisticated evil Christians may fall when they mask their avarice with religion. But these two portions of the play should not be overemphasized as they have recently been; they should be kept in proper relation to the whole. Just as there are treacherous Indians who deliver the Mexican kingdom to the Spaniards, so there are evil Spaniards who are bringing ruin on their own country. Their injustices against the Indian king and others will not go unpunished, Cortez warns, after releasing Montezuma from the rack and kneeling before that king in tears:

Cort. If this go free, farewel that discipline
Which did in Spanish Camps severely shine:
Accursed Gold, 'tis thou has caus'd these crimes;
And into *Spain* wilt fatally be brought,
Since with the price of Blood thou here are bought.

(V.ii. 132–37)

Thus, Cortez prophesies that some disaster will come to Spain if the "Accursed Gold" that was the "price of Blood" is brought there and the evildoers go unpunished. Perhaps Dryden is alluding to the subsequent decline of Spain's international power, and tracing that decline to those injustices perpetrated in the New World.

It is worth noting that Cortez has substantially altered by the end of the play from his ebullience in the first scene of Act I, where he states that wealth belongs to the "bravest Nation" or Spain, which comes "boldly" to the New World with "four hundred foot and forty horse." The Spanish do not, however, "boldly" attack the Indians and conquer, since the Indians are betrayed by other Indians. Instead of courage, most of Cortez' officers exhibit greed and sensuality. Cortez realizes during the course of the play not only that Indians may be treacherous but that his Spanish soldiers are capable of even more heinous deeds—and in the name of religion. Cortez is a normative Christian and as such condemns other Christians—particularly churchmen—who seek only power and wealth and will not stop at religious persecution to attain their goal.

Although the Indian state virtually falls into the lap of the Spaniards in this play, the event can also be seen as a personal success for the hero Cortez, whose moral superiority is acknowledged by the Indians, and as a victory for the Christian God over those heathen deities who have kept a "long possession" of the earth "far from Heaven" (II.i.29–30). The superiority of Cortez can be seen in his prevention of the massacre of the helpless Indians in Act I, his giving the same instead of harsher terms of peace after an Indian defeat, his freeing of the prisoner Guyomar (Montezuma's son), his agreement to stop the war for Cydaria's sake (though he is prevented by the Indian Orbellan), and—in spite of Montezuma's attempt on his life in Act III, scene iv—his saving the Indian king from the rack in the last act. In all his actions, then, Cortez has joined, to use Cydaria's phrase, a "will confin'd" with "boundless power," and thus deserves victory:

> *Cyd.* Heaven has of right all Victory design'd,
> Where boundless power dwells in a will confin'd;
> Your *Spanish* Honour does the World excel.
>
> (II.iii.63–65)

A larger divine plan for the expansion of Christianity is suggested in the second act, in which Montezuma visits an Indian priest and hears an "Earthy Spirit" prophesy. The spirit announces that the "powers below" are fleeing before the Christian God: "A God more strong, who all the gods commands,/ Drives us to exile from our Native Lands." The Spanish are called a "Nation loving Gold" by the same spirit; these must rule the land unless Montezuma destroys his enemies in the one day of power that will be granted him. It is another spirit (Kalib) that tells the King about this day of power and warns him that it will "never come again" if he lets it pass. That day comes in Act III, scene iv, but Montezuma lets it go for the sake of a more complete revenge:

> In that small time [two days], I shall the Conquest gain
> Of these few Sparks of Vertue which remain:
> Then all who shall my head-long passion see,
> Shall curse my Crimes, and yet shall pity me.
>
> (III.iv.129–32)

Montezuma thus disregards the prophecy and brings on his own disaster through his "head-long passion" for blood. His desire for revenge has been implanted in him chiefly by his imperious mistress Almeria, Zempoalla's daughter. The Spaniards are comparatively harmless (except in the torture chamber) measured against these self-destructive Indians.

Like Montezuma and Acacis in *The Indian Queen,* both Cortez and Guyomar represent norms in the play: they are respectively the passionate and the correct hero. Cortez puts love before his obligation to his king in Act II, when he accedes to Cydaria's plan to end the hostilities. Like Antony, he feels some shame but argues thus: "Men can but say Love did his reason blind,/ And Love's the noblest frailty of the mind" (II.ii.70–71). Cortez errs on the side of passion at the start, but he later attains proper balance of external and internal obligations, civil law and natural bonds. He does not let love blind his reason when he lets his would-be assassin Orbellan return to the Indian camp (III.iii), even though the latter means to wed Cydaria.

Like Acacis, Guyomar is at first a model of calm and exact virtue. He shows his "piety" by saving his father's life in preference to that of his mistress when both are in danger. When Cortez takes him prisoner and frees him in Act II, scene iii, Guyomar calls the Spanish leader "Brother" and promises to try to win the king's consent to the terms of peace, particularly since Cortez has not altered them after the recent Indian defeat. Guyomar fails to negotiate a peace, but he repays his debt to Cortez by saving him from assassination by Orbellan (III.ii) and by protecting him from immediate death when Cortez is his prisoner (III.iv). In the latter scene, Guyomar, like Acacis, passionately offers to die for his friend and stands between Montezuma's sword and Cortez: "You see I Live but to dispute your will;/ Kill me, and then you may my Pris'ner Kill" (III.iv.105–06). Thus, Guyomar disobeys his father and king for the sake of his commitment to Cortez; though his disobedience is nonviolent, it is a great departure from the "exact virtue" he displays in Act II, scene iii, where he follows Aeneas-like "piety."

Although John A. Winterbottom asserts that Guyomar is the norm in *The Indian Emperour*,[32] it is more likely that Cortez and Guyomar are two different halves of the hero at the start of the play. As we observe them developing toward wholeness—Cortez by controlling his passion, Guyomar by learning to display it—we find them sharing a common political philosophy. The Indian warrior argues that kings should not be judged by subjects, especially by "Those who to Empire by dark path aspire," and who "plead a call to what they most desire" (IV.ii.78–79). Cortez, in like manner, explains that "Monarchs may err, but should each private breast/ Judge their ill Acts, they would dispute their best" (II.ii.30–31). Although in Act II Cortez disobeys his king temporarily by calling off the war and Guyomar resists his father and king to save Cortez' life, both are loyal subjects to the end. They fight neither for gain nor power, but take their reward on trust from fate. Guyomar, in rejecting Alibech's unwittingly treasonable plot in Act IV, tells her that he will be true to his principles "And leave my Fortune to the gods and you"; and Cortez, in setting free his rival Orbellan, cries, "To Arms, to Arms, Fate shows my Love the way." Neither of them would, finally, win his mistress by any dishonorable deed.

Odmar, unlike Cortez and Guyomar, wants the reward of Alibech's love without effort or merit. In the first part of the play, he claims her as his birthright. Later, he is willing to betray his father and king if only Alibech will reward his "Successless Courage." Odmar accepts with alacrity the treasonable scheme which Guyomar rejects in Act IV. Like Abdalla in *The Conquest*, he obeys his mistress as if he had no will of his own:

> *Odm.* To save our Lives our Freedom I betray—
> —Yet since I promis'd it I will obey;

---

32. "The Place of Hobbesian Ideas, p. 669.

> I'le not my Shame nor your Commands dispute:
> You shall behold you Empire's absolute.
>
> (IV.iii.132–35)

Odmar, however, perpetuates this treachery not for love's sake but for revenge. Guyomar wins a victory over the Spanish in the same scene, and Montezuma gives him the hand of Alibech. The envious Odmar now claims that conscience is the "foolish pride of doing well," and he determines to pursue revenge: "Sink Empire, Father Perish, Brother Fall,/ Revenge does more than recompence you all" (IV.iii.61–62).

That Odmar's love for Alibech is merely lust is evident by the fact that he attempts to rape her when she scorns him upon his arrival with the victorious Spaniards. Just as Traxalla clamors for "justice" from Zempoalla at the end of *The Indian Queen* and is rewarded with death, so Odmar falls to talking about justice when he is prevented by Vasquez from harming Alibech: "Thus Lawless Might does Justice overthrow." Vasquez rightly reproves him as a traitor and kills him in combat. Odmar is a hero manqué in this play; he paints all his actions in glowing colors, and it is only toward the end of the play that his baseness is actually revealed. Even at his death he still speaks of "justice" and "love" when he has betrayed his people and attempted to rape his brother's wife. He and Orbellan, the would-be assassin of Cortez, are the Indian counterparts of Vasquez and Pizarro.

Almeria is another extreme Indian character. Like her mother Zempoalla, she regards "Repentance" as "the Vertue of weak minds," and after her brother Orbellan's death she is obsessed with the idea of revenge. Just as her mother's love for Montezuma had saved him from death in the earlier heroic play, so now Almeria's sudden passion for Cortez makes her preserve his life. These sudden passions in the heroic plays are essentially Dryden's version of deus ex machina; the characters themselves often attribute their unrequited passion to fate.

Although John Loftis argues that the theme of Indian cruelty is not a predominant one in the play,[33] the actions of Odmar, Orbellan, and Almeria should suffice to disprove his statement. Moreover, the fact that the Taxallan Indians attempt to kill Montezuma and his courtiers in the temple is significant. The bloody sacrifice of five hundred captives has just been completed when the Taxallans attack, yet, after the skirmish, Montezuma is ready to sacrifice more slaves if Cortez so desires:

> If then thou art that cruel god, whose eyes
> Delight in Blood, and Humane Sacrifice,
> Thy dreadful Altars I with Slaves will store,
> And feed thy nostrils with hot reeking gore.
> (I.ii.236–39)

When Montezuma lets his "day of power" go by for the sake of his revenge, he promises such a conquest of the Spaniards that witnesses will curse him (III.iv.132). Dryden suggests by means of all these details that the Indians are heir to all the vices which beset the children of Adam elsewhere.

If *The Indian Emperour* opens when the Indians have just performed a bloody sacrifice, it ends when the Spaniards have tortured Montezuma on the rack. Thus, the play opens and closes with two forms of abuse in the name of religion. This last scene is more permeated with evil than the first because it is not fear of a cruel god that drives the tormentors but a love

---

33. Comparing *The Tempest* with Dryden's *The Indian Emperour*, Loftis notes that the former "reveals a searching interest in the comparative examination of natural and civilized morality—but not the interpretation of the native in terms of a rationalistic primitivism." Dryden's interpretation of the conquest, Loftis argues, follows the lines of Montaigne's essays "Of the Canibales" and "Of Coaches," where the latter gives "an idealized conception of the Indians as rational primitives, a conception of the Spaniards as cruel and bigoted, a use of the contrast between the races to emphasize at once the liabilities of civilization, and the relativity of social, moral, and even by implication religious beliefs" (Commentary to *The Indian Emperour*, pp. 308, 311).

of gold. The Christian priest reaches the height of wrath at the thought that Montezuma is hiding his gold:

> Mark how this impious Heathen justifies
> His own false gods, and our true God denies:
> How wickedly he has refus'd his wealth,
> And hid his Gold, from Christian hands, by stealth:
> Down with him, Kill him, merit Heaven thereby.
>
> (V.ii.5–9)

This motif of Christian avarice can be traced throughout the play. In the first act, Vasquez tells Montezuma that the Spanish king wants his sceptre and his "useless Gold," and Pizarro puts a religious mask on this demand by claiming papal authority. Montezuma replies that the king "poorly begs" a metal he despises and that the pope, who may give "Empires in Heaven," cannot do so on earth, for heaven "bestows the Crowns that Monarchs wear."

Cortez does not participate in the opening discussion concerning the terms of peace; he is, in fact, away courting Cydaria. Dryden thus conveniently dissociates his Spanish hero from the quest for gold. When Pizarro and the Spanish priest torture Montezuma in Act V, they are going beyond their orders, since Cortez stops them indignantly. Before dismissing the Spaniards as uniformly avaricious and hypocritical, then, we should recall the many generous actions of Cortez.

The attempted conversion of Montezuma to Christianity in Act V brings on an exciting debate between the proponent of natural reason—the Indian Emperor—and the upholders of papal authority. Although various critics have thought that Dryden evinced some anticlericalism here, it is important to note that he is simply putting forth the standard Protestant version of the power-hungry Romish clergyman. The priest is much more interested in making Montezuma crumble under his authority than in converting him. He exhorts the Indian to give up his "carnal reason" and refer himself "to our Unerring Head." He threatens him with eternal damnation instead of speaking to him of Scripture:

> *Chr. Pr.* Those Pains, O Prince, thou sufferest now
>   are light
> Compar'd to those, which when thy Soul takes flight,
> Immortal, endless, thou must then endure:
> Which Death begins, and Time can never cure.
>
> (V.ii.39–42)

Montezuma, on the other hand, pleads that there must be "One equal way to bliss" and that "all must know enough for happiness," a proposition with which Thomas Aquinas, among other Christian theologians, would agree, and a tenet which Dryden himself embraced in *Religio Laici*.[34] Finally, it is the doctrine of papal infallibility which Montezuma rejects, not Christianity:

> *Mont.* Man and not erre! what reason can you give?
> *Chr. Pr.* Renounce that carnal reason, and believe.
> *Mont.* The Light of Nature should I thus betray,
> 'Twere to wink hard that I might see the day.
>
> (V.ii.90 93)

It would be a misreading of Act V to suppose that Dryden is lining up arguments against Christianity here. One need only compare this attempted conversion of Montezuma with the conversion of Apollonius wrought by Catharine in *Tyrannic Love* to see that Dryden is satirizing the Roman Church's emphasis on authority rather than reason. Catharine does not contradict reason but enlightens it with faith, whereas the Christian Priest tries to stifle natural reason by means of fear and blind obedience, his notion of religion resembling that of

---

34. T. P. Dunning has shown that a considerable number of Christian theologians have, throughout Church history, believed in the salvation of the heathen, of the just man who has not been formally baptized; see "Langland and the Salvation of the Heathen," *MAE, 12* (1943), 45–54.

Abessa and Corceca in Spenser's *Faerie Queene*.[35] Dryden's
view is that a Christian ought to have a faith beyond but not
contradictory to natural reason, that he ought not to be simply
cowed by fear of hell or bullied by authority into sheep-like
subjection.

Since faith is a question of reason and private conscience,
the only method by which one may obtain a conversion would
be rational discourse. The theme of conversion by persuasion
seems to underlie *The Indian Emperour*. When Pizarro tells
Montezuma in Act I that the Spaniards have arrived in order
to extend religion, the king replies:

> He who Religion truely understands
> Knows its extent must be in Men, not Lands.
>
> (I.ii.297–98)

In other words, one may not convert a land by mere conquest.
Unlike Hobbes, who thinks that a will to obedience is the
underlying factor in belief, Dryden thinks it is individual persuasion or conviction.

Since the Roman Catholic faith would have been thought
by Dryden at this time to be a religion demanding from its
adherents blind subservience to authority, it is appropriate
that he should attack the Spanish priest for his use of physical
force and temporal power in extending his religion. Both Montezuma and Cortez deplore this intermixing of religion with
political and military matters. Montezuma refers to such
priests who think they are equal to, yet independent of, the
king as "Those ghostly Kings" who "would parcel out my
pow'r,/ And all the fatness of my Land devour" (I.ii.315–16).
Cortez, too, calls them "Enemies of Crowns":

> And you—
> Who sawcily, teach Monarchs to obey,
> And the wide World in narrow Cloysters sway;
> Set up by Kings as humble aids of power,

35. Spenser, *The Faerie Queene*, Book I, canto iii.

You that which bred you, Viper-like devour,
you Enemies of Crowns—
(V.ii.125–30)

A good contrast to this view of power-hungry Christian clergy
is the view we have of Catharine, in *Tyrannic Love,* effecting
numerous conversions while spurning all opportunities to regain her temporal crown and even looking forward to martyrdom. Thus, Dryden's position on Church-State relationships
seems to be that the Church ought to submit to the authority
of the sovereign in temporal matters, that it ought not to seek
wealth and political power, but that in purely spiritual matters it should be independent. This position does not essentially alter even after his conversion to the Roman Church.

Although Montezuma is the spokesman for natural reason
in the debates with the Christian Priest, Vasquez and Pizarro
in the first and last acts, he does not always act according to
reason. Dryden shows the limitations of natural religion by
making him subject to a weak passion for Almeria. This passion so undermines his concern for state affairs that he resembles the dull sensualist Boabdelin of *The Conquest.* When he
visits the Indian prophet in Act II, he is more anxious to hear
about the success of his love than of his war. Only when he is
told that Almeria will never love him and that the Indian
Queen Zempoalla will receive him in the shades below does
he show signs of despair, exclaiming that he is "weary of this
flesh." Before discovering the fate of his love he speaks with
brave resignation about the possibility of military defeat:

> *Mont.* Mourn they who think repining can remove
> The firm decrees of those who rule above;
> The brave are safe within, who still dare dye,
> When e'er I fall I'le scorn my destiny.
> Doom as they please my Empire not to stand,
> I'll grasp my Scepter with my dying hand.
> (II.i.41–46)

Nevertheless, he mourns his fate at his first military setback:

> Ill Fate for me unjustly you provide,
> Great Souls are Sparks of your own Heavenly Pride,
> That lust of power we from your god-heads have,
> You'r bound to please those Appetites you gave.
>
> (II.iii.38–41)

He cannot face life as a vassal king and commits suicide as a last act of courage and kingship. His death is not unlike Zempoalla's in the previous play, and his despair over the loss of power stands in sharp contrast to the patience he exhibited in *The Indian Queen* and to the perseverance in suffering which all the heroes of these plays display. Montezuma despairs because he confuses his own essential importance with that of his crown: "Kings and their Crowns have but one Destiny:/Power is their Life, when that expires they dye" (V.ii.226–27).

Although he is a spokesman for natural reason, then, Montezuma is not the normative character in *The Indian Emperour*. He is too weak in his love and despairing about his loss of power. On the contrary, his son Guyomar, who with Cortez is representative of the norm, does not despair after the Spanish victory but retires with his bride to the barren mountains where "The Sand no Gold, the Mine no Silver yields:/ There Love and Freedom we'l in Peace enjoy" (V.ii.371–72). Cortez has offered to share his throne with Guyomar, but, as M. W. Alssid observes, this Indian and his bride are like "the pagan spirits in the Incantation scene," in that "they relinquish Mexico to stronger gods, recognizing the inevitability of Cortez's universally significant conquest."[36]

Tyrannic Love

In *Tyrannic Love* Dryden has still another kingdom disintegrate and pass with ease into the hands of Christians. This

---

36. "The Perfect Conquest: A Study of Theme, Structure and Character in Dryden's *The Indian Emperour*," *SP, 59* (1962), 558.

time, however, the conquest is spiritual rather than military. Maximin, a champion of the old order, actually undermines what is best in the old Roman tradition: he is a usurper and a tyrant who wants to take away the last few privileges of the senate; he persecutes Christians in the name of the national religion but is himself impious and scornful of the gods. The irony which underlies the whole play is that Maximin thinks he is in control of all the Romans about him, yet he is the blind instrument by which Christianity gains a foothold in the imperial court.

Tyrannic Love has been the object of recurrent criticism on account of the "notorious rants" of Maximin, an extreme law-breaker who is presented here as the antithesis to the deposed queen, St. Catharine. Dryden himself states that the "part of *Maximin,* against which these holy critics so much declaim was designed by me to set off the character of S. Catharine."[37] The tension between these two larger-than-life characters is fundamental in the design of the play; even the normative characters, Porphyrius and Berenice, are means between these extremes. The third pair of characters—Placidius and Valeria—is in sharp contrast to the first: Valeria is a martyr to fate, a tragic figure, whereas Catharine is a martyr to faith; and Placidius is a power-seeker who helps to overthrow the old order, whereas Maximin is the overweening possessor of power.

In the portrayals of Maximin and Catharine, one finds evidence of Dryden's distinctive skill as a dramatist. Maximin, a murderer and usurper of the throne of his benefactor, tries to deprive the senate of some of its traditional powers in order to further his expansionist military designs; Catharine, on the other hand, is a dethroned monarch who refuses to receive the crown of Egypt when the Emperor offers it: "The Deity I serve, had he thought fit,/ Could have preserved my crown unconquered yet" (III.i., p. 409). Maximin sets himself up as the equal of the gods and deprives his subjects of freedom of

37. Preface, *Tyrannic Love,* Watson, *1*, 139.

conscience, hoping to make them "puppets danced upon a
wire" (IV.i., p. 430); but Catharine is happy with the "humble
quiet of possessing naught" and seeks only to move others by
calm persuasion and by example. Although Catharine is accused of frenzy—indeed all zealous Christians are accused of a
"pious madness of the mind"—she is consistently reasonable:
"Nor pride, nor frenzy, but a settled mind,/ Enlightened from
above, my way does mark" (II.iii., p. 403). Maximin, on the
contrary, sounds increasingly like a madman as the play progresses; he frenetically tries to find that "power o'er wills,
which heaven n'er found" and speaks of matching wolf to
lamb—that is, going beyond natural limits. When the two
monarchs meet face to face in Act III, Catharine comments on
Maximin's "furious anger" and "impious love" and suggests
that for all his apparent freedom he is but a slave:

> Such power in bonds true piety can have,
> That I command, and thou art but a slave.
>
> (III.i., p. 411)

Catharine and Maximin stand at opposite poles, also, on the
issue of freedom of conscience. Maximin thinks Christians are
blinded by an "execrable superstition," but he persecutes them
chiefly for reasons of statecraft. He deprives them of liberty of
conscience because he fears that an innovation in religion may
disturb the stability of the state. In Hobbesian fashion, he
thinks that a uniform public worship is essential. Maximin, in
short, is an Erastian. Because he knows his claim to the throne
is contestable, he hangs on desperately to the status quo:

> That silly crowd, by factious teachers brought
> To think that faith untrue, their youth was taught,
> Run on, in new opinions, blindly bold,
> Neglect, contemn, and then assault the old.
> The infectious madness seizes every part,
> And from the head distils upon the heart.

And first they think their prince's faith not true,
And then proceed to offer him a new;
Which if refused, all duty from them cast,
To their new faith they make new kings at last.
(II.iii., p. 402)

Paradoxically, the greatest lawbreaker in the play, the usurper Maximin, makes religious conformity the test of political loyalty. Religion, for him, is merely an extension of the state's power, rather than a set of private convictions, since he can scoff at heaven at one time and later ask the philosopher Apollonius, "Dar'st thou of any faith but of thy prince's be?" (II.iii., p. 405).

Catharine, on the contrary, makes religion a matter of private conscience. She stands in contrast, therefore, not only to Maximin but to the Christian priest in *The Indian Emperour* who tried to bully Montezuma into becoming a Christian. She converts Apollonius by convincing him that his moral precepts "but reach the actions"—have a mere external application— whereas Christian morality reaches "the mind." She shows the danger of Stoicism, in which the scorn of reward leads to a barren pride. When she describes the virtuous man, she shows him solitary and standing, like Chaucer's Troilus, on some immutable eighth sphere:

Thence you may see
Poor human kind, all dazed in open day,
Err after bliss, and blindly miss their way.
(IV.i., p. 434)

Her moral doctrine, then, is a matter of reasoning and controlling one's own passions. When a miracle occurs before her death, Catharine tells Maximin that a greater miracle is occurring within him: "A power controls thee which thou dost not see;/ And that's a miracle it works in thee" (V.i., p. 455).

In their attitudes toward external sources of law, Maximin and Catharine are also at different ends of the spectrum. Originally a Thracian shepherd, Maximin gained the crown by murdering his benefactor, Berenice's brother, and then forcing Berenice to marry him. In rebelling against the king, Maximin showed contempt for civil law, and in murdering his benefactor, he offended against natural law. Now that he is emperor he scorns the traditional form of government and wants to curb the senate. In the first scene of the play, he argues that the Roman senators are simply "not fit an empire to increase." An allusion to Brutus in one of Berenice's speeches brings a larger frame of reference to bear on Maximin's past actions. Berenice tells Porphyrius that Brutus' action may have been good on the one hand because he slew a tyrant, but on the other hand it was evil, for he slew a benefactor as well, one to whom he was bound in trust. She warns her lover not to follow Brutus and thus implicitly compares her husband to Caesar, who also undermined ancient liberties and had imperialistic designs.

Catharine, on the contrary, disregards external sources of law only to follow a higher, divine law. In spite of her compassion for the plight of Berenice, she is not moved to escape martyrdom and thus save the Empress. Berenice reasons that if Catharine flees, Maximin's passion for her will subside; she argues that if to escape were a sin, "Heaven had shut up your flight from Maximin." Catharine, recognizing a conflict of "pity" and "piety," is torn between the "private interest"— saving the life of Berenice—and the "will of heaven"—suffering martyrdom for faith. Later, she is torn between "nature" and "grace" when her mother Felicia in turn pleads with her to appease Maximin by showing some signs of relenting. Felicia argues that heaven would not have given her (Felicia) such fear, would have inspired her with "firmer thoughts" to prepare her for her own martyrdom. Catharine does not wish others to become martyrs; rather she concludes that heaven can save them without her help. She reproaches Berenice for weaving glosses on heaven's will and her mother for "shiver-

ing on the bank . . . When we should plunge into eternity."
Thus, Catharine follows her conception of a higher law beyond the laws of natural compassion and love of parent.

Like Acacis, Ozmyn, and Aureng-Zebe, all exemplary characters who go from a calm virtue to a passionate disobedience
of parent and king for the sake of conscience, Catharine rises
from a simple, rational faith to a passionate one:

> Thus with short plummets heaven's deep will we sound,
> That vast abyss where human wit is drowned!
> In our small skiff we must not launch too far;
> We here but coasters, not discoverers, are.
> Faith's necessary rules are plain and few;
> We many, and those needless, rules pursue;
> Faith from our hearts into our heads we drive,
> And make religion all contemplative.
> You on heaven's will may witty glosses feign;
> But that which I must practice here is plain,
> If the All-great decree her life to spare,
> He will the means, without my crime, prepare.
>
> (IV.i., p. 439)

Catharine's obedience to the promptings of faith rather than
reason just prior to her martyrdom is not so much a distrust of
reason as a rising beyond it to a sense of mystery, to Sir Thomas
Browne's *oh altitudo*. Earlier, in her discourse with Apollonius, she stressed calm reason: "But where our reason with
our faith does go, / We're both above enlightened, and below"
(II.iii., p. 403). Now, in the face of death, she is painfully aware
of how small human knowledge is compared to that "vast
abyss," heaven's will, and so she follows her heart.

Maximin and Catharine are extremes because both of them
move outside the sphere of civil and natural laws, Maximin
for the sake of god-like power on earth and Catharine for the
sake of an otherworldly crown. Whereas Maximin becomes
increasingly blasphemous as the play progresses, calling his

son's death "destiny's preposterous crime" and declaring that "All that was worth a prayer is gone," Catharine becomes more and more diffident about what she calls "glosses" on the divine will, such as Berenice's and her mother's. Maximin comes to think he is the "spirit of the world"; Catharine compares herself to a small skiff.

Berenice and Porphyrius stand between the extremes of Catharine and Maximin and represent a more easily attainable virtue. Porphyrius is a passionate hero who gives up a multitude of worldly advantages for love, and Berenice, in the tradition of Dryden's heroines, is an effective check on the hero's passions, constantly reminding him of his obligations. Porphyrius is not only the foremost military leader, the Emperor's favorite, and heir to the Roman empire after Charinus' death, but he is also loved by Maximin's only daughter. Like Antony, torn between empire and an apparently hopeless or profitless love, he chooses to share Berenice's exile and disgrace:

> gazing round about, I see
> Nothing but death, or glorious misery;
> Here empire stands, if I could love displace;
> There, hopeless love, with more imperial grace;
> . . . I'll turn my face to love, and there I'll fall.
>
> (III.i., p. 416)

In the second act, when Porphyrius is ready to rebel against Maximin for her sake, Berenice warns him that though he thinks heaven sends him as "its instrument":

> Heaven ne'er sent those who fight for private ends.
> We both are bound by trust, and must be true;
> I to his bed, and to his empire you.
>
> (II.i., p. 399)

Heeding her warning, Porphyrius gives back all his honors and declares himself a foe before leading an attack against Maximin. He is prevented from killing Maximin because Berenice cries out from the scaffold; she thus prevents the hero from becoming a regicide and spares Maximin's life in spite of his condemnation of her.

Porphyrius' political ideas represent the norm in this play. He upholds the senate against Maximin when he says: "Traitor's a name, which, were my arm yet free,/The Roman senate would bestow on thee" (V.i., p. 459). He also champions the cause of religious toleration in the state; in a memorable speech he suggests that religious conviction binds the believer with necessity:

> If for religion you our lives will take,
> You do not the offenders find, but make.
> All faiths are to their own believers just;
> For none believe, because they will, but must.
>
> (IV.i., p. 441)

When Maximin retorts that such freedom of conscience is a weapon in a "rebel's hand," Porphyrius points out that the monarch may set limits to the political expression of a citizen's belief: "Those who ask civil power and conscience too,/Their monarch to his own destruction woo."

Valeria and Placidius are, like Catharine and Maximin, in complete opposition to each other, and yet that opposition helps to define them as characters. Placidius is an opportunist; Valeria, Maximin's daughter by a former wife, is a tragic figure who sees herself as a "secret martyr," owning "no cause" (IV.i., p. 431). She shows no anger but only mourns her unlucky stars when Porphyrius fails to requite her love. Shortly before her suicide she declares that "there's a fate,/Which hinders me from being fortunate." She thinks it would be fruitless to appeal to the gods because her "father's crimes" are heaped on her head (V.i., p. 462). Like other star-crossed characters in the heroic plays (Acacis in *The Indian Queen*, Montezuma in *The Indian Emperour*, Abdelmelech and, to some

extent, Ozmyn and Benzayda in *The Conquest of Granada,*
and Melesinda in *Aureng-Zebe*), Valeria provides a touch of
chiaroscuro in an otherwise brilliantly lit canvas. Dryden's
optimistic vision of a gradual secular redemption of the world
seems contradicted by these fatalists. They commit suicide as
though they were offering themselves as sacrifices to hostile
supernatural forces that must be appeased. Nevertheless, the
outcome of each play suggests that they were mistaken and
that a benevolent providence guides human history. They
despair that the circumstances about them will ever improve.
Nevertheless, the outcome of each of the plays is proof that
they ought to have waited patiently for deliverance.

Placidius is a courtier whom, in his own opinion, "deep arts
of state could ne'er beguile." His shrewdness leads him in
Acts I and IV to visit the necromancer in order to act with the
greatest advantage to himself by manipulating the gods. It is
ironic that this crafty politician, who regards Christians as a
faction selling "their duty at a dearer rate" (II.iii., p. 402),
should sell himself "to ruin for a smile" and betray the trust of
his king for the sake of Valeria. The discrepancy between
Placidius' idea of himself and his true state becomes clearer as
we near the climax. Placidius will help Valeria save the life of
Porphyrius whom he knows she loves, only for a "price" or
"ransom"—her vow to be his own wife. Valeria calls him a
usurer, one who thrives on "extortion" and "mere reward"
(V.i., pp. 444–47). After using him to liberate Porphyrius, she
voids the bargain by committing suicide. Thus, Placidius has
given up his political advantages for an unrequited passion
which he himself describes in terms of a commercial transaction.

In *Tyrannic Love,* the two most worldly characters, those
who are farthest from normative Christian virtue, kill each
other. Moreover, the mutual assassination is unmotivated
by any rational consideration. Placidius has, appropriately
enough, voiced an Epicurean belief in chance as the pattern of

life; he joins religious superstition (necromancy) with the materialism of Epicurean philosophy. The gods, he argues, are indifferent to man because they wish to live in perfect quiet. Catharine reproves Placidius on this point and connects him with Lucretius:

> This doctrine well befitted him, who thought
> A casual world was from wild atoms wrought:
> But such an order in each chance we see,
> (Chained to its cause, as that to its decree,)
> That none can think a workmanship so rare
> Was built, or kept, without a workman's care.
>
> (III.i., p. 410)

Catharine rejects the notion that chance governs the world and speaks of "order," "cause," and "decree" or law with regard to the universe.

Maximin, the victim of Placidius, is Hobbesian not only in the practical aspects of his rule but in its theory. He argues that he cannot commit sin or be convicted of crime because he holds the power; power is what makes the gods divine, and it is the only source of right. A typical speech of Maximin shows the derivation of this idea from Hobbes:

> Our Gods are Gods, 'cause they have power and will;
> Who can do all things, can do nothing ill.
> Ill is rebellion 'gainst some higher power:
> The world may sin, but not its emperor.
>
> (V.i., p. 456)[38]

Maximin's need to keep everyone about him in tyrannical

---

38. Hobbes, II. xxxi., p. 234. Elsewhere, Hobbes points out that man is governed by a "perpetual fear" that "must needs have for object something." If the object is not seen, then it must be "some *power,* or agent *invisible:* in which sense perhaps it was, that some of the old poets said, that the gods were at first created by human fear" (I, xii., p. 70). Thus, Hobbes would seem to suggest what Maximin states flatly, that God reigns not so much because He is all-good but because man stands in awe of His power.

subjection is evident in his relationship to his daughter; he tells Valeria: "Children to serve their parents' int'rest live;/ Take heed what doom against yourself you give." He goes on to say that free will can exist only in the king:

> I'll find that power o'er wills, which heaven ne'er found.
> Free will's a cheat in any one but me;
> In all but kings, 'tis willing slavery;
> An unseen fate which forces the desire;
> The will of puppets danced upon a wire.
> A monarch is
> The spirit of the world in every mind;
> He may match wolves to lambs, and make it kind.
>
> (IV.i., p. 430)

Thus, Maximin places human law, the power of the king, above natural and divine laws. To a Restoration audience, he would have been understood to espouse a Hobbesian viewpoint and, to a lesser extent, the viewpoint of the divine-right apologist, Sir Robert Filmer. Filmer, after all, does not give much allowance for freedom of conscience when such freedom interferes with an explicit command of the monarch.[39]

By letting Placidius and Maximin deteriorate to the point of killing each other, Dryden passes judgment on these two attitudes toward life. The first, that chance governs life and that the gods are indifferent to man, leads Placidius to be shrewd at the start, but this superficially reasonable conduct gives way to irrational impulsiveness in a moment of real crisis. The second, that only a monarch can exercise free will and can decide between right and wrong, is disproved by Maximin's enslavement to passion and by his frenzied self-contradictions.

Parallel to the incantation scene of *The Indian Emperour* and to the visit of Zempoalla to the Indian priest in *The Indian Queen*, there is a scene of necromancy in *Tyrannic*

---

39. Filmer, *The Anarchy*, in *Patriarcha*, p. 297.

Love. Nigrinus, whose prophecy of disaster for the Emperor had been recounted in the first act, is called upon in Act IV to send a lewd dream to Catharine and tempt her to love Maximin. Like the earlier scenes of prophecy, this section is well integrated with the problem of free will versus destiny which all the characters discuss and upon which they have varied opinions. Nigrinus calls up an earth demon who is constituted "all of purest atoms of the air," and who is about to tempt Catharine with a carnal dream when an angel comes to protect her with a flaming sword. Unlike the earth demon, who takes orders from Nigrinus, this angel receives his mandate from "that great will which moves this mighty frame" (IV.i., p. 425). Nigrinus is forced to confess that "No charms prevail against the Christians' God" (IV.i., p. 427). This masque-like portrayal of the superiority of the Christian God over heathen deities corresponds to the characterization of Catharine as superior to her captors. What Dryden implies is that the virtuous Christian is impervious to subliminal demonic forces which would deprive him of his free will; only by his own choice can he commit sin. Moreover, providence keeps watch over the virtuous, and the angel armed with a flaming sword represents the supernatural aid which such a person can expect in a moment of crisis. The scene of necromancy contradicts Valeria's idea that the gods are deaf to human cries; it substantiates Catharine's claim that the world can neither have been built or continue to exist "without a workman's care" (II.i., p. 410).

The Conquest of Granada

In the ten-act play entitled *The Conquest of Granada* Dryden once more focuses his attention on the disintegration of a non-Christian kingdom and its betrayal from within. Although many of the events in the play are taken from the ninth book of Madeleine de Scudéry's *Almahide*, Dryden, in Kathleen Lynch's words, "amplifies" these events and "reshapes" them.[40] He does so to illustrate what seems to be his distinctive view of historical change: that justice is restored on earth through the instrumentality of lawless and ambitious men who act unwittingly to bring on their own destruction and the success of the virtuous.

Granada is betrayed by discontented Moors as a result of dissension and factious hatred within the state. It is therefore delivered to, not conquered by, the Christians. In the same way that Lyndaraxa delivers her country, so Odmar betrays the Indians in *The Indian Emperour* and Placidius frees Porphyrius and Berenice by assassinating Maximin in *Tyrannic Love*. Similarly, the strife between Traxalla and Zempoalla in *The Indian Queen* helps to bring about the downfall of that tyrant. What distinguishes *The Conquest* from these previous plays is that Dryden concentrates in this play on the disintegrating kingdom; all the characters of major importance in the play are Moors residing in Granada. There is no Cortez or Catharine in *The Conquest* to represent an explicitly Christian point of view. Instead of an interplay between Christians and non-Christians, Dryden creates a tension between the Abencerrages and the Zegrys, two Moorish factions, the former loyal to the Muslim state but leaning to Christianity in matters of belief and morals, and the latter disloyal to the monarch but fiercely Muslim and anti-Christian in sentiment. Paradoxically, it is the Zegrys, so violently in support of Islam, who betray the country to the Christians. The Abencerrages, for all their sympathy to Christianity, fight alongside the Muslim king until they are defeated; that king is "slain by a Zegry's hand" (Pt. II, V.ii., p. 156).

The fact that Granada is betrayed by the intolerant Zegry faction makes *The Conquest*, in its larger design, an argument for tolerance and freedom of conscience. Even though a group of citizens, like the Abencerrages, may not have the same re-

---

40. "Conventions of Platonic Drama," p. 458.

ligion as that established or espoused by the monarch, this does not mean that such a group would be politically disloyal in time of war. It is those who are intolerant and factious and ungoverned by moral considerations who may well betray the country. The Zegrys, Dryden indicates throughout the play, are power-hungry and desirous of wealth; their factious championship of Islam (one might read Puritanism) makes them hate the Abencerrages (one might read Papist sympathizers), but only to advance their own party, not to promote the common good.

Throughout the play it is clear that if the Moors were united behind Almanzor and Boabdelin, they could easily resist the Christians; similarly, if all the Indians had remained united behind Guyomar in *The Indian Emperour,* the Spaniards would have been overcome. Granada falls because the Zegrys engineer its defeat, just as Mexico falls because Odmar frees the Spanish officers and leads them to conquest. Heaven works through the treachery of Zegrys and Indians to bring "conquering crosses" into Mexico and Granada.[41]

Dryden examines the Christian title to Granada in the first act by means of a debate between the Duke of Arcos and Boabdelin. According to the Spanish Duke, the Christians have a "just and rightful claim"; the Muslims are usurpers and have been so for eight hundred years. According to the law of monarchical succession, the kingship ought to go to the "successors of Rodrique" who have always held the Asturias and Portugal and whose kingdom of Granada was lost by forcible conquest. This argument would be close to that of Sir Robert Filmer, who would argue that if the successor of the

41. The phrase "conquering crosses" is used by Almanzor at the end of *The Conquest* when he is about to lead the Christian army against the remaining Moors in Spain: "Then, wave our conquering crosses in the air,/ And cry, with shouts of triumph." This motif of "conquering crosses" pervades three of Dryden's heroic plays, *The Indian Emperour, Tyrannic Love,* and *The Conquest of Granada.*

true king were still known after this lapse of time, he would
have a claim to the throne.[42]

When Boabdelin, however, boasts that the "noblest title"
springs "from force," that brute strength "first made kings,"
the Duke of Arcos shifts his ground and argues in Hobbesian
terms, claiming that a contract exists between Boabdelin and
Ferdinand because the former has accepted military and financial aid from Ferdinand. At first Boabdelin tries to say that
the contract is null and void because he was forced to agree to
it; the Duke speaks of the contract thus:

> To gain your freedom you a contract signed,
> By which your crown you to my king resigned,
> From thenceforth as his vassal holding it,
> And paying tribute such as he thought fit;
> Contracting, when your father came to die,
> To lay aside all marks of royalty.
>
> (I.i., p. 28)

Boabdelin, it is true, was a captive at the time he agreed to the
contract. But Hobbes has pointed out in his discussion of a
contract that if one party accepts benefits from another on the
basis of a contract, then he is bound to it.[43] Dryden's theory
of government is, as was explained in the first chapter,
grounded on the idea of contractual obligation; one ought not
to rebel violently or attempt to undermine a government from
which one has received benefits. Boabdelin's acceptance of
soldiers and money from Ferdinand even during a time of civil

42. Filmer asserts that "no time bars a King," because the right to a kingdom
is one of the "gifts that have their original from God or nature and no man can
make a law of prescription against it" (*Directions for Obedience to Governours,*
p. 233).

43. In Part I, chapter xiv of the *Leviathan,* Hobbes asserts that a pact or
covenant is made when one party performs his part of a contract while the
other is trusted to do his part later. In such cases, Hobbes argues, "he that is to
perform in time to come, being trusted, his performance is called *keeping of
promise,* or faith; and the failing of performance, if it be voluntary, *violation
of faith*" (p. 87).

insurrection constitutes an acknowledgment of the binding nature of the contract between them.

The opening debate on the Christian claim to Granada indicates, then, that the Spanish Christians have a good claim both from the point of view of monarchical succession and from the Hobbesian contractual viewpoint. Boabdelin's last position is that Ferdinand may take what he can of his kingdom by force of arms. Arcos agrees, but regards this as a usurious transaction: "The estate was his; which, yet since you deny,/He's now content, in his own wrong, to buy" (I.i., p. 29). Almanzor completely misses the point and thinks that the Christians are usurious here:

> Thus, as some fawning usurer does feed,
> With present sums, the unwary unthrift's need,
> You sold your kindness at a boundless rate,
> And then o'erpaid the debt from his estate;
> Which, mouldering piecemeal, in your hands did fall
> Till now at last you came to swoop it all.
>
> (I.i., p. 28)

In Almanzor's view Ferdinand has behaved like an economic imperialist who attaches strings to his foreign aid. That Almanzor is probably rash in his judgment of Ferdinand is shown by the fact that he chooses sides with hardly a thought, at least at the start of *The Conquest*. In Act I, scene i, he decides to favor Abdalla and dethrone Boabdelin without a care for justice: "True, I would wish my friend the juster side;/ But, in the unjust, my kindness more is tried."

The theme of broken contracts pervades the entire play.[44]

44. The theme of broken contracts also pervades the *Iliad*, for a Trojan breaks the truce in Book III just as the king of Granada breaks his agreement with Ferdinand; in both cases, the broken contracts lead to hostilities. Similarly, Agamemnon breaks his agreement with Achilles over the reward just as Boabdelin and Abdalla break theirs with Almanzor. To underline this parallel between his heroic play and the *Iliad*, Dryden likens Almanzor to the "sullen Achilles" when he sits on the shore and waits for a ship to take him to Africa.

Boabdelin has not only failed to keep one contract with Ferdinand, but he fails to keep another with Almanzor when he denies him the right to free his prisoner, the Duke. Abdalla, like Boabdelin, fearing for the security of the state, breaks faith with Almanzor and deprives him of his right to free another prisoner, Almahide. Boabdelin wants the Duke of Arcos safely incarcerated and Abdalla wants to please the Zegry chieftain Zulema by giving him Almahide. Because they do not respect Almanzor's freedom of action, both of them help bring on dissension in the state and eventual disaster. Dryden suggests here, as he does in his portrayal of other arbitrary monarchs in the heroic plays, that a sovereign who cannot keep his word to his subjects brings on disaffection and rebellion, often in his noblest and most worthy leaders.

At the start of Part II of *The Conquest,* Dryden gives his audience a brief glimpse of the disintegration of Granada from the Christian viewpoint. Ferdinand remarks that "heaven and earth" are joined for the overthrowing of the "Moorish tyrants"; he asserts that "All causes seem to second our design" (Pt. II, I.i., p. 85). He describes the life cycle of empires in a memorable passage:

> When empire in its childhood first appears,
> A watchful fate o'ersees its tender years;
> Till, grown more strong, it thrusts and stretches out,
> And elbows all the kingdoms round about.
> The place thus made for its first breathing free,
> It moves again for ease and luxury;
> Till, swelling by degrees, it has possessed
> The greater space, and now crowds up the rest;
> When, from behind, there starts some petty state,
> And pushes on its now unwieldy fate;
> Then down the precipice of time it goes,
> And sinks in minutes, which in ages rose.
>
> (Pt. II, I.i., p. 85)

The disintegration of Granada is not simply the result of a Christian siege. The Moorish kingdom is ready to sink down "the precipice of time." Isabel remarks that Granada suffers under the "double bands" of religious and political tyranny; a restoration of Christian rule will restore Spain "to freedom and truth faith . . . Its old religion and its ancient lord."

The larger historical design of *The Conquest,* therefore, involves the expansion of Christianity in Europe, this time at the expense of Islam instead of heathendom. Although Ferdinand remains in the shadows in this play, he is perhaps the normative king. He is a heroic lover, releasing the prisoners Ozmyn and Benzayda at the request of Isabel, yet he is also a practical ruler who has made Boabdelin his vassal king by contract and now is willing, in response to the latter's rebellion, to make a like contract with Lyndaraxa, provided she open the gates of Granada to the Christians. Thus, Ferdinand gains the Moorish city with little bloodshed. He is a Machiavellian prince in the sense that he has virtù as well as virtue.

The strife between the Abencerrages and the Zegrys is another basic element in the design of *The Conquest.* The Zegry intolerance toward the other faction is expressed by Hamet in the first act: "Their mongrel race is mixed with Christian breed; / Hence 'tis that they those dogs in prison feed" (I.i., p. 24). Abdelmelech defends the kindness of the Abencerrages to the Christian prisoners on the basis of a law of compassion to all men, regardless of creed:

> *Abdelmelech.* Our holy prophet wills, that charity
> Should even to birds and beasts extended be:
> None knows what fate is for himself designed;
> The thought of human chance should make us kind.
>
> (I.i., p. 24)

As a consequence of their intolerance, the Zegrys are unforgiving, factious, dissembling, quarrelsome. They ambush the Abencerrages in Act I, just as the Taxallans had ambushed

Montezuma at the start of *The Indian Emperour*. Ozmyn, an Abencerrage warrior, is quick to forgive: "Though injured first, yet I will first seek peace" (I.i., p. 23). In Act II we discover that at an earlier date Tarifa, a Zegry, had attacked Ozmyn with a "steel-pointed dart" during a tourney with "blunt" canes. When Ozmyn killed Tarifa in self-defense, he began a worse feud between the two houses, a feud which is only enhanced by the difference of religious belief. The Zegrys care nothing for reason, but exhibit a predatory nature; they argue that "Reason's a staff for age, when nature's gone" (II.i., p. 35). Zulema sums up the opportunistic point of view of his clan when he tells Abdalla to seize the crown:

> Man makes his fate according to his mind,
> The weak low spirit fortune makes her slave;
> But she's a drudge when hectored by the brave:
> If fate weaves common thread, he'll change the doom,
> And with new purple spread a nobler loom.
>
> (II.i., p. 36)

In spite of this predatory inclination, the Zegry faction dissembles in the second act, hiding its revengeful purpose under the mask of friendship for the Abencerrages. After the betrothal of Abdelmelech, an Abencerrage chieftain, to Lyndaraxa, a Zegry, Abdalla announces: "The two fierce factions will no longer jar,/ Since they have now been brothers in the war" (II.i., p. 30). Immediately thereafter, the Zegrys convince Abdalla that he must usurp the throne and further their plans.

The strife between the factions is one of the chief reasons why Granada cannot mount an effective defense against the Christians. Almanzor warns Boabdelin to unite his subjects and "pour their common rage upon the foe," and Boabdelin himself says that "this intestine strife" takes one more prop from "our weak foundations." Yet the factions continue to grow farther apart until the Zegrys are fighting with the Christians against the Abencerrages and Boabdelin. Party loyalty thus replaces loyalty to the king among the Zegrys. Even so, the contrast between the two parties is not black and white; one of the exemplars of virtue is a Zegry—Benzayda—and two Abencerrage leaders are far from faultless—Abenamar and Abdelmelech.

Although the factions are never reconciled politically, they are brought together on the individual level. The lovers Ozmyn and Benzayda must first go into exile because of the feud between their families, but they are later reconciled to both their fathers. Ozmyn shows remarkable tolerance by carrying a shield in defense of Selin, the father of Benzayda and a Zegry who had formerly condemned him to death and who is now fighting on the Christian side. Ozmyn will not carry a sword or join Selin's "party," and he even declares that Selin errs in choosing his side. Nevertheless, his anxiety for the personal safety of Benzayda's father leads him to accompany the old leader on the battlefield. Ozmyn gives an example of tolerance by valuing individual relationships as highly as his political allegiance, and yet keeping the two obligations distinct.

The two normative characters in *The Conquest* are Ozmyn and Almanzor, the correct hero and the passionate hero, respectively. The contrast between the two appears in the opening description of a bullfight: Ozmyn kills the bull precisely according to the rules, but Almanzor breaks every rule because the bull and the situation are exceptional. Ozmyn bows to each lady, his "well-taught courser" kneeling low; Almanzor is nonchalant, "Observed by all, himself observing none" (I.i., p. 21) Ozmyn kills nine bulls with "never-erring fury," and he seems a "dext'rous rider." Almanzor, on the other hand, rides with "graceful pride" and slays one enormous, wild bull with *sprezzatura:*

> Not heads of poppies (when they reap the grain)
> Fall with more ease before the laboring swain,
> Than fell this head.
>
> (I.i., p. 21)

After this opening contrast, the gradual union of the two heroes can be traced throughout the play. Ozmyn rises above a slavish obedience to externally imposed rules; he disobeys his parent, leaves his country's safety in other hands, and goes into exile with Benzayda. Like Guyomar, Catharine and Acacis, he rises above mere correctness in behavior to a passionate application of virtuous ideals. On the contrary, Almanzor, like Cortez, Porphyrius, and Montezuma of *The Indian Queen,* learns to bridle his lofty passions for the sake of the common good. His original vision of himself as an irresistible natural force, an earthly god, is belied by the trials he must face: he is reduced to bondage, sent into exile, and finally defeated in battle. In adversity he begins to control his impulses to revenge and love; he curbs his will and puts the safety of Granada above private considerations. Out of Almanzor's humiliation—his military and political defeat—comes his redemption: he is discovered by his father, the Duke of Arcos, given a noble title by Ferdinand, and, because of Boabdelin's death, promised the hand of Almahide.

Lyndaraxa and Boabdelin stress the "marks of sovereignty," but Almanzor understands the essence of kingship. He is so true to his word that it stands "like fate" (III.i., p. 37); he protects the "oppressed" because it belongs "to a king's office to redress the wrong" (I.i., p. 25), and declares that he is "as free as nature first made man." Lyndaraxa's definition of a king stands in sharp contrast; it serves to explain Boabdelin's idea of kingship as well as hers:

> A king is he, whom nothing can withstand;
> Who men and money can with ease command.
> A king is he, whom fortune still does bless;
> He is a king, who does a crown possess.
>
> (V.i., p. 68)

Almanzor recognizes Ferdinand as a true king in the last act of *The Conquest:* "Something so kingly, that my haughty mind/ Is drawn to yours, because 'tis of a kind" (Pt. II, V.ii., p. 159).

Although Almanzor thinks he can scorn society and be a king in nature, he fails to realize that his proud independence is accompanied by some baser impulses. He often acts as though he were divine justice, placing on the throne of a nation whomever he pleases and removing him when he no longer seems deserving. The reason for such unwarranted use of his strength is that Almanzor is on a personal quest for one kind of reward—not financial gain or power, but honor. When he is treated dishonorably, his wrath knows no bounds. At one point, Boabdelin calls him a "beast of prey" and man's "common foe":

> Since, then, no power above your own you know,
> Mankind should use you like a common foe;
> You should be hunted like a beast of prey;
> By your own law I take your life away.
>
> (I.i., p. 25)

In his relations with the Xeriff brothers of Morocco, described in Act I, Almanzor first fought for the elder brother and placed him on the throne; when this king "disdained" Almanzor's services, he toppled the throne and placed the younger in power. In Granada, similarly, Almanzor first overthrows Boabdelin and places his brother Abdalla on the throne, then defeats the second king and replaces him with Boabdelin; this time both brothers are ungrateful. Unlike Lyndaraxa who is seeking the crown for herself, Almanzor disrupts the political order to salve his wounded pride and to elevate to the kingship him who has least offended against his sense of his just deserts.

It is Almanzor's impatience, Almahide declares, which betrays him into fruitless rebellions: "Rash men, like you, and impotent of will,/ Give chance no time to turn, but urge her still" (V.ii., p. 78). Instead of always taking the initiative, he ought to wait patiently for the operations of divine justice in history. Moreover, he must learn to look within himself for happiness, to be content with the "conscience of an act well done."

Almahide reprimands Almanzor for "piratical" behavior in *The Conquest* because his actions as a lover correspond to his political deeds. When Almahide becomes his prisoner in Act III, he grants her freedom in his kingly manner, but he later complains that she has not rewarded him sufficiently. He claims that he is "starved to death," that he cannot live on "bare praises" and must have "alms"; he has let go "rich merchandise" captured through piracy only to buy it again "justly." His lady retorts that he now uses her "as pirates do; / You free me; but expect a ransom too" (IV.ii., p. 65). He tells Boabdelin that he "bought" Almahide with "blood and dangers," yet when that king offers him any other reward, he angrily replies that his services are not for sale (V.ii., p. 74). Finally, Almanzor sets a snare for his lady's chastity in the fourth act of Part II only to be called "little" and "mercenary." Almahide teaches him to control the pirate and the "beast of prey" within him. She argues that the only possible reward for his great actions is the "secret joy of mind" that belongs to "great souls" (Pt. II, IV.iii., p. 139).

She herself does not refuse him for the sake of mere reputation but for that honor which is "the conscience of an act well done." The only sphere of free will, she suggests, is within the mind; if one follows the dictates of conscience and refrains from heeding the appetites, then one is free, for "All appetite implies necessity" (Pt. II, IV.iii., p. 137). Earlier in the same scene, Almanzor doubts whether any free will exists; his mother's ghost has appeared and spoken of the future, so that subsequent events seem predestined:

> O Heaven, how dark a riddle's thy decree,
> Which bounds our wills, yet seems to leave them free:
> Since thy foreknowledge cannot be in vain,

Our choice must be what thou didst first ordain.
Thus, like a captive in an isle confined,
Man walks at large, a prisoner of the mind:
Wills all his crimes, while Heaven the indictment draws,
And, pleading guilty, justifies the laws.

(Pt. II, IV.iii., p. 136)

In previous heroic plays, where an Indian priest or a necromancer forecasts the future, the same question of prescience and free will is raised. The answer which Dryden suggests to the problem of free will can be summed up in Almahide's words just quoted: "All appetite implies necessity." Only those who give way to their appetites and stop following the dictates of conscience becomes instruments in the downfall of a kingdom and commit crimes of rebellion and regicide. The Abencerrages and even the Christians are not as responsible for Granada's fall as the Zegrys, because the latter act on the premise that "peace of mind were bravely lost" to win a crown (II.i., p. 35). Those who follow the dictates of conscience and who keep their peace of mind, may witness all the events that have been foretold and even participate in these events without incurring guilt. Free will, for Dryden, lies in right action, not in the breaking of laws; in *Astraea Redux* Dryden says that providence sent the patient Monck as an instrument to free England from the "real bonds false freedom did impose." The theme of excessive freedom can be traced through all the heroic plays, for all those who break internal and external laws are in "real bonds," are controlled by necessity rather than by free will.

Almanzor and Almahide are contrasted as a couple to Ozmyn and Benzayda. The first two often exercise their free will, imposing it on circumstances about them, but the others regard themselves as the victims of fate. The motif of piracy in the play serves to sharpen this contrast. Almahide calls her lover a pirate when he seeks to extort certain signs of affection from her, but Benzayda calls fortune a pirate:

> Blind queen of Chance, to lovers too severe,
> Thou rulest mankind, but art a tyrant there!
> Thy widest empire's in a lover's breast:
> Like open seas, we seldom are at rest.
> Upon thy coasts our wealth is daily cast:
> And thou, like pirates, mak'st no peace at last.
>   (Pt. II, III.ii., p. 115)

This motif recurs in a speech by Abenamar in the next act, when he finds that not only has Ozmyn, his son, returned into his power to save the life of Selin, but also that Benzayda has come to offer herself in place of her father Selin. Abenamar thanks "fortune" for delivering those he sought into his hands: "My own lost wealth thou giv'st not only back,/ But driv'st upon my coast my pirate's wrack" (Pt. II, IV.i., p. 125).

The story of Ozmyn and Benzayda is an extended allusion to that of Romeo and Juliet. The lovers belong to the two opposing factions of Granada, and the family feud has been heightened by the recent killing of Tarifa; they are star-crossed in their union, yet they bring about the eventual reconciliation between their houses. Benzayda falls in love with Ozmyn, who is at this time a prisoner of the Zegry clan, though she has been ordered to execute him. She tells the fettered Ozmyn that "sure at our births,/Death with our meeting planets danced above" (IV.ii., p. 62). When the two go into exile, they leave all to "providence and chance" (V.i., p. 72). They are quickly captured by the Christians, and Benzayda attributes this to fate:

> Fate aims so many blows to make us fall,
> That 'tis in vain to think to ward them all:
> And, where misfortunes great and many are
> Life grows a burden, and not worth our care.
>   (Pt. II, I.i., p. 88)

As misfortunes continue to fall upon them, Ozmyn and Benzayda think they are doomed. The turning point for them

comes when they offer up their lives to atone for the hatred
between their families. A reconciliation with Benzayda's
father occurs in Part II, Act II, because Ozmyn offers to die for
the old Zegry. Again, both Ozmyn and Benzayda try to ransom Selin from Abenamar with their lives and Selin, in turn,
offers his life for theirs. In view of this generosity, Ozmyn's
father is softened and filled with shame. This situation paral-
els that in the eighth story, tenth day, of the *Decameron*. In
that tale Boccaccio relates how the heart of a judge was moved
when several persons offered themselves up to be punished for
the same crime. Because the story of Ozmyn and Benzayda is
so close to that of Romeo and Juliet, this happy ending comes
as a surprise. Its function seems to be to emphasize the rational-
ism and optimism in Dryden's point of view. Self-sacrificing
virtue, he shows, will eventually be rewarded.

Besides the two normative couples we have discussed, there
are extreme characters such as Boabdelin, Lyndaraxa, Abdalla,
and Abdelmelech who play an important part in *The Conquest*. In fact, they are just as important as the normative
figures, since it is in the interrelationship of all the characters
that the meaning and design of the play can be observed. Most
critics emphasize the role of Almanzor, but he can hardly be
evaluated properly without placing him near his foil, Ozmyn,
and contrasting his idea of internal kingship with that of external kingship espoused by Boabdelin and Lyndaraxa.

The two extremes of established tyrant and aspiring rebel
are drawn in considerable detail: Boabdelin is the Hobbesian
tyrant, while Lyndaraxa lives up to Hobbes' idea of man in the
state of nature, for she is avidly in pursuit of power and is
checked only by that natural law which Hobbes stresses—
self-preservation.[45] Boabdelin thinks he controls his subjects,

---

45. So important is self-preservation to Hobbes that he makes it the basis of
the law of nature, asserting that "A LAW OF NATURE, lex naturalis, is a
precept or general rule, found out by reason, by which a man is forbidden to
do that, which is destructive of his life, or taketh away the means of preserving

but he is in fact sensual and ineffectual. Similarly, Lyndaraxa desires the freedom which she thinks only a monarch can have, yet she is willing to sell her body to Abdalla, whom she despises, or to any other man for the sake of a crown: "I will be constant yet, if Fortune can;/ I love the king,—let her but name the man" (IV.ii. p. 54). However brilliant their speeches often are, both Lyndaraxa and Boabdelin are would-be heroes.

Self-deceived in his notion of a king's power, Boabdelin complains that the senators "too slowly grant" funds for his wars or "saucily refuse to aid my want." He concludes that only absolute monarchy is effectual:

> But kings, who rule with limited command,
> Have players' sceptres put into their hand.
> Power has no balance, one side still weighs down,
> And either hoists the commonwealth or crown;
> And those, who think to set the scale more right,
> By various turnings but disturb the weight.
> (Pt. II, I.ii., p. 90)

Like Maximin in *Tyrannic Love* Boabdelin wants to rule without the voice of the people because he thinks he can be more successful in his wars and create greater stability in the state. Dryden undercuts this theory by showing that it is just that tyrannical wielding of power that brings on rebellions and disrupts the political order. The notion of absolute monarchy espoused by Sir Robert Filmer and Hobbes appears, consequently, to be impractical in the application. Ferdinand and Isabel condemn the Moorish government as a tyranny in the second part of the play and, since they are the normative

---

the same; and to omit that, by which he thinketh it may be best preserved" (I, xiv., p. 84). Filmer points out that Hobbes, by arguing that a man "cannot lay down the right of resisting them that assault him by force to take away his life," has stated a doctrine that is "destructive to all government whatsoever." In Hobbes' idea of self-preservation, therefore, Filmer sees a source of anarchy (*Observations Concerning the Originall of Government,* p. 248).

monarchs here, their opinion can safely be said to be Dryden's. Throughout *The Conquest* and in his other heroic plays, Dryden suggests what he clearly asserts in "To My Honour'd Kinsman":

> A Patriot, both the King and Country serves;
> Prerogative, and Privilege preserves:
> Of Each, our Laws the certain Limit show;
> One must not ebb, nor t'other overflow:
> Betwixt the Prince and Parliament we stand;
> The Barriers of the State on either Hand:
> May neither overflow, for then they drown the Land.[46]

In spite of his theory of absolute kingship, Boabdelin is forced to bend to his people's will during rebellions and tumults. In the first section of the play, he "begs" and "entreats" the warring factions to lay down their arms. In the second section, on the occasion of a popular uprising for the recall of Almanzor, Boabdelin complains: "In tumults people reign, and kings obey" (Pt. II, I.ii., p. 91). Dryden indicates that it takes a tumult or a riot to make a tyrant listen to his subjects' voice. Boabdelin is also a dull sensualist who finds the task of ruling "weary toil," mere "business," and "importunate affairs" (V.ii., p. 81). He speaks of "soft peace" at the start of the play and is looking forward to the joys of love at a time of siege. He goes to battle at the end of the first act moaning that kings are "slaves of state." Shortly after his marriage, he says he is "gorged and glutted," that marriage is a "chain" for the bodies when the "hearts are loose" (Pt. II, III.i., p. 109, and I.ii., p. 92). This king who claims absolute, tyrannical power is in reality an impotent sensualist; Almahide calls him a "vulgar good," or cheap merchandise.

Lyndaraxa's ambition resembles that of Boabdelin, for she wants to be "without control." In order to reach that state, however, she makes herself a slave of opportunity: "I know

46. "To My Honour'd Kinsman," ll. 171–77.

not what my future thoughts will be:/ Poor women's thoughts
are all *extempore.*" She voices scorn for those who produce
"Beforehand a long chain of thoughts" because hers vary with
each success or failure (IV.ii., p. 59). Before beginning his
career as a rebel and usurper, Abdalla pleads with her that she
"may be happy with a private man"; unlike Almahide who
would like the "private greatness" of being Almanzor's wife,
she holds her love "As in some weather-glass" and will let it
rise for whoever possesses the crown. Her love for Abdalla
begins to rise when he seizes the crown, but when he loses it,
she remarks: "I love a king, but a poor rebel hate" (V.i. p. 69).
Whereas fate is a "pirate" for Ozmyn and Benzayda, it is a
"lottery" for Lyndaraxa:

> O lottery of fate! where still the wise
> Draw blanks of fortune, and the fools the prize!
> These cross, ill-shuffled lots from heaven are sent,
> Yet dull Religion teaches us content.
>   (Pt. II, III.ii., p. 116)

Later, when she seems to have created her own destiny by
betraying Granada to receive the crown from Ferdinand, she
is stabbed to death by Abdelmelech. She regards fate as a rebel
at this point, because she is the queen that ought to control it:
"Sure destiny mistakes . . . Dying I charge rebellion on my
fate" (Pt. II, V.ii., p. 158).

The essential fault of Lyndaraxa, as of other would-be
heroes in Dryden's heroic plays, is that she regards historical
circumstances as being shapeless unless the strong individual
can give them shape; if there is a providence in history, it is as
inefficient and as blind to merit as a lottery. Montezuma, in
The Indian Emperour, points out a similar fault in some of the
Spanish invaders. They perform fasts and penances to atone
for their sins and therefore sin "cheaply": "First injure
Heaven, and when its wrath is due,/ Your selves prescribe it
how to punish you" (I.ii.303–08). The normative characters in

each play accept historical conditions, such as a tyranny or a state of siege, as a context within which to behave virtuously and to endure patiently until providence makes some changes. They do not have the warrant, Dryden implies, to act in place of providence and forcibly change their environment. They must give shape to their own lives, rather than to the world about them. Thus, Dryden's vision of the world is essentially untragic, the opposite of that vision found in the plays of Euripides, Shakespeare, and other tragedians. This is a comic view in the large sense, because, in spite of the foreordained course of history, there is enough scope for the free exercise of virtue on the part of individuals that these may deserve happiness.

Abdalla and Abdelmelech are also extreme characters, parallel to Lyndaraxa and Boabdelin and equally distant from the normative characters Ozmyn and Almanzor. Abdelmelech is weak and dull like Boabdelin, while Abdalla is full of surface action and runs helter-skelter like Lyndaraxa. Boabdelin and Abdelmelech are impotent because they act with too little vigor, whereas Abdalla and Lyndaraxa accomplish nothing because they are too wild and variable.

Abdalla resembles Traxalla in *The Indian Queen* and Odmar in *The Indian Emperour* but is drawn with much more subtlety. In this character one can see the serious version of such fools as Sparkish and Fopling Flutter in Restoration comedy. Wycherley's Sparkish is so complaisant toward his mistress that he encourages her to flirt with an ardent admirer, and Etherege's Fopling Flutter thinks that his French dress and affected manners will win Loveit. In the same way, Abdalla loves with "hoodwinked eyes" even though he knows of Abdelmelech's ardent love and of the response it evokes in Lyndaraxa: "Your love I will believe with hoodwinked eyes; —/ In faith, much merit in much blindness lies" (Pt. II, II.iii., p. 105). He expects to win Lyndaraxa with only the accoutrements and clothing of a monarch: "'Tis plain that she . . .

would, even in my arms, lie thinking of a throne" (II.i., p. 35). Abdalla becomes so dehumanized in his pursuit of Lyndaraxa that he begins to resemble the speaker of Swift's "Digression on Madness" in *Tale of a Tub;* he creams off the surface of things because he is afraid of the corruption underneath, and he finds joy in thus being "well-deceived." Throughout the play Abdalla appears consciously to choose deception; he will "love, be blind, be cozened till I die" (III.i., p. 39).

Although Abdalla betrays his brother, king, and country for Lyndaraxa, his love is not requited. He justifies his continued devotion by reflecting that "'Tis only pride, to be beloved again" (Pt. II, II.i., p. 99). In an explicit allusion to Antony, Abdalla glorifies himself out of all proportion when he goes to meet Lyndaraxa after a defeat: "I fly, like Antony from Actium,/ To meet a better Cleopatra here" (V.i., p. 67). He is greeted as a "saucy slave" and "poor rebel" by his lady, surely a ludicrous comedown from Cleopatra's manner of receiving Antony; he is not allowed into her fortress, but must go to "Christian dogs" for safety. He complains in a manner reminiscent of Othello: "I have loved too well." The final judgment of Abdalla is passed by Lyndaraxa herself as she stands over his corpse and calls him a "whining, tedious, heavy lump of love!"

The character of Abdalla would serve to show that Dryden's norm for love in these heroic plays is not *frauendienst.* Those who betray their country or king for the service of a woman, Traxalla, Odmar, and Placidius, are also sensualists and fools in their love. Although some critics have argued that love and service to women constitute one of the great virtues in Dryden's heroic plays, such a view is untenable once the plays have been carefully examined.

Abdelmelech, the dull and weak lover of Lyndaraxa, does not go so far as to fight against his king for her sake, but his unwarranted trust in her gives her the opportunity to betray Granada. Even when he sees her "last baseness" over Abdalla's corpse, he says he must fly solitude and "herd, like wounded deer, in company." He realizes, like Abdalla, that his lady is simply deceiving him, for he refers to the Circe myth: "These arts have oft prevailed, but must no more:/ The spell is ended, and the enchantment o'er" (Pt. II, IV.ii., p. 131). Yet he remains under her spell; even though she would have made him her Bajazet, he complains (like Abdalla) that he loves "too well" and stabs himself as well as her:

> Thy blood I to thy ruined country give,
> But love too well thy murder to outlive.
> Forgive a love, excused by its excess,
> Which, had it not been cruel, had been less.
>
> (Pt. II, V.ii., p. 158)

Abdalla's and Abdelmelech's weakness in love can be contrasted to Almanzor's common sense. When this normative character thinks that Almahide has been faithless, he decides to champion her publicly "for my honour's sake" but to "leave her, when she's freed; and let it be/ Her punishment, she could be false to me" (Pt. II, V.i., p. 144). The norm that Dryden suggests, then, is that a right-thinking man ought not to serve a faithless lady. Nor should a woman subject herself to an untrue man: in *Aureng-Zebe,* Indamora advises Melesinda that she has no obligation to commit suicide to rejoin her faithless husband; Indamora represents a common sensical, independent attitude within the love relationship, just as Almanzor and Almahide do.

   The Conquest is one of the best examples of Dryden's fusion of apparently turbulent historical change with the actually immutable "laws of justice." In the preface to *An Evening's Love* (1671), Dryden remarks that in tragedy, "where the actions and persons are great, and the crimes horrid, the laws of justice are more strictly to be observed [than in comedy]; and examples of punishment to be made to deter mankind from the pursuit of vice."[47] Again, speaking of *All for Love,* Dryden says of Antony and Cleopatra that they were "famous patterns

<hr />

47. Watson, *1,* 151.

of unlawful love; and their end accordingly was unfortunate."[48] If the character had been one of "perfect virtue," he goes on, he "could not, without injustice, be made unhappy." Thus, Dryden regards the serious play as a court where final justice is dispensed, surely a great departure from Shakespeare and a sharp contrast to Otway. Dryden shows what ought to be under the appearance of an actual historical incident.

It is possible to regard *The Conquest* chiefly as a "kind of continuous discourse on heroism" and a "dramatization of the *idea* of a hero,"[49] but a more exciting way to read this play, as well as Dryden's other serious plays, is to regard it as a model of all historical and political change. Dryden suggests that the fall of Granada is like the fall of most great kingdoms: these are torn by rival parties, preyed upon by ambitious, vain courtiers, and governed by dull, sensual tyrants. The "laws of justice" are carried out in this play because all the virtuous inhabitants of Granada find their way to the Christian court. Almahide is converted, Almanzor discovers Christian parents, and Ozmyn and Benzayda, whom Dryden has called "patterns of exact virtue," are welcomed by the Christian monarch after their capture in Part II, Act I. Dryden thus shows that the change from Muslim tyranny to Christian rule has occurred in such a way that justice has prevailed.

Aureng-Zebe

In his last heroic play Dryden achieves a new simplicity of surface with a new depth of characterization. *Aureng-Zebe,* Lewis N. Chase observes, is "nearer the Racine manner, calmer, more correct, with simpler plot, and characters truer to nature, the supernatural machinery omitted, and the dialogue not so extravagant."[50] One reason for the play's appearance of calm and simplicity is that nearly all the characters belong to

48. Ibid., p. 222.
49. Waith, p. 157.
50. P. 34.

the same ruling family. In previous heroic plays there were two large factions pitted one against the other: Incas against Aztecs in *The Indian Queen,* Christians against Indians in *The Indian Emperour,* Christians against heathens in *Tyrannic Love,* and Zegrys against Abencerrages in *The Conquest.* In *Aureng-Zebe,* on the contrary, brother is pitted against brother, stepmother against stepson, and father against son. Dryden has shifted the scene from a large political forum to an intimate view of India's ruling family. He has also shifted his interest from the theme of conquest and Christian expansion to the problem of succession within a single realm. Finally, there is no Christian character here; since *The Indian Queen,* Dryden had either used a Christian character as a normative figure or, as with Almanzor and Almahide, had moved his normative characters toward the Christian world.

Part of the simplicity of *Aureng-Zebe* arises from the fact that there is only one hero. Previous heroic plays, as I have shown, had a double norm, a passionate hero and a correct one who grew more like each other as the plays progressed. To some extent, Aureng-Zebe is a descendant of such correct heroes as Acacis, Guyomar, Ozmyn, and Catharine, but his passionate nature ought to be recognized too. Like the impulsive heroes of previous plays, he often struggles against his desire to restore justice around him by means of violence; moreover, he must frequently overcome his own sense of despair. At the end of Act I, after nearly using his sword against his father's messenger and being checked by his lady, Aureng-Zebe puts up his weapon and exclaims: "Strong virtue, like strong nature, struggles still; / Exerts itself, and then throws off the ill." This statement is not that of a calm or precise type of hero.

Morat has been thought by some critics to be the descendant of the passionate heroes of earlier plays. But Morat is, in every respect, far less sympathetic than Montezuma, Cortez, Porphyrius, and Almanzor. All these heroes were prompted by a love of justice and honorable fame; Morat, on the other hand, is a power-seeker. Moreover, his rebellion against his father is a far more serious crime than that of the mercenary generals Almanzor and Montezuma against the ungrateful monarchs who had used their services. Whereas Porphyrius has no imperial ambitions, even though the crown is lawfully within his grasp, Morat turns against his brothers for the sake of imperial dreams: "My arms from pole to pole the world shall shake,/ And, with myself, keep all mankind awake" (III.i., p. 309). He also turns against his parents for the sake of Indamora, even though his love is unlawful in view of his marriage to Melesinda. Just before his death, Morat is partly redeemed when he gives up his political ambitions out of love for Indamora. He continues, nevertheless, to neglect his faithful, despairing wife, and so could hardly be a normative figure. That he should be wiped off the scene before the end of the play is a final indication that he does not deserve to live on and prosper in a just world. Morat is savage like the Almanzor who appears early in *The Conquest*, but he has not much of the latter's nobility.

It has been said that Aureng-Zebe has "all the extraordinary powers of the hero, but instead of using them for his own aggrandizement, he tries to ensure the safety of the state no matter what the cost in personal sacrifice."[51] And yet, this statement is misleading because "the state" in this play is represented by Aureng-Zebe's father, so that civil law and parental law are merged. It might be said that, like Guyomar, Aureng-Zebe follows "Piety" as well as civil duty. Reuben A. Brower has drawn a just comparison between Aeneas and Aureng-Zebe in this matter of piety.[52] Aureng-Zebe's dilemma can be reduced to a simple conflict between moral obligations: he can obey his father and king by giving up Indamora and accepting the crown, or he can fulfill his obligation to his betrothed by saving her from his father's clutches. The dilemma cannot be resolved by mere force of arms; Aureng-Zebe refuses to employ

51. Winterbottom, "The Development of the Hero," p. 162.
52. "Dryden's Epic Manner and Virgil," *PMLA*, 55 (1940), 127.

Solyman's troops against his own father when these are offered
to him in the second act. Because he is obliged to await Indamora's and his own deliverance patiently, Aureng-Zebe is
tempted to despair:

> *Aureng-Zebe.* When I consider life, 'tis all a cheat;
> Yet, fooled with hope, men favour the deceit;
> Trust on, and think to-morrow will repay:
> To-morrow's falser than the former day;
> Lies worse, and, while it says, we shall be blest
> With some new joys, cuts off what we possess.
> Strange cozenage! None would live past years again,
> Yet all hope pleasure in what yet remain;
> And, from the dregs of life, think to receive,
> What the first sprightly running could not give.
> I'm tired with waiting for this chemic gold,
> Which fools us young, and beggars us when old.
>
> (IV.i., p. 320)

Imprisoned and tempted to such despair, Aureng-Zebe resembles the just men who face severe trials in Scripture. Robert E.
Moore remarks that Aureng-Zebe is "more typical of the underlying gravity of Dryden's genius" than corresponding heroes in
earlier heroic plays,[53] and it is true of the play as a whole that
Dryden takes a grave and almost homiletic tone.

The design of *Aureng-Zebe* might be summed up as the
problem of the Indian succession. While all the brothers of
Aureng-Zebe are vying for the throne of India, he alone prefers virtue before empire; thus, he alone deserves the crown,
and, out of the chaos of civil war a new order must emerge in
which Aureng-Zebe will be heir to the crown. An unjust Indian
law compounds the difficulties in the play, for it is decreed that
the younger sons are "doomed to die" at the time of succession:
"Less ills are chosen greater to avoid,/ And nature's laws are
by the state's destroyed" (I.i., p. 278). This civil law is of course

53. P. 22.

contrary to nature, and Aureng-Zebe's brothers are actually fighting for self-preservation as well as for the crown. Darah is the eldest son and, according to the opening discussion of the brothers' characters, neither he nor Sujah is fit to be emperor; the former is revengeful and lacking in diplomacy, while the latter is a bigot who thrives on a "foreign interest" (I.i., p. 279). In some opening remarks by courtiers, Morat is described as "insolent" and envious. Aureng-Zebe is thought to be "more temperate" and "weighed," but though he surely is temperate in action, later soliloquies and conversations reveal that he is highly passionate in disposition.

In a vain attempt to avoid a conflict over the succession, the Emperor had sent his sons to distant provinces. In the opening scene, however, all the sons except Aureng-Zebe are at war, and "Fortune labours with the vast event." The fickle crowd awaits "servilely" for fate to name a king. Thus the Emperor's precaution in sending his sons far away has been to no avail: "What Heaven decrees, no prudence can prevent" (I.i., p. 277). The design of *Aureng-Zebe* seems, in this light, to suggest that heaven itself chooses the successor to a throne. Aureng-Zebe has been designated heir to the throne by destiny rather than by simple birthright, and the civil war between his brothers' factions is simply a means to provide for his accession.

Ironically, the Emperor himself thinks that chance rules the world and that birthright is of no consequence in the succession. A linear descendant of Maximin, the Hobbesian emperor of *Tyrannic Love,* the father of Aureng-Zebe is an arbitrary, tyrannical ruler and a sensualist as well. He takes a Lucretian point of view of life and regards children as the "blind effect of love and chance,/ Formed by their sportive parents' ignorance" (III.i., p. 309). He thinks birthright is a gift he may confer upon whichever son has the most merit:

> One then may be displaced, and one may reign,
> And want of merit render birthright vain.
>
> (III.i., p. 310)

When the Emperor disregards birthright, however, and decides on "merit," he chooses the rebellious and power-hungry Morat for his successor. He punishes Aureng-Zebe, for like Lear, he mistakes his offspring's honesty for want of love. Like Lear, too, he is sent packing by the ungrateful child he rewards. Morat tells him: "Of business you complained; now take your ease; / Enjoy whate'er decrepit age can please" (IV.i., p. 328). The extended allusion to *King Lear* seems to reach a climax in the Emperor's following soliloquy:

> Too late my folly I repent; I know
> My Aureng-Zebe would ne'er have used me so.
> But, by his ruin, I prepared my own;
> And, like a naked tree, my shelter gone,
> To winds and winter-storms must stand exposed
> alone.
>
> (IV.i., p. 329)

Dryden has made a full-blown Epicurean out of the Emperor, not only in the popular sense by making him a lover of "ease," but in the philosophical sense by making him voice a theory of indifferent gods and of second causes such as that propounded by Placidius in *Tyrannic Love*. Dryden appears to create a fusion between Hobbesian ideas of government and Lucretian or Epicurean philosophy; he suggests that tyrants who wish to impose their absolute sway on their subjects and to deny them freedom of conscience are often trying to maintain a strict, external order which they conceive to be the only alternative to anarchy. Zempoalla in *The Indian Queen* and Lyndaraxa in *The Conquest* desire to impose order on a disorderly world, where the "wise" draw blanks in the "lottery" of fate. In *Aureng-Zebe* the Emperor imagines himself a Lucretian god and suggests that heaven does not intervene to restore justice on earth:

> 'Tis a base world, and is not worth our care;
> The vulgar, a scarce animated clod,

Ne'er pleased with aught above them, prince or God.
Were I a god, the drunken globe should roll,
The little emmets with the human soul
Care for themselves, while at my ease I sat,
And second causes did the work of fate;
Or, if I would take care, that care should be
For wit that scorned the world, and lived like me.

(III.i., p. 309)

After the Emperor has resigned his wearisome crown in order
to fill his remaining years with pleasure, he discovers the limitations of his view of life. He repents of his tyrannical behavior
toward Aureng-Zebe and says that "Heaven's justice" is working through Morat. Having thus been redeemed to a proper
sense of values, the Emperor is overcome with shame and attempts suicide; he is prevented by Aureng-Zebe and, unlike
Lear, restored to his former position at the end of the play.

Although Aureng-Zebe learns to wait for deliverance
through the workings of providence, and the Emperor thinks
he can act in the place of fate and determine the succession by
arbitrary command, Melesinda sees herself as the helpless victim of an unkind destiny. She tells Indamora that her mind
"foretells" an unhappy future: "Short is my life, and that unfortunate" (III.i., p. 306). Part of that unhappy destiny is of
her own choosing, however, since she lives entirely for her husband and compares herself to a flower drooping at the absence
of the sun when Morat is away (III.i., p. 306). Indamora's sensible relationship with Aureng-Zebe stands in sharp contrast
to Melesinda's clinging helplessness. Melesinda has very little
influence on Morat, for he will not be moved by her tears to
spare his brother's life, even when she warns him that the
"doom" he has prepared for another may be his own: "Weigh
well the various turns of human fate,/ And seek, by mercy, to
secure your state" (III.i., p. 316).

In contrast to Indamora, who treats Aureng-Zebe coldly
when the prince has a fit of jealousy, Melesinda is unable to
disguise her feelings or to control Morat, hence her final des-

pair. Although she is related to earlier tragic characters like Valeria in *Tyrannic Love* and Acacis in *The Indian Queen,* Melesinda is cast in a far more sentimental mold. She is closer to an Otway heroine than to her heroic counterparts in Dryden; she wanders about in misery after her husband, saying: "In pity stay some hours, till I am dead" (IV.i., p. 326). Her husband's love for Indamora does not make her angry or revengeful toward her rival; she is far too weak for a choleric response. Morat dies in Indamora's arms, but he asks his wife's forgiveness and tells her to live. Indamora too counsels Melesinda to live, arguing that she has "no right" to die for an unkind husband. But Melesinda, protesting always that "Heaven looks careless on" at human misery gives her life to rejoin Morat: "Adorned with flames, I'll mount a glorious bride" (V.i., p. 352).

In contrast to Melesinda's weakness and despair in the face of difficulties are her husband's tempestuous attempts to control fate and her mother-in-law's revengeful and passionate behavior. In a more intimate, less political setting than that of his previous heroic plays, Dryden thus shows a variety of human responses to a state of disorder and injustice. Morat and his mother are distinguished, even though both are lawbreakers, by the fact that the son has a "brute soul," is either amoral or below morality, whereas the mother is conscious of making a moral choice and seems therefore more culpable. In the civil strife which surrounds them, both pursue power and private gain rather than the restoration of justice.

Morat may have some surface resemblance to Almanzor, but he is much more like Marlowe's Tamburlaine in his amorality and political ambitions. Almanzor boasted that he needed no kingdom to be a king, but Morat wishes to shake the world "from pole to pole" by force of arms (III.i., p. 309). Morat states that he is not like a "private man" who can "be swayed by honour or by love," but Almanzor, even in spite of his early contempt for love, showed none of this contempt for "honour." Morat's ingratitude toward his father is based on his theory that power is the summum bonum—"You cancelled duty when you gave me power" (IV.i., p. 327)—and on the notion, too, that what makes the gods divine is their power— "Since 'tis to that they their own greatness owe/ Above, why should they question mine below? (IV.i., p. 329). This view of the gods is also held by Zempoalla and Maximin, the usurpers in heroic drama. Aureng-Zebe reproves his brother, saying: "You speak, as if you could the fates command" (III.i., p. 311). Indeed, Morat reaches a point of near-insanity when he boasts, "I'm in Fate's place, and dictate her decrees" (IV.i., p. 324), and goes on to compare himself with the gods.

It is fitting that in a play dealing with private, moral issues rather than political ones Dryden should introduce the theme of conversion or repentance several times. The Emperor has a change of heart and asks Aureng-Zebe's forgiveness; Arimant alters from a cold follower of the Emperor's commands to a man of conscience; and Morat gives up his political ambitions and asks his wife's forgiveness at his death. Morat's "brute soul" is considered fit by Aureng-Zebe to reign in "woods and wilds"; yet he is tamed by his love for Indamora and persuaded by her to "bid Fortune carry back her bribe." The scene of Morat's conversion is parallel to the temptation scene in Part II, Act IV of *The Conquest.* Just as Almahide reproved Almanzor for being "mercenary" in asking payment for his services to her, so Indamora tells Morat that " 'Tis base to seize on all, because you may;/ That's empire, that, which I can give away" (V.i., p. 338). Unlike Almanzor, Morat is determined at the end of the scene to pursue his unlawful love, even though he agrees to give up his political ambitions:

> 'Twas not for nothing I the crown resigned:
> I still must own a mercenary mind;
> I, in this venture, double gains pursue,
> And laid out all my stock, to purchase you.
>
> (V.i., p. 338)

Morat, then, retains his "mercenary mind" until death and merely gives up the crown to "purchase" Indamora's love, like Antony in *All for Love*. At his death, he speaks of having been "Puffed with the pride of Heaven's own gift, frail life," of having been swelled with "ambitious spirit," but he still clings to Indamora rather than to his wife. Almanzor goes farther and is redeemed more fully, for he agrees never to disturb Almahide's virtue again, but to let their love be, in her words, "image-like, to heighten piety."

Nourmahal, unlike her son and husband, shows no signs of contrition. She is not like the avenging ladies and power-seekers of earlier heroic plays, however, for her words and acts have more to do with private morality than with her proper relationship to the state. Dryden implicitly likens her to Phaedra, for she falls in love with her virtuous step-son, is rejected, and later dies by suicide. Nourmahal differs from Phaedra, on the other hand, in that she is much less a victim of passion than an active pursuer of self-gratification. She is more of a queen bee than a woman swayed by passion. Nourmahal asserts that "no sex confines the soul" and that she will simply use Aureng-Zebe to quench her flames and then kill him:

> *Zayda.* He's dead, whose love had sullied all your
> >reign,
> And made you empress of the world in vain.
>
> *Nourmahal.* No; I my power and pleasure would divide:
> The drudge had quenched my flames, and then had died.
> I rage, to think without that bliss I live,
> That I could wish what fortune would not give.
>
> >(V.i., p. 342)

Nourmahal's view of the male sex is the perfect antithesis to her husband's and Morat's view of the female; Morat tells her, for example, "When man's at leisure, study how to please,/ Soften his angry hours with servile care" (IV.i., p. 324). In Act II Nourmahal plays the role of a shrewish wife, reproaching her husband for his new love and for his impotence: "Must I your cold long-labouring age sustain,/ And be to empty joys provoked in vain?" The Emperor at first tries to placate this "pompous chastity" and "clamorous virtue." But she proceeds from reproving his "withered hands" and "false desire" to threatening him at a political level: "Then, as the greatest curse that I can give,/ Unpitied be deposed, and, after, live!" (II.i., p. 297). It is ironic that, after showing contempt for her husband's impotent passion for Indamora, Nourmahal should herself follow the path of adultery and incest.

Unlike her predecessors in heroic drama, Nourmahal is is aware of her "crime" in loving Aureng-Zebe and even asks herself if this passion is heaven's means of saving the Prince or if it is simply a result of her depravity:

> Whether this passion from above was sent,
> The fate of him Heaven favours to prevent;
> Or as the curse of fortune in excess,
> That, stretching, would beyond its reach possess;
> And, with a taste which plenty does deprave,
> Loathes lawful good, and lawless ill does crave.

> (III.i., p. 314)

In spite of her "clamorous virtue" in Act II, she argues in Act IV that "Promiscuous love is Nature's general law." Thus, she comes to resemble the Emperor in almost every respect, even though she starts from an opposite pole. He is a tyrannical husband who thinks that "Man is by nature formed your sex's head,/ And is himself the canon of his bed" (II.i., p. 298), and she is a rebellious wife who wants to make of man a "drudge" to quench her "flames." Both see marriage as a wearisome bondage, the Emperor because "there's a godlike liberty in love," and the Empress because to follow one's lust is to "gloriously offend," like the gods. Both would coerce the object of their lust, would be content to have the body without the heart.

The proper relationship between a man and a woman,

Dryden suggests, is that of Aureng-Zebe and Indamora. They are possessive enough of each other to exhibit jealousy, but not enough to die for love; when Indamora is informed of Aureng-Zebe's death she still shrinks from suicide. The two episodes of jealousy in Acts IV and V are meant to show that these lovers have equal "maistrie." When Aureng-Zebe demands an explanation to clear away his jealous distrust, Indamora behaves coldly and declares her "scorn" for his "mean suspicions." Aureng-Zebe is not merely a well-bred, platonic lover; he finds it extremely difficult to submit to his lady in Act V, just as he found it difficult to submit to his father in Act I. When the Prince put up his sword at the end of Act I, he remarked that "Strong virtue, like strong nature, struggles still." A similar struggle occurs in Act V:

> She's guiltless, and I should submit; but oh!
> When she exacts it, can I stoop so low?
> Yes, for she's guiltless; but she's haughty too.
> Great souls long struggle ere they own a crime;
> She's gone; and leaves me no repenting-time.
>
> (V.i., p. 351)

Although in a weaker moment, distraught by jealousy, Aureng-Zebe resembles his father and is willing to settle for the body rather than the heart of Indamora, arguing that "Brutes are more blest, who grossly feed on joy" (V.i., p. 350), he later realizes her innocence and kneels for forgiveness. The relationship between Aureng-Zebe and Indamora, then, is a union of bodies and minds, rather than simply one of flesh.

Arimant's description of Aureng-Zebe as one who is "by no strong passion swayed,/ Except his love" is far from complete. Aureng-Zebe seems calm at the start of the play because he possesses a "parent's blessing, and a mistress' love" (I.i., p. 279). As soon as those rewards are taken from him, however, Aureng-Zebe begins to struggle with his own tendency to use force against unjust authority and to fall into despair. When both

his father and mistress are cold to him in the first act, he complains of his "distempered mind" and of "despair." It is with
difficulty that he puts away his sword and stands "the blameless
pattern of a son" when Arimant, following the Emperor's
orders, places Indamora under arrest.

In the second act, Aureng-Zebe falls into the same despair
about virtue being rewarded in this world as Montezuma does
in *The Indian Queen* (II.iii. 48–51). Even so, he refuses the
troops of Solyman and of Dianet which are offered to him on
separate occasions as means of restoring justice in the Indian
capital; Aureng-Zebe will not "buy an empire at so base a
rate," will not offend against parental and civil laws to gain a
throne (II.i., p. 303). Again, in Act IV, he ponders the thought
that life is a "cheat" and does not reward virtue, yet he quickly
refuses the wealth which Nourmahal offers as the price of
incest; he turns her away with passion:

> Hence, hence, and to some barbarous climate fly,
> Which only brutes in human form does yield,
> And man grows wild in Nature's common field.
>
> (IV.i., p. 322)

Thus, Aureng-Zebe shows his passionate nature from the moment that those rewards which belong to him, his father's
blessing and Indamora's love, are taken away. Then he falls
into jealous rages, fits of discouragement and moods of sensual love when "Love mounts, and rolls about my stormy
mind,/ Like fire, that's borne by a tempestuous wind" (IV.i.,
p. 333). Yet he overcomes his passion when he is about to act.
In this sense, Arimant's description may be taken as accurate;
Aureng-Zebe is not "swayed" into unlawful action by his
strong passions. His character can be summed up as a passionate nature in a state of equipoise.

That there is a unique emphasis on moral instruction in
Aureng-Zebe seems clear when we compare the last scene of
this play with that of *The Indian Queen:* both scenes have a

pair of contrasting suicides. In *The Indian Queen,* Acacis immolates himself as an act of protest against his mother's cruelty toward his Peruvian friends; Zempoalla, on the other hand, kills herself because all her power and possessions are gone and only in this way can she exercise some control over her fate. In *Aureng-Zebe* Melesinda, who dies by fire to rejoin her husband in the next world, is portrayed as mounting to heaven "Adorned with flames"; she needs no fuel to burn, for her love is "Rich in itself, like elemental fire." Nourmahal commits suicide by poison, and her suffering suggests diabolical torments. Morat's ghost appears to her blowing fire into her with bellows; she suffers, unlike Melesinda, in a restless and despairing manner, giving occasional signs of her revengeful nature: "Now I'm a burning lake, it rolls and flows;/ I'll rush, and pour it all upon my foes." The suggestion that Nourmahal is suffering the pain of the damned makes this suicide more instructive in the traditional sense than that of Zempoalla. These suicides and the scenes of repentance in *Aureng-Zebe* indicate that Dryden is more concerned with the individual and with moral issues here than with political and historical questions.

In the second part of *The Conquest,* also, Dryden emphasized private morality at the expense of larger political issues; the scenes of reconciliation between Ozmyn and Benzayda and their respective families, the scene of Almanzor's temptation of Almahide to unlawful love, the slander against Almahide's character perpetrated by Zulema, all these situations would seem to divert the audience from the larger political and historical issues of the play and instruct them in private morality.

Thus, in *Aureng-Zebe* and in the second part of *The Conquest,* Dryden seems to have substantially altered the nature of the heroic play. At the surface the subject is still political and historical, but most of the conversations and actions seem fitted to private persons as well as to monarchs, rebels, and usurpers. In *Aureng-Zebe,* especially, the central issue is whether Aureng-Zebe can, in the manner of Job, withstand a series of temptations and the loss of all his rewards. He even has three chief temptations as does Christ in the desert. The first temptation (to fight Arimant, the Emperor's man, and save Indamora) has the guise of a natural obligation, but he restrains himself out of piety to his father. The second temptation has the guise of filial obedience (to give up Indamora to his father and inherit the throne immediately), but Aureng-Zebe remains loyal to his love. The last temptation, that of incest with Nourmahal, seems, like the demand of Satan that Christ worship him, nakedly evil. When Aureng-Zebe refuses the pleasures and rewards which Nourmahal offers him, he is given a cup of poison which he determines to drink like the "dying Socrates." The essential design of *Aureng-Zebe*, then, is the testing of a virtuous man to see if he is worthy of succeeding to the throne. In addition, the situation which fate brings about for Aureng-Zebe's testing provides opportunities for other characters, like Morat, the Emperor, and Arimant, to regain a proper sense of values.

Even though four characters in this play are in love with Indamora, it would be a misreading of *Aureng-Zebe* to argue that love is the dominant theme. As in previous heroic plays, love provides a situation, a catalyst to make every character reveal himself and act according to his nature; love, as Placidius asserts in *Tyrannic Love*, arouses gentle fires in souls that are gentle but tempests in stormy minds. In spite of all her admirers, Indamora is practically helpless and in captivity throughout the play; it is only by equivocation, by a harmless flirtation with Morat that she saves Aureng-Zebe's life for a short while. She is more witty and charming than any of her predecessors in heroic drama, especially in her flirtations and in her treatment of Aureng-Zebe's jealousy, but she does not bring about the dénouement.

By the time Dryden wrote *Aureng-Zebe*, he was ready to abandon heroic drama for a different kind of play. Moody

Prior remarks that by 1677 "the day of the heroic play in rhymed couplets was over. In that year Nathaniel Lee wrote *The Rival Queens* in blank verse, and Dryden also abandoned the couplet in *All for Love* which appeared a few months later."[54] It is not merely the rhymed couplet, though, that Dryden left behind when he stopped writing heroic plays; his plays were never again so thoroughly schematized, so fugue-like in the arrangement and interrelationship of characters. In his next serious play, Dryden focuses on two "famous patterns of unlawful love," Antony and Cleopatra; if this had been a heroic play, there would have been at least one normative couple to whom these unlawful lovers would have stood in contrast. In *Aureng-Zebe* Morat behaves like Antony in that he gives up an empire for love and neglects his wife, but there is an explicit norm in the character of Aureng-Zebe. In *All for Love,* on the contrary, the norm is implicit. Therefore, the conceptual wholeness of heroic drama is missing; Dryden presents would-be heroes without heroes, brings forth characters who respect either civil law or natural law, but none who learn to respect both.

54. P. 177.

4

Dryden's Dramatic Technique

In the preface to *An Evening's Love* (1671), Dryden asserts that "serious plays" depend not much "on observation."[1] This assumption is a cornerstone of Dryden's aesthetics, for, as the previous reading of the heroic plays indicates, his art is a rational construct, derived from complex mental processes rather than from observation of actual experience. Dryden would have been supported in his idealist theory of art by Davenant and Hobbes, but opposed by Shadwell. Davenant thinks that poets "describe Mankinde" not so much as they see it but as they are "perswaded or guided by instinct," and Hobbes argues that the "manners of men" which poets represent are "feigned, as the name of Poesy imports, not found in men."[2] Shadwell, on the contrary, thinks that a poet and

1. Watson, *1*, 155. John M. Aden notes that in Dryden's distinction between judgment as "an effect of observation" and wit as a "sharpness of conceit," wit must signify "something like conception in the sense of poetical insight, the inner vision as opposed to the merely outward vision, creativity as opposed to reproduction." Hence, Aden concludes that in this preface Dryden's notion of creativity seems to move "away from that of the representational and toward the ideal" ("Dryden and the Imagination: the First Phase," *PMLA, 74* [1959], 37, 38). Even in the preface to *The Rival Ladies* (1664), however, Dryden seems far from a representational idea of creativity, since the entire process which he describes there takes place within the confines of the dramatist's mind and consists in pushing "images" or "ideas" of nature into the light.

2. Sir William Davenant, "Preface to *Gondibert, An Heroick Poem*," (1650), in *Critical Essays of the Seventeenth Century*, ed. J. E. Spingarn (Oxford, 1909), 2, 3. Thomas Hobbes, "Answer to Davenant's Preface to *Gondibert*," (1650), in *Critical Essays, 2*, 56. The relationship between Hobbes and Dryden on the matter of aesthetics is described at some length by Clarence DeWitt Thorpe in "The Psychological Approach in Dryden," *The Aesthetic Theory of Thomas Hobbes* (Ann Arbor, Mich., 1940), pp. 189–220.

dramatist ought to work from actual observation; such "Observation" is necessary "even in the highest Tragedies," for the dramatist must "have observed the Customs of Courts and the manner of conversing there"; he even contends that if a humor does not "resemble some man or other" it is "monstrous and unnatural," thus suggesting that the artist should imitate existence, not essence.[3] The extended debate between Dryden and Shadwell, which culminates in *MacFlecknoe*, is basically a quarrel between artists espousing opposite theories of art.

Dryden's notion of a serious play during the 1660s and 1670s is well summed up in the definition of a play proposed by Lisideius in the *Essay of Dramatic Poesy*: "it ought to be *A just and lively image of human nature, representing its passions and humours, and the changes of fortune to which it is subject, for the delight and instruction of mankind*."[4] That this deceptively simple definition is Dryden's own is attested first by the fact that it is "well received" by the other participants in the discourse; only Crites quibbles (in character) that the definition is not "altogether perfect" since it includes other forms of poetry than the dramatic.[5] Secondly, Dryden claims it as his own in "A Defence of *An Essay of Dramatic Poesy*": "This I have plainly said in my definition of a play: that it is a just and lively image of human nature, etc. Thus, the foundation, as it is generally stated will stand sure, if this definition of a play be true."[6]

This definition is as thoroughly schematized as any of Dryden's heroic plays; its elements have been arranged symmetrically, so that "just" and "lively" are in tension, "passions" and "humours," "delight" and "instruction," and "human nature" (characters) and "changes of fortune" (circumstances).

---

3. Thomas Shadwell, "Preface to *The Humorists*" (1671), *Critical Essays*, 2, 159, 157.
4. Watson, *1*, 25.
5. Ibid.
6. Watson, *1*, 122.

The words "lively," "passions," and "delight" suggest motion, spontaneity, or the spark of wit, while the words "just," "humours," and "instruction" suggest regularity, a predictable order and the weight of judgment. Like the heroic play, which contains symmetrical pairs of characters representing opposite points of view, this definition of a serious play is basically a series of conceptual opposites.

The phrase "image of human nature" which appears in Dryden's definition is more difficult to interpret than one might suppose, for the word "image" in Dryden's critical prose usually has the connotation of idea, essence, or first principle. As the following discussion will illustrate, Dryden repeatedly calls his characters "patterns," "ideas," and "images." He insists that these images of human nature, as well as images of other creatures, be boldly and sharply etched, consistent, and completely intelligible. Such a preoccupation with essence rather than existence is not surprising in a playwright of ideas who insists that poetry must "*be* ethical" even if it only resembles "natural truth."[7] For Dryden, moreover, history is an illustration of moral philosophy, and satire is "of the nature of moral philosophy."[8]

In the preface to *Annus Mirabilis* (1667), Dryden speaks of images that are "well wrought" and beget admiration. He compares the poet who embellishes his images to Venus "breathing beauty upon her son Aeneas," suggesting that the poet heightens what is observable.[9] The poet's images, however, are more than heightened imitations; they are more sharply delineated, more symmetrically arranged than their counterparts in nature. Dryden speaks more than once of placing the images of a Venus and of a lazar near each other because there is "imitation of nature" in either extreme.[10]

7. Ibid., p. 120.

8. Watson, 2, 8, 122.

9. "An Account of the Ensuing Poem," Watson, *1*, 99, 101.

10. "Preface to *Tyrannic Love*" (1670) and "An Account of the Ensuing Poem" (1667), Watson, *1*, 140, 101.

Venus and a lazar, from a mimetic point of view, would constitute an exaggerated portrayal of reality. Such a black and
white contrast, however, would appeal to a playwright of
ideas. Dryden has a tendency to juxtapose the beautiful and
the distorted, the admirable and the absurd, the saintly and
the irreligious in his plays. He conveys such sharp images of
heroes, tyrants, and rebels that he catches few of the subtle
nuances of empirical reality.

Dryden mentions the fact that Lucretius has "used this word
"image" oftener than any of the poets,"[11] and suggests that he
is therefore using the word deliberately, with full awareness of
its meaning in classical literature. At first glance, Dryden's
use of the word "image" to denote the essence or first principle of a thing seems to have little in common with that of
Lucretius, who refers to images as the floating outer skins of
things, as insubstantial shapes which are thrown off the surface of objects.[12] But Lucretius also asserts that "at any given
time, every sort of film is ready to hand in every place: they
fly so quickly and are drawn from so many sources. And, because they are so flimsy, the mind cannot distinctly perceive
any but those it makes an effort to perceive."[13] Thus, Lucretius leaves room for the imagination by showing that the mind
can choose to see whatever image or combination of images
it wants to see at any given time; the centaur, for example,
is the combination of two floating films, or images. Dryden,
similarly, thinks that to a great mind, all the images of nature
are at hand; he praises Shakespeare because "All the images
of nature were still present to him" and Cromwell because
"all the rich Idea's" of human nature were present in his "own

11. "The Author's Apology for Heroic Poetry and Poetic Licence," prefixed
to *The State of Innocence* (1677), Watson, *1*, 204.

12. Lucretius, *The Nature of the Universe,* Book IV, trans. Ronald Latham
(Aylesbury, 1955), p. 131.

13. Lucretius, p. 153. Dryden quotes a passage from this very section of
Lucretius in his "Apology for Heroic Poetry"; he speaks of "the conjunction of
two natures which have a real separate being," such as the centaurs whom
Lucretius describes.

large brest."[14] Both Dryden and Lucretius would agree, therefore, that the mind can choose to see any image, whether or
not it is actually present to the senses, and that these images
convey the identity of certain objects (for example, the centaur), whether or not these are in existence.[15]

Imaging, for Dryden, is a creative process that occurs within
the confines of the dramatist's mind. In the preface to *The
Rival Ladies* (1664), he speaks of the fancy moving the "sleep-
ing images of things toward the light, there to be distinguished,
and then either chosen or rejected by the judgment."[16] Elsewhere he writes that the imagination runs like a "nimble span-
iel" within the memory, the storehouse of images, for the
"species or ideas of those things which it designs to represent."[17] The more "comprehensive" the mind, the greater the
store of images it holds, and the closer approximation there is
between its contents and that nature which is outside of the
mind. Shakespeare did not need to look outwards; he "looked
inwards" to find nature; similarly, Cromwell understood his
followers by "intuition" rather than by tedious observation.[18]
For Dryden, as for Lucretius, the mind's view of images is
analogous to, but separate from, the senses' view of them.[19]

Dryden never makes it entirely clear whether the images
stored in such vast quantities in the poet's mind are the result
of reading and experience or whether they are innate, perhaps

14. Watson, *1*, 67; also, "Heroique Stanzas" (1659), in *Works*, California
edition, *1*, st. 26, ll. 101–04, p. 14.

15. Lucretius, p. 153.

16. "To Roger, Earl of Orrery," Watson, *1*, 2.

17. "An Account of the Enusing Poem," Watson, *1*, 98. Dryden borrowed
this metaphor from Hobbes. Hobbes, in the "Answer to Davenant," gives us an
insight into his and Dryden's view of memory: "For memory is the World
(though not really, yet so as in a looking glass)" wherein judgment gravely
examines "all the parts of Nature" and Fancy "finds her materials at hand"
(*Critical Essays, 2*, 59).

18. "Heroique Stanzas," ed. Hooker, st. 26, l. 102.

19. Lucretius asserts that the vision beheld by the mind "closely resembles"
that beheld by the eyes; just as the impact of films on the eyes accounts for
external vision, so some "flimsier" films hit the mind's eye (Book IV, p. 153).

inherent to reason. What is certain is that the images stored in the mind are true and constant referents; they represent the essence of reality and therefore cannot but correspond to the world outside the mind. Dryden, like Dante at the start of Canto II of the *Inferno,* seems confident that Memory, the mother of the Muses in classical mythology, cannot err: "che ritarrà la mente che non erra." Louis I. Bredvold, in "The Tendency toward Platonism in Neo-Classical Esthetics," seems to describe Dryden particularly when he writes of seventeenth-century artists that "the Nature which was then thought to be imitated by art will be much better understood from Cicero than from Hobbes and the scientists."[20] The passage he cites from Cicero contains a use of the word "image" in exactly the sense that Dryden understands it:

> When Phidias undertook a statue of Jupiter or Minerva, he did not select a model and follow it strictly, but in his mind he had an extraordinary ideal type of beauty. . . . For, as in the arts of sculpture and painting there is something perfect and excellent which is not perceived by the eye but which is derived from an ideal image in the mind, so we perceive the true type of eloquence with our minds and not with our ears.[21]

Dryden often uses the word "image" to denote a character; at other times he uses the word "pattern." Both words imply that the character is conceptualized rather than drawn from life. He defends his character Philocles, a central figure in *Secret Love* (1668), from the attack of critics, arguing that he never intended him for a "perfect character" since the Queen in that play is the "one great and absolute pattern of honour"; he adds that the "variety of images" is "one great beauty of a play," hence the poet must combine perfect and imperfect characters.[22] One senses that all the characters in the play have

20. *ELH, 1* (Sept., 1934), 94, 98.
21. Ibid.
22. "Preface to *Secret Love*" (1668), Watson, *1*, 106.

been placed along an abstract, ethical continuum ranging from foolish to imperfect. In his discussion of *The Conquest of Granada,* similarly, Dryden calls Almanzor a "more exact image of human life" because of his frailties;[23] Almahide, Ozmyn, and Benzayda, on the other hand, are the "patterns of exact virtue" in the play.

Dryden again uses the words "pattern" and "image" to designate character in the preface to *Tyrannic Love.* There he speaks of "patterns of piety" and "lively images of piety," such as Saint Catharine who can "second the precepts of our religion." Their irreligious, blasphemous foils—Maximin, for example—do not promote disbelief since they are not patterns to be imitated.[24] Antony and Cleopatra are called "patterns of unlawful love" in the remarks on *All for Love,* and Dryden says he considered giving the poem *Eleonora* the title *The Pattern,* since the lady for whom the panegyric was written was "the pattern of charity, devotion, and humility; of the best wife, the best mother, and the best of friends."[25]

For Dryden, a character is successful if he is thoroughly intelligible and consistent, attributes undoubtedly suitable for a play of ideas. The audience should be able to predict what the character will do: "If the inclinations be obscure, 'tis a sign the poet is in the dark, and knows not what manner of man he represents to you; and consequently you can have no idea, or very imperfect, of that man; nor can judge what resolutions he ought to take; or what words or actions are proper for him."[26] What Dryden demands of a character is entirely in accord with Aristotle and Horace; the former asks that charac-

23. The dedication of *The Conquest* to the Duke of York, quoted in part by Watson, *1,* 163 n.; "Of Heroic Plays," Watson, *1,* 165.

24. "Preface to *Tyrannic Love*" (1670), Watson, *1,* 140.

25. "Preface to *All for Love*" (1678), Watson, *1,* 222; "To the Earl of Abingdon," prefixed to *Eleonora* (1692), Watson, *2,* 62. In the "Preface to *Don Sebastian*" (1690), Dryden states that there is not only a "general moral" in his play but "also another moral, couched under every one of the principal parts and characters, which a judicious critic will observe" (Watson, *2, 50*).

26. "The Grounds of Criticism in Tragedy" (1679), Watson, *1, 250.*

ters be "consistent and the same throughout," and Horace states that a poet should "keep a part, as first defined, consistent in its every stage."[27] Hobbes too asserts that a figure in a heroic poem should maintain "to the end the same character" which he had in the beginning.[28] By making his characters thoroughly intelligible and consistent, however, Dryden cannot fully individualize them, and so perhaps he must, to use Lewis N. Chase's phrase, "present abstract human qualities" rather than men and women.[29]

To assail Dryden's characters for being psychologically unreal would be to misunderstand their effectiveness in heroic drama. Moody Prior has remarked with some justice that these characters are "very good for their purpose; that, in fact, for the kind of work in which they exist they could not be other than they are."[30] In plays of ideas such as Dryden creates, with their complex interrelationship of action, discourse, and character, it is necessary that characters be stripped down to their essence so that they become manageable vehicles for the exposition of points of view.

When Dryden sets out to write a play that is an "image of human nature," then, he is not so much trying to mirror forth a reflection of the world about him as attempting to reveal some essential, timeless qualities of human nature. If examined singly, his characters will not reveal the subtleties of Shakespeare's creations, but when examined all together in their fugue-like interrelationships, they have an exciting metaphysical complexity.

THE IMPORTANCE OF DESIGN

Dryden's chief norm for drama is exactitude and wholeness

27. Horace, *The Art of Poetry* (Book II, Epistle III), in *The Poems of Horace*, trans. A. Hamilton Bryce (London, 1907), p. 280. Aristotle, *Poetics*, in *The Basic Works of Aristotle*, ed. Richard McKeon (New York, 1941), p. 1469.
28. Hobbes, "Answer to Davenant's Preface," *Critical Essays*, 2, 64.
29. *The English Heroic Play*, p. 51.
30. *The Language of Tragedy*, p. 164.

of design. He is not fascinated by imagination merely as an instrument of discovery; undisciplined originality would not have gained much credit with him. Nor does he pay much tribute to style, insisting that words, like the coloring of a painting, are mere surface and of no value if the design is badly wrought. What he does lavish praise upon and what he himself excels in is disposition, the interrelation of parts within a whole. He often censures ancient as well as modern French dramatists for "narrowness" of plot and "fewness of persons."[31] An abundance of distinct characters and a large, historically significant action would be, for Dryden, major ingredients in a good play.

Because the architectural merit of a play, its draftsmanship, is more important to Dryden than the novelty of its content or the language in which it is executed, he makes continual use of an architectural metaphor to designate the various parts of a play. Ben Jonson once compared the fable of a play to the place where a building is to be erected,[32] and Davenant called *Gondibert* "this new Building" with such distinct parts as "the outward frame, the large rooms within, the lesser conveyances, and now the furniture."[33] Dryden makes more elaborate use of the metaphor. He employs it first of all to distinguish the work of fancy from that of judgment in the making of a play. In the preface to *Secret Love* (1668), Dryden calls judgment the "master-builder" which restrains fancy and is its proper "surveyor," and contrasts judgment to self-love, which would

31. Eugenius, in the *Essay of Dramatic Poesy*, mentions often that the plots of the tragedies of the Ancients are "narrow, and the persons few" (Watson, *1*, 37), and Neander attacks French plays for "dearth" of plot and lack of variety in characters. In Part II of "Heads of an Answer to Rymer," Dryden shows that ancient tragedy was deficient because of "the narrowness of its plots, and fewness of persons" (Watson, *1*, 212). Throughout his critical writings, Dryden makes fullness and variety of design one of his chief norms for tragedy.

32. Ben Jonson, *Timber, or Discoveries*, in *Critical Essays of the Seventeenth Century, 1*, 60.

33. Davenant, "Preface to *Gondibert*," pp. 1, 17, 20.

let fancy run astray.[34] Judgment is in charge of the "fabric and contrivance" of the play and may determine "without deception" whether the finished piece is faithful to the model or "pattern." Fancy, on the other hand, gave judgment the "perfect idea" of the pattern which the master builder now follows.[35] In *An Essay of Dramatic Poesy* (1668), Neander also calls judgment the "master-workman" in charge of raising a building. In the construction of a play, this builder needs "many subordinate hands, many tools to his assistance," including "history, geography, or moral philosophy." The master builder even needs verse, for this is a "rule and line by which he keeps his building compact and even."[36]

Also by means of the architectural metaphor, Dryden distinguishes the plot, characters, manners, and thoughts in a play. He consistently compares the plot or fable with the underground parts of a building, or the foundation; this part should be sturdy, for on its solidity rests the entire building. Dryden, defending English dramatists against Rymer's attacks, says that they "can raise passions as high on worse foundations" than those of the Ancients, whose plays were "more correctly plotted."[37] In the preface to *An Evening's Love* (1671), Dryden states that his "characters are raised" on the "foundation" of a borrowed story.[38] In still another piece of criticism, Dryden points out that the plot is below ground and will not immediately strike the eye of the viewer, while the manners and thoughts of the characters are "above ground."

> After the plot, which is the foundation of the play, the next thing to which we ought to apply our judgment is

34. Watson, *1*, 105.
35. Ibid.
36. Ibid., p. 35. Eugenius also refers to the architectural image; he claims that the Ancients were "building an house without a model" when they wrote plays without a predetermined number of acts.
37. Watson, *1*, 215.
38. Ibid., *1*, 155.

the manners, for now the poet comes to work above
ground: the ground-work indeed is that which is most
necessary, as that upon which depends the firmness of the
whole fabric; yet it strikes not the eye so much as the beauties or imperfections of the manners, the thoughts, and
the expressions.[39]

The plot being, therefore, the base of his building, Dryden
goes on to make the characters and their manners the sides
of the edifice. Whereas the plot is hidden and subterranean,
the characters are very much in view; hence Dryden calls his
drama an "image of human nature," rather than the "mimesis
of an action," as Aristotle defines a play.[40]

In creating his characters, Dryden follows three criteria:
variety, greatness, and probability. The characters are so much
a part of the entire architectural design that Dryden wants to
give several characters, not one or two, a rank of the first mag-
nitude. *In Tyrannic Love,* for example, Maximin, Catharine,
Placidius, Valeria, Berenice, and Porphyrius are almost of the
same importance; their interrelationship creates the design of
the play. Dryden gives a mild censure to his predecessor Davenant when he says that "what was wanting to the perfection
of his *Siege of Rhodes* . . . was design, and variety of characters."[41] Dryden's own way of making characters, of putting up

39. "The Grounds of Criticism in Tragedy," prefixed to *Troilus and Cressida* (1679), Watson, *1*, 247. In some later references to the metaphor of architecture, Dryden writes that the building, or work of art, must be carefully
finished in every part to assure its perpetuity: "even the cavities ought not to
be filled with rubbish which is of a perishable kind, destructive to the strength,
but with brick or stone though of less pieces, yet of the same nature, and fitted
to the crannies ("To John, Marquess of Normanby" [1697], Watson, 2, 224).
His praise of Congreve written in 1694 again suggests the architectural image;
Congreve starts with "Firm Doric pillars" and crowns them with the "fair
Corinthian" ("To Mr Congreve, on his *Double-Dealer*," Watson, 2, 170).

40. *Poetics,* p. 1461. Aristotle says that tragedy is not an imitation of persons but of action, hence his position would be exactly opposite to that of
Dryden.

41. "Of Heroic Plays: An Essay," Watson, *1*, 159.

the sides of his building, is most aptly described by Neander in
the *Essay of Dramatic Poesy:*

> But this hinders not that there may be more shining char-
> acters in the play: many persons of a second magnitude,
> nay, some so very near, so almost equal to the first, that
> greatness may be opposed to greatness, and all the persons
> be made considerable, not only by their quality but their
> action. 'Tis evident that the more the persons are, the
> greater will be the variety of the plot. If then the parts
> are managed so regularly that the beauty of the whole be
> kept entire, and that the variety become not a perplexed
> and confused mass of accidents, you will find it infinitely
> pleasing to be led in a labyrinth of design, where you see
> some of your way before you, yet discern not the end till
> you arrive at it.[42]

In his heroic plays, Dryden effects this opposition of greatness
to greatness by making all of his characters able champions of
distinct points of view, without regard to their position on the
ethical continuum. Even the rebels and tyrants have the appearance of heroes and are like "statues which are placed on
high" which are "made greater than the life, that they may
descend to the sight in their just proportion."[43] But even
though Dryden insists that his images, or characters, should
be "admirable" and "wonderful," he adds that they must be
more than "barely possible."[44] In his defense of Almanzor
as a character within the bounds of probability, he says, " 'tis
at last charged upon me that Almanzor does all things; or, if
you will have an absurd accusation, in their nonsense who
make it, that he performs impossibilities." Dryden compares
the actions of his character not only with the historical account
of Almanzor, but with accounts of Caesar and other generals

42. Watson, *1*, 61.
43. Ibid., p. 88.
44. "The Grounds of Criticism in Tragedy," Watson, *1*, 245.

who stood alone before an army or quelled a mutiny by their single authority. He adds that Almanzor is far from always victorious, since he is made a prisoner "and, at the last, defeated, and not able to preserve the city from being taken."[45]

Dryden's love of design leads him to compare the dramatist with an architect and the poet with a watchmaker, a lapidary, and a gunsmith.[46] Bonamy Dobrée asserts that "it is the sheer artificiality of his plays which gives them their high place." He finds a "sense of the architectural," a "hard structure" which compensates the reader for the absence of natural passion.[47] In the "Heads of an Answer to Rymer," Dryden lists the parts of a "tragic or heroic" poem in a way which suggests the importance of structure:

    I.   The fable itself.

    II.   The order or manner of its contrivance in relation of the parts to the whole.

   III. The manners or decency of the characters in speaking or acting what is proper for them, and proper to be shewn by the poet.

   IV. The thoughts which express the manners.

    V.   The words which express those thoughts.[48]

The implied norm in this list is propriety in the design; all the parts must be fitted properly to the whole, so that characters who are appropriate to the fable speak "what is proper for them," and the thoughts are properly expressive of their manners, and the works of their thoughts. Every part is neatly tied in, "like the links of a curious chain," as Dryden himself notes.[49]

John M. Aden finds an "artistic dualism" in Dryden and believes that the poet conceived "of art as a thing with interior

---

45. "Of Heroic Plays," Watson, *1*, 166.
46. "Preface to *An Evening's Love*" (1671), Watson, *1*, 155.
47. *Restoration Tragedy*, p. 96.
48. Watson, *1*, 217.
49. Ibid.

and exterior aspects."[50] Dryden's critical writings will surely give credence to that statement, while giving frequent proof that the interior aspect of a work is its design, the disposition of the parts. Dryden distinguishes the interior and exterior aspects of a work of art in the "Preface to *Fables Ancient and Modern*": "Now the words are the colouring of the work, which, in the order of nature, is last to be considered. The design, the disposition, the manners, and the thoughts, are all before it."[51] The architectural merit of a work of art, not its fine array of words, should, in Dryden's view, determine its rank.

DELIGHT, ADMIRATION, AND INSTRUCTION

Dryden's serious drama, especially his heroic drama, offers, then, an *"image of human nature"* that is particularly well wrought in terms of design. The purpose of this drama is to delight and instruct, according to Dryden's definition which Lisideius states in *An Essay of Dramatic Poesy* and the poet repeats in the "Defence of *An Essay*."[52] At other times, however, Dryden mentions that "admiration" and "concernment" are the effects he hopes to achieve. These ends are not irreconcilable, since admiration, as Dryden uses the word, easily takes in both delight and instruction, while concernment replaces the pity and fear which Aristotle submits are the proper effects of tragedy.

Since Dryden lets each character wear the mask of a hero in the heroic plays, it is not immediately evident that the plays are instructive. Maximin is just as eloquent as Catharine, and the Emperor has lines which are comparable in beauty to those of Aureng-Zebe. The proponents of government under law and of tyranny are equally witty. It is in the design of the plays that the instruction lies. First, the dramatist shows the

50. p. 28.
51. Watson, 2, 275.
52. Watson, *1*, 25, 122.

"laws of justice" at work in the plot, by dealing out rewards to the virtuous and punishments to the rest. The poet-dramatist has fortune at his command, "with which wisdom does often unsuccessfully struggle in the world."[53] Secondly, the dramatist creates two kinds of characters—"patterns" for imitation and "patterns" for avoidance; by thus raising intellectual admiration and contempt in the viewer, the dramatist hopes to instruct him and make him more discerning of true merit in human nature.

Some critics of heroic drama hold that this drama is not instructive; Moody Prior, for example, thinks that one chiefly finds "emotional and dialectical displays" in such works.[54] Bonamy Dobrée, on the other hand, sees here a triumph of "the little justice of little men. Virtue must be rewarded here and now: Aureng-Zebe must have his throne and his Indamora because he is so good a son."[55] Another critic who finds fault with the poetic justice meted out by Dryden is Margaret Sherwood. She argues that it takes a greater faith to "believe in the divine significance of events as they actually are, fairly considered, with desire to learn the truth from them [than] from an a priori notion."[56] From this viewpoint, however, it would seem that the story of Job, "fairly considered," ought to have an unhappy ending, for Dryden, like the biblical historians, is not so much concerned with the tragic lives faced by isolated individuals, as with the larger, historically significant, universal patterns of existence. From this eighth-sphere point of view, he shows that the good are generally and in the long run rewarded. In writing a play of ideas, moreover, he would surely find it useful to fit the facts to his scheme of values and thereby to show that a sound point of view does succeed in practice.

53. "To Roger, Earl of Orrery," Watson, *1*, 4.
54. P. 158.
55. P. 31.
56. *Dryden's Dramatic Theory*, p. 20.

Dryden's interest in poetic justice can be traced throughout his critical writings, beginning with *An Essay of Dramatic Poesy*. In that essay Eugenius censures the Ancients for having "often shown a prosperous wickedness, and an unhappy piety" and contends that they have lacked in instruction;[57] Lisideius, moreover, praises the French for observing the laws of justice, for mending "the intrigue of fate" and dispensing "with the severity of history, to reward that virtue which has been rendered to us there unfortunate."[58] In the "Heads of an Answer to Rymer," Dryden states that since the "reformation of manners" is the desired effect of tragedy, then "the punishment of vice and reward of virtue are the most adequate ends of tragedy, because most conducing to good example of life."[59] If the poet cannot follow the rules of poetic justice, he should at least render "virtue always amiable, though it be shown unfortunate; and vice detestable, tho' it be shown triumphant."[60] For the sake of public instruction, therefore, Dryden would favor a somewhat rationalistic approach to life in serious drama, in the sense that nearly every character should succeed according to his deserts. He makes an exception to this rule in such characters as Acacis, Abdelmelech, Valeria, and Melesinda; these tragic figures are either committed to a political party that heaven does not favor or bound by love to one who is not deserving of their loyalty. Each of these characters thinks of fate as pitiless and commits suicide just before the end of the play. They interpret heavenly justice from a narrow, personal point of view instead of a larger, historical one.

In addition to illustrating the laws of justice, the dramatist, in Dryden's view, ought to provoke admiration in the viewer. According to G. Gregory Smith, the critical word *"admiration"* was first established by Minturno, who added it to "delight"

---

57. Watson, *1*, 38.
58. Ibid., p. 47.
59. Ibid., p. 218.
60. Ibid., p. 213.

and "instruction" as a third function of poetry; hence, "its critical place is with 'instruction' and 'delight' in the general definition of the purpose of Poetry."[61] In France of the 1640s, Corneille had made admiration the accepted goal of the dramatist; he attempted to raise admiration in his audiences by displaying moral strength, a composite of Roman *virtus* and Christian resoluteness, in men who were so superior that they achieved repeated victories over their passions. Instead of holding the mirror up to the man who is confused and swayed by the lower forces in his nature, Corneille showed the rare but still existent man who is capable of exalted deeds, strength of will, and perseverance in the pursuit of honor or nobility.[62] Dryden follows Corneille not only in valuing admiration as the chief emotion to be raised by serious drama, but in arguing his theories in discourses and in prefaces to his plays. Like Corneille, Dryden creates characters who have very strong passions and who learn to channel them constructively without weakening them. Corneille writes that such a glorious triumph over passion surpasses what can be found in ancient drama:

> et la haute vertu dans un naturel sensible à ces passions, qu'elle dompte sans les affaiblir, et à qui elle laisse toute leur force pour en triompher plus glorieusement, a quelque chose de plus touchant, de plus élevé et de plus aimable que cette médiocre bonté, capable d'une faiblesse, et même d'un crime, où nos anciens étaient contraints d'arrêter le caractère le plus parfait des rois et des princes dont ils faisaient leurs héros.[63]

The low idea of virtue—"cette médiocre bonté"—in ancient tragedy permitted the dramatist to present even his normative

---

61. *Elizabethan Critical Essays* (London, 1959; reprinted from the edition of 1904), *1*, 392.

62. J. Calvet, *Manuel illustré d'histoire de la littérature française* (Paris, 1955), pp. 248–52.

63. Pierre Corneille, "Examen" attached to *Le Cid*, ed. F. M. Warren (Boston, 1895), p. 11.

characters as subject to weaknesses and base impulses, but the Christian dramatist, Corneille shows, must provide loftier images of virtue commensurate with his view of free will.

In the "Defence of *An Essay*," Dryden writes that a "bare imitation" of life will not serve to "affect the soul, and excite the passions, and, above all, to move admiration (which is the delight of serious plays)." He goes on to distinguish tragedy and comedy on the ground that admiration is the delight of the former, satire of the latter.[64] He even substitutes "admiration, compassion, or concernment" for "fear and pity" when he translates Aristotle's words concerning the purpose of tragedies, implying that there is an element of fear or awe in his idea of admiration.[65] Sir Philip Sidney had also altered Aristotle's words to the same effect, so that it is possible that Dryden derived his critical use of the word "admiration" from this English source rather than from Minturno.[66]

Baxter Hathaway remarks that Dryden's notion of tragedy is an important one for the history of tragic theory. "Admiration," this critic explains, "is the important passion which tragedy should evoke. Tragic fear is supplanted, shrewdly enough perhaps, by concernment. Here the fear is not for ourselves, but for the safety and well-being of the central figure of the play."[67] This concernment for the central characters is a detached type of reaction, one might infer, compared to

64. Watson, *1*, 114.

65. *An Essay of Dramatic Poesy*, Watson, *1*, 46; and "Heads of an Answer to Rymer," Watson, *1*, p. 213. In the former, Dryden's character Crites makes the uncontested statement that Aristotle has defined the end of tragedies to be "admiration, compassion, or concernment," while in the second critical work, Dryden suggests that pity and terror, "in a larger sense," can be said to comprehend "concernment for the good" and "detestation for the bad." In both cases there is a definite alteration of Aristotle's meaning with the result that the audience does not fear for itself or pity the man driven by his own sins and by fate; instead, the audience has the detached and intellectual responses of "concernment," "detestation," and, in the earlier work, "admiration."

66. Watson notes that Sidney in his *Apology*, "replaces 'fear' with 'admiration' and that the heroic play presupposes such a definition," *1*, 46 n.

67. "John Dryden and the Function of Tragedy," *PMLA, 58* (1943), 670.

the fear on one's own account which Aristotle and other theo-
rists of the drama have envisaged. Certainly, this is a more
suitable reaction to a play of ideas than tragic fear.

Dryden's idea of a serious play changes somewhat after he
ceases writing heroic plays. After 1677 he begins to describe
the serious play as distinct from the epic, whereas, at the time
he wrote heroic plays, he tended to merge the two genres.
Thus, admiration is at this time the reaction caused by an epic
only, whereas pity is that caused by a serious play. Tragedy
must now simply purge the passions; its purpose is to "raise
and afterwards to calm the passions, to purge the soul from
pride, by the examples of human miseries, which befall the
greatest."[68] The epic, on the other hand, ought to raise the soul
and harden it to virtue,[69] an effect formerly attributed to
heroic drama. Dryden's remarks on the epic hero in the preface to Virgil are reminiscent of his discussions of Almanzor
and other dramatic heroes, for he speaks of raising the viewer's
admiration by means of a hero, some of whose qualities are
"proposed to imitation":

> The shining quality of an epic hero, his magnanimity,
> his constancy, his patience, his piety, or whatever charac-
> teristical virtue his poet gives him, raises first our admira-
> tion; we are naturally prone to imitate what we admire;
> and frequent acts produce a habit. If the hero's chief
> quality be vicious as, for example, the choleric and ob-
> stinate desire of vengeance in Achilles, yet the moral is
> instructive . . . The courage of Achilles is proposed to

68. "To John, Lord Marquess of Normanby," Watson, 2, 226–28; this attitude on tragedy can be seen in the preface to *Troilus and Cressida*, "The
Grounds of Criticism in Tragedy," where Dryden writes that pity for the misfortunes of the virtuous and fear lest we too suffer from such turns of fortune
are the passions to be moved by tragedy; hence, Dryden seems more preoccupied
with the effect of tragedy upon the emotions of the audience after 1677. Words
like "tender" and "distressed" which appear in the latter essay with respect to
tragedy would have been out of place in reference to heroic drama.

69. "To John, Lord Marquess of Normanby," Watson, 2, 224.

imitation, not his pride and disobedience to his general, nor his brutal cruelty to his dead enemy, nor the selling of his body to his father. We abhor these actions while we read them; and what we abhor we never imitate.[70]

Admiration, which was at an earlier point the "delight of serious plays," is here the delight of epics and a means of instruction, because either the epic hero is a pattern for imitation or "the moral is instructive" by showing the ill consequences of his faults.

Instruction and delight, two of the ends of tragedy, often seem to overlap in Dryden's thinking. He first makes them merge in the effect of admiration, whereby the viewer is delighted and edified at the same time, and later describes them not as opposing principles within the framework of a poem, but as complementary ends of the creative process. For example, in the "Heads of an Answer to Rymer," Dryden states that the "chief end" of the poet is to please, but the "great end" of the poem is to instruct.[71] Similarly, in the preface to his translation of *De arte graphica*, Dryden remarks that the aim of the poet is to "make sure of pleasing and that in preference to instruction," but he immediately adds that the "chief design of poetry is to instruct."[72] Dryden, consequently, has substantially altered the conventional relationship between delight and instruction. Instead of delight being the sugarcoating for the bitter pill of instruction, as it is in Sidney, it is the poet's psychological motivation. The poet needs first and foremost, Dryden implies, to delight others; delight is the private incentive to creation. Moral instruction, on the other hand, is the poet's public stance; his product is instructive even though his desire is to delight. This theory appears to be a remarkable psychological advance over its predecessors in criticism. In

70. Ibid., p. 228.
71. Watson, *1*, 219.
72. Watson, 2, 186.

sum, Dryden has focused attention on the creative process by making delight and instruction part of a sequence rather than conflicting principles within a poem. In the same way, he systematically undermines the conventional relationship between wit and judgment, making them work in sequence during creation.

When Dryden states that the poet's business is to please, he is not suggesting that he distort reality. "Nothing but nature," he asserts, "can give a sincere pleasure; where that is not imitated, 'tis grotesque painting; the fine woman ends in a fish's tail."[73] Again, he remarks that "you rarely meet with anything in Virgil but truth, which therefore leaves the strongest impression of pleasure in the soul."[74] The poet, whose aim is to delight his audience, must therefore be a conscientious truthteller. If he succeeds in delighting somewhat more than he does in instructing, he will have ministered to the audience's "private pleasures" by such characteristics as "agitation of spirits," "impetuosity," lofty and sonorous expressions.[75] If, on the other hand, he succeeds in instructing somewhat more than in delighting, he will have acted like a "minister of state," fulfilling a public obligation by putting folly to shame and insinuating "virtue rather by familiar examples than by the severity of precepts."[76] Just as delight is the private aim of the poet, so it creates private pleasure in the viewer, and just as instruction is the public stance of the poet, it promotes the general good of the audience.

When Dryden suggests that he would "choose to be loved better," because he delights, rather than to be "more es-

---

73. "To John, Lord Marquess of Normanby," Watson, 2, 229.

74. "A Defence of *An Essay of Dramatic Poesy*," Watson, *1*, 121.

75. *A Discourse Concerning Satire* (1693), Watson, 2, 130–32. These phrases are used to describe Juvenal, but apply to the impetuous half of all the other pairs of writers whom Dryden describes in his critical writings.

76. Ibid. These expressions describe Horace, but could be applied to the more correct and rule-minded half of the numerous pairs of writers Dryden mentions.

teemed," because he instructs,[77] he leads one to suppose that he would prefer to be like Juvenal, Shakespeare, and Homer, rather than like Horace, Jonson, and Virgil. Even here, however, the distinction is not simple. Juvenal is a more severe chastiser of vice, yet more delightful than Horace.[78] Juvenal's ability to delight his readers, therefore, is not founded on any absence of moral instruction; it is rather the product of his vehement and fiery temper which stands in contrast to Horace's magisterial restraint.

Evidently, Dryden loves Juvenal and Shakespeare above Horace and Ben Jonson for the fire and passion with which they convey their moral instruction, and he places Homer at a higher rank in his affection than Virgil. In a passage explaining why "the Grecian is more according to my genius than the Latin poet," Dryden calls Homer "violent, impetuous, and full of fire," adding that he is "rapid in his thoughts," and that he takes "all the liberties."[79] On the other hand, he esteems or admires Horace, Jonson, and Virgil for the superlative artistry with which they convey their moral instruction. Just as he distinguishes the passionate and the correct form of heroism in the heroic plays and provides pairs of heroes, such as Montezuma and Acacis, Cortez and Guyomar, Almanzor and Ozmyn, so he divides literary creativity into its passionate and correct forms. Both forms are normative, for both are morally instructive and delightful; it is a question of degree, not kind, which distinguishes the two forms. Dryden seems in this way to over-

77. Ibid., p. 132.

78. Ibid., pp. 128–29. Dryden writes that "Juvenal, excepting only his first satire, is in all the rest confined to the exposing of some particular vice; that he lashes and there he sticks." And again, he notes that Juvenal "exhorts to particular virtues, as they are opposed to those vices against which he declaims," whereas Horace attacks fools and fops and attempts to make men wiser rather than better.

79. "Preface to *Fables Ancient and Modern*" (1700), Watson, 2, 274; Dryden emphatically restates this point two pages later where he writes: "This vehemence of his, I confess, is more suitable to my temper; and therefore, I have translated his first book with greater pleasure than any part of Virgil."

lap delight and instruction when he says of Juvenal and Horace: "I am profited by both, I am pleased with both; but I owe more to Horace for my instruction, and more to Juvenal for my pleasure."[80]

Dryden's view of the purpose of drama and poetry resembles in part the views of Davenant and Sidney, while it stands in contrast to that of Milton. Davenant, like Dryden, distinguishes the purpose of the poet from the purpose of the poem. But Dryden declares that the artist's "chief end" is to delight others, while Davenant says it is to pursue fame; and Dryden calls the "great end" of poetry moral instruction, while Davenant thinks poetry can aim no higher than the giving of "collateral" help to "Religion, Armes, Policy, and Law" in order to bring about a "peaceful obedience to Superiors."[81] For Davenant the summum bonum is a social one; he even defines virtue as "prerogative of blood, which is seldom unassisted with education, or greatnesse of minde."[82] He evidently regards social stability and stratification into classes as goals to be achieved apart from any consideration of individual abilities and ambitions. Dryden, however, has wrought human nature "to an higher pitch" in heroic drama in order to show it with more exactitude, to reveal it free of accidents and deformities, other than those which come of free choice, to conceptualize it rather than to differentiate the aristocratic and the common man. Like Ben Jonson, Dryden would scorn those upper-class gallants who differ from clowns only "in clothes, not in judgment or understanding."[83] Conversely, he would not despise a great man without a title, since he portrays the tyrannical Inca king in *The Indian Queen* as doing just this and living to regret it.

Davenant asserts that he expects "Princes and Nobles," or

80. *A Discourse Concerning Satire*, Watson, 2, p. 127.
81. Davenant, "Preface to *Gondibert*," pp. 35, 44.
82. Ibid., p. 14.
83. Jonson, *Timber*, in *Critical Essays, 1*, 19.

the "Chiefs" of society, to read his works and to be "reform'd and made Angelicall by the Heroick."[84] Dryden, likewise, mentions that tragedy instructs persons who are "greater" than those instructed by comedy, but it is not clear that by the word "greater" he is referring to a higher social class; he might very well be designating men of superior mind and ability.[85] In the heroic plays, Almanzor and Montezuma are more admirable than those holding the titles and crowns; Almanzor, in fact, suggests that he can be kingly in the context of nature and need not rule a realm.

Lewis N. Chase argues that heroic drama is "thoroughly anti-democratic" in sentiment, noting in particular that there is "no appearance of a representative of the people" and that the characters are all "of illustrious birth."[86] It is certain, however, that to some extent Dryden uses noble birth as a metaphor for human nature wrought to a "higher pitch," for mankind as it ought to be rather than as it is. Since Dryden has created plays of ideas in which characters, dialogues, and actions are strictly schematized, he need not reflect the society about him as much as humanity in the abstract. Whereas Davenant claims openly to be addressing only the nobility and gentry in his poetry, because the "common Crowd" ought "to be corrected by laws, where precept is accompanied with punishment,"[87] Dryden shows no overt partiality to upper-class audiences in his critical writings.

Both Davenant and Dryden resemble Sir Philip Sidney in regarding their characters as images or patterns which are at once delightful and instructive. Davenant is opposed to overt instruction in a work of art, but he concedes that "Images of Vertue" in heroic poetry are so "amiable" that they are always "gently and delightfully infusing" rather than "inculcating

84. P. 45.
85. "A Parallel betwixt Painting and Poetry," Watson, 2, 193.
86. Pp. 138–40.
87. "Preface to *Gondibert*," p. 14.

Precepts."[88] Sidney set a precedent for both seventeenth-century poets by regarding his heroic characters as patterns for imitation: "the loftie Image of such woorthies, most inflameth the mind with desire to bee woorthie, and informes with counsaile how to bee woorthie."[89] Sidney, moreover, asserts that characters ought to be clearly delineated and consistent; he would favor no 'ambiguity, no chiaroscuro in his images of human nature: "If the Poet do his part aright, he will shew you in *Tantalus Atreus,* and such like, nothing that is not to be shunned; in *Cyrus, Aeneas, Ulisses,* each thing to be followed."[90] This view of characters is somewhat simpler than that of Dryden, for the latter creates imperfect heroes in Almanzor, Porphyrius, and Montezuma. The rashness and the fiery temper of each of these individualistic heroes are not meant to be imitated. On the whole, though, Dryden, like Sidney, thinks that the poet should make "notable images of vertues, vices" and give an "image of that whereof the Philosopher bestoweth but a woordish description."[91]

Dryden, moreover, follows Sidney in making admiration the passion to be evoked by heroic drama, and in arguing that the poet should let his audience think that he merely intends to amuse them. Delight is the vehicle of moral enlightenment; it is "al the good, fellow *Poet* seemes to promise," but he shows his audience "the form of goodnes, (which seene, they cannot but love) ere themselves be aware, as if they tooke a medicine of Cheries."[92] By making his instruction more covert the poet would make its effect more certain.

Unlike Davenant and Dryden, Milton favors overt instruction and is more concerned with catharsis than with "well raised admiration." In his definition of a tragedy prefixed to

88. Ibid., p. 46.
89. Sir Philip Sidney, *The Defence of Poesie,* in *The Prose Works of Sir Philip Sidney,* ed. Albert Feuillerat (Cambridge, 1962), *3,* 25.
90. Sidney, p. 16.
91. Ibid., p. 14.
92. Ibid., p. 21.

Samson Agonistes (1671), Milton substitutes three adjectives for Dryden's single word "instruction": "gravest, moralest, and most profitable." "Tragedy," he writes, "as it was antiently compos'd, hath been ever held the gravest, moralest, and most profitable of all other Poems: therefore said by *Aristotle* to be of power by raising pity and fear, or terror, to purge the mind of those and such like passions, that is to temper and reduce them to just measure with a kind of delight, stirr'd up by reading or seeing those passions well imitated."[93] Milton suggests in his definition that "antiently compos'd" tragedies were grave and moral, yet Dryden has Eugenius point out in the *Essay of Dramatic Poesy* that the ancients lacked poetic justice and therefore lacked instruction, because they showed a prosperous wickedness or a suffering virtue.[94] Since Dryden himself seems to favor using poetic justice as a vehicle for instruction, he would favor the modern type of instruction. Thus Dryden and Milton would certainly be at opposite poles on the matter of what is "most profitable," Dryden wishing to designate the virtuous by showing them as prosperous at the end of the plays (always excepting those virtuous characters who despair and commit suicide), and Milton giving more explicit moral instruction while showing the virtuous suffering without hope of a tangible reward.

Dryden wants to show images of human nature that will raise admiration or detestation in the viewer, but Milton wants human passions "well imitated" so that the viewer may be stirred to a response of pity and fear. The response Dryden expects is at once more detached and more intellectual. Milton would purge the passions of the viewer while instructing him; Dryden, on the other hand, would "affect the soul" by images of heroic virtue and of the folly of would-be heroes. Like Carlyle in *Heroes and Hero-Worship,* Dryden works on the

93. "Preface to *Samson Agonistes*" (1671), in *The Works of John Milton* (New York, 1931), *1*, Pt. II, p. 331.
94. Watson, I, 38.

premise that men must be lifted, not tempered to virtue; they must learn to admire rather than to expend their emotions.

Dryden's view of tragedy is distinct from Aristotle's partly for the same reason that it is distinct from Milton's. In his definition of a serious play he replaces Aristotle's pity and fear with the more cerebral delight and instruction. Aristotle makes tragedy the mimesis of an action; Dryden makes it an image of human nature, putting the action at the subterranean base of his building where it will not strike the viewer's eye. For this reason, Dryden follows the "laws of justice" in his plot and thus rearranges his action to suit the ethical design of the play. While Aristotle would have the dramatist imitate a serious, great, and complete action, Dryden would have him portray a conceptualized human nature, with typical vicissitude and suffering in the plot ending in the reward of the good and the punishment of the foolish. For Aristotle, the essence, the "life and soul" of a tragedy is the plot;[95] for Dryden, it is the design, the interrelation of fable, characters, thoughts, manners, and words.[96]

The realm of originality for the dramatist, in Dryden's view, would be in the design, the disposition of parts, and the intricate scheme of values underlying the work. Dryden, to use Sidney's expression, emphasizes the "skill of the artificer" and prefers to see the poet as maker rather than as prophet.[97] He describes the poet in his critical writings as an architect, watchmaker, lapidary, and gunsmith. Milton seems to be at the opposite pole when he speaks of the poet at "sacred to the gods" and "their priest":

> Diis etenim sacer est vates, divumque sacerdos
> Spirat & occultum pectus, & ora Jovem.[98]

95. *Poetics,* p. 1460.
96. "Heads of an Answer to Rymer," Watson, *1*, 217.
97. Sidney, p. 6.
98. Milton's *Elegia Sexta* to Charles Diodati, in *The Works of John Milton, 1*, Pt. I, pp. 212–13.

Milton sees "what religious, what glorious and magnificent use might be made of poetry, both in divine and human things."[99] Dryden, on the other hand, sees poetry as connected to moral philosophy rather than to religion, at least at the time he is writing heroic plays. Like Euripides in Aristophanes' *The Frogs,* Dryden could boast that he excels in "Superlative artistry, craftsmanship, and the skill of a talented teacher/ To make men better by counsel sage."[100]

DRYDEN'S POETIC NORMS

If the foregoing remarks on Dryden's dramatic technique make him appear too much of a meticulous craftsman, then it may be necessary to glance at another side of this poet. He often shows scorn for writing that is dryly correct, or faultless and dull. In one instance he confesses that even if he sees "the more material faults of writing" in his work, he has no "leisure to amend them," since it is "enough for those who make one poem the business of their lives to leave that correct."[101] When he separates poets and dramatists of past ages into the fiery and the correct, he frequently hints that he is of the fiery, impetuous sort, for he finds Homer "more according to my genius" than Virgil, and he characterizes the former with rapidity of thought, violence, and impetuosity.[102] Even though design has clear priority with Dryden, it must still be a design with breadth, excitement, and the kind of effervescence associated with Baroque art.

The norms for dramatic poetry are expressed as a duality in the *Essay of Dramatic Poesy.* Shakespeare and Jonson are parallel to Almanzor and Ozmyn, the normative pair in *The Conquest,* because they represent what is fiery and what is

99. *Of Education,* to Master Samuel Hartlib (1644), in *The Works of John Milton, 4,* 286.
100. Aristophanes, *The Frogs,* in *The Complete Plays of Aristophanes,* ed. Moses Hadas (New York, 1962), p. 400.
101. "A Defence of *An Essay of Dramatic Poesy,*" Watson, *1,* 111.
102. "Preface to *Fables Ancient and Modern,*" Watson, 2, 274.

justly designed in drama. Shakespeare describes human passions, while Jonson writes of humours; Shakespeare delights, Jonson instructs; Shakespeare excels in the "variety and greatness of characters," but Jonson surpasses him in his "intrigues," and his well-knit action.[103] Shakespeare reveals a preponderance of wit, Jonson, of judgment. Thus, the definition of a play which Dryden gives at the start of the *Essay* finds its perfect expression in no one dramatist, but in these two English dramatists combined. Taken together, Shakespeare and Jonson give a *"just and lively image of human nature, representing its passions and humours, and the changes of fortune to which it is subject, for the delight and instruction of mankind."*

The aberrations from the norm in Dryden's dramatic criticism are also parallel to aberrations from virtuous behavior in heroic plays. The dull sensualist Boabdelin and the excessively active Lyndaraxa find their counterparts in the dull poet and the unrestrained wit. Crites describes the dull poet as standing at one "extremity of poetry," because he is a "very Leveller" who fills his verse with "pretty expletives."[104] Lisideius describes the other extreme as a wretched punster, one who is always "wresting and torturing a word into another meaning," surely a prefiguration of MacFlecknoe himself.[105] As the *Essay* progresses, those who imitate the Ancients in a servile way are shown to verge on dullness, while those who follow the Moderns and care only for innovations are shown to lean toward uncontrolled wit. Crites, for example, prescribes "much labour and long study," a strict observance of the unities, and "elegant" language. At the other extreme, Eugenius advises the artist to study nature, to strive for "easy" rather than "elegant" language; he praises the Moderns for novelty of plot and for

---

103. Watson, *1*, 65. Dryden makes an almost identical statement about Shakespeare and Jonson twenty-five years later in the *Discourse concerning Satire*, Watson, 2, 73; his dramatic norms, like some other literary norms he posits, have thus remained constant throughout most of his critical writings.

104. Watson, *1*, 21.

105. Ibid.

care in showing poetic justice, as well as for portraying whole characters rather than types.[106] Later on in the *Essay,* the French and English dramatists are contrasted on the same basis, and the French emerge as faultless but dull in their observance of decorum, while the English seem unrestrained in their search for "variety and copiousness."

Neander suggests that the good dramatist ought to find a mean among all the opposites presented. Although he speaks for English dramatists as opposed to French, he concedes that both may be to blame: "if we are to be blamed for showing too much of the action, the French are as faulty for discovering too little of it: a mean betwixt both should be observed by every judicious writer."[107] Dryden gives no positive advice on how to combine the dual norms; his method is to show Scylla and Charibdis—the extremes of dullness and excessive wittiness.

A last opposition of extremes in the *Essay* may well remind one of Swift's opposing Yahoos and Houyhnhnms. Dryden contrasts writers who are not "fit to write" to faultless writers who are "no where to be found."[108] The norm can never be perfectly achieved; it can only be the object at which we aim. The heroic couplet, he argues, will help English poets to approximate the norm, for their tendency is to excessive wit and variety and the couplet will put clogs on their fancy, leaving greater room for judgment.

Dryden's norms for satire are parallel to his norms for drama. Like Shakespeare and Jonson, Juvenal and Horace represent a dual norm. Dryden is "pleased" and "profited" by both, but he distinguishes them into the "tragical" and the "comical" spirit, respectively.[109] Juvenal is a severe chastiser of vice, whereas Horace is rather pedestrian in style, urbane

---

106. Ibid., p. 40.
107. Ibid., p. 63.
108. Ibid., p. 91.
109. *A Discourse Concerning Satire,* Watson, 2, 140.

and subtle in raillery. The two satirists have different objects: Juvenal lashes particular vices with vehement indignation, while Horace mildly admonishes human folly in general. The two have divergent manners: Juvenal is "pointed," Horace "polite." Both are contrasted to the satirist Persius, who exhorts his readers too openly to Stoic morality, and balances his judgment with too little wit.[110] Thus, approximately twenty-five years after the *Essay of Dramatic Poesy*, Dryden compares two normative poets in a manner similar to his earlier comparison of Shakespeare and Jonson. Earlier, he suggested that a balance of the lively and the just would be best for the dramatist, that he should strive for a via media between the passionate writing of Shakespeare and the more correct design of Jonson. In the *Discourse* he advises modern satirists to attack a particular object in the manner of Juvenal, yet maintain a polite manner in the way of Horace. Boileau combines Juvenal, Horace, and Virgil to form the "most beautiful and most noble kind of satire. Here is the majesty of the heroic, finely mixed with the venom of the other; and raising the delight which otherwise would be flat and vulgar, by the sublimity of expression."[111] Virgil provides the model of an elegant surface, while the two satirists give patterns of what is just and lively in their genre.

The heroic play must instruct by means of a fable that contains the "laws of justice" and characters that are patterns for imitation; similarly, the satire must instruct by attacking such persons as are public nuisances, remaining at the same time within the bounds of courtesy. At the start of the *Discourse*, Dryden suggests the norm by referring to the "good sense" and "good nature" of the satirist Dorset.[112] He then turns to the absence of these qualities in his libelers, critics who have attacked

110. Ibid., p. 119. Dryden says of Persius that "he rather insulted over vice and folly, than exposed them like Juvenal and Horace."
111. Ibid., p. 149.
112. Ibid., pp. 74, 78.

Dryden's character and poetry without "wit" and "morality."
He argues that to attack such critics effectively one would need
both a faultless manner of writing and a sense of justice.[113]
The satirist needs, on the one hand, "good sense" and "wit"
in selecting the guilty party he will attack and in choosing to
emphasize particular faults, and, on the other, he needs "good
nature" and "morality" in keeping his indignation within
bounds, and in maintaining a sense of his common humanity
with the object of his satire.

This dual norm underlies the entire evolution of satire.
Dryden points out that the first satires were "scoffing and ob-
scene," or lacking in moral restraint, as well as "gross and rus-
tic," or lacking in wit.[114] When satirists improved, their work
became "full of pleasant raillery, but without any mixture of
obscenity." The desire of the satirist to criticize the follies or
vices of others, a desire which is as "depraved" as man's own
fallen nature, bears "better fruit," Dryden shows, when it is
guided by intellectual and moral considerations.[115] The best
satire will be "sharp" and full of venom to satisfy the wit, but
"well-mannered" to fulfill the requirements of "good nature"
or morality.

Similarly, the evolution of the drama, as recounted in the
Essay of Dramatic Poesy, is toward greater moral content, as
Eugenius points out, as well as toward more variety in plot
and characterization. Wit is shown in the lively portraiture
of human nature, while moral judgment is displayed in the
well-designed plot in which each character receives his just
reward or punishment.

Dryden's idea of a serious play not only corresponds in large
part with his idea of a satire, but it is related to his view of
history, translation, epic, and lyric poetry. In his discussion of
history, for example, Dryden finds a normative pair of his-

113. Ibid., p. 78.
114. Ibid., pp. 106–07.
115. Ibid. p. 97.

torians just as he found normative pairs of dramatists and of satirists. Polybius has the "great comprehension and the larger soul," he asserts, but Tacitus has the "more close connection of his thoughts"; the first, like Shakespeare, has a natural genius, while the second shows greater learning and regularity, like Jonson.[116]

In his preface to *Ovid's Epistles* (1680), Dryden contrasts just and lively translators much as he contrasted the correct French dramatists and the more fiery English in the *Essay of Dramatic Poesy.* Those who render a word-for-word translation tend to be dull and "servile," while those who imitate too freely are "libertine." He suggests here, as Neander does in the *Essay,* that a via media should be sought between these extremes: "Imitation and verbal version are, in my opinion, the two extremes which ought to be avoided; and therefore, when I have proposed the mean betwixt them, it will be seen how far his argument will reach."[117] The perfect balance or middle way between Shakespeare and Jonson, Juvenal and Horace, transliteration and imitation may be unattainable; Dryden simply states that one ought to strive for it.

Dryden contrasts three pairs of epic writers in his *Discourse Concerning Satire;* these pairs are arranged chronologically, and the last one comes closest to the implied normative pair, Homer and Virgil. Statius and Lucan are unsatisfactory because the first has too unbounded an imagination and the second displays "heat and affectation."[118] Both are in contrast to Virgil: Statius is a "blustering tyrant" and Lucan has the vice of "ambition," whereas Virgil has true "majesty" and "stateliness." As in the heroic plays, so in epic writing the tyrant and the ambitious rebel are contrasted to the true image of a king. Ariosto and Tasso are also unsatisfactory epic poets, the first having a "luxurious" style and lacking a just design,

116. "The Character of Polybius and his Writings" (1693), Watson, 2, 69.
117. "Preface to Ovid's *Epistles*" (1680), Watson, *1*, 271.
118. Watson, 2, 82.

and the second having a "dry" and "flatulent" style with forced conceits.[119] Milton and Spenser, on the other hand, have the "genius and learning to have been perfect poets"; Milton "endeavours everywhere to express Homer," while Spenser has studied Virgil to advantage. Milton, however, sometimes runs into "a flat of thought," while Spenser lacks "uniformity" of design.[120]

Thus Dryden has schematized the history of the epic, just as he has schematized the history of drama and of satire, into a series of pairs. Within each pair of writers, one tends to be correct in design and more suave in manner, but sometimes dull, predictable, or narrow; the other tends to be fertile and lively, but in danger of falling into excesses, such as unrestrained imagination and irregular design. Whether Lisideius and Neander contrast the French and English dramatists, or Dryden contrasts Horace and Juvenal, this basic tension remains constant.

Even in lyric poetry, Dryden divides those poets who have understood the "sweetness of English verse" into two groups: Denham is "correct," and Waller is "even, sweet, and flowing"; on the other hand, Cowley is "copious," "full of spirit," and Suckling is a "courtly" wit.[121] The first two are more exact poets, who would err on the side of dullness, and the other two are lively poets who might let their wit carry them away.

Too great an emphasis has been placed on Dryden's skepticism in the past few decades of criticism and too little on his tendency to conceptualize and schematize everything from political and ethical behavior to aesthetic pursuits. He appears skeptical because he rarely gives positive advice on how to reach the golden mean; yet by stacking the cards, by suggesting the extremes to be avoided and the norms to be combined, he

119. Ibid.
120. Ibid., pp. 83–84.
121. *An Essay of Dramatic Poesy*, Watson, *1*, 24.

effectually guides his reader or audience in making the proper choice.

Like the scientists of his period, Dryden opposes "not only the dogmatism of credulity and tradition but also the dogmatism of unbelief." These scientists, according to Moody E. Prior, do not accept skepticism as an end in itself but as "an essential element in good method, as an attitude of mind necessary in any investigation destined to lead to truth and certainty."[122] Dryden does not dogmatically preach one mode of writing or behavior, but by means of his pairs of heroes, dramatists, satirists, and epic writers, he suggests that norms do exist even if a single representative or pattern of absolute perfection cannot be found.

Dryden's skeptical method can best be illustrated by means of his comparison between Seneca and Plutarch, for what he says of the latter applies with peculiar force to himself.[123] Seneca is "censorious," "still searching for some occasion to vent his gall," glad to "reprehend vice," and so imperious as to impose his opinions when he teaches; he is "haughty and ill-bred" in manner. On the contrary, Plutarch is "candid," "frequent in commending what he can," endeavoring to teach others but refusing "not to be taught himself," and for this reason "always doubtful and inquisitive"; Plutach's virtue is, then, "humbled and civilized." Both writers are instructive, but the latter is alluring and genial besides.

Dryden's mixture of skeptical method and neat, deductive schemes of values may seem an odd one, but the poet himself noticed a similar mixture in Plutarch when he described this historian as "a Platonician, at least an Academic, that is, half Platonist half Sceptic."[124] Francis Bacon was not far from such a mixture when he told his followers to begin in doubt so that

122. Moody E. Prior, "Joseph Glanvill, Witchcraft, and Seventeenth-Century Science," *MP, 30* (1932–33), 191.
123. "The Life of Plutarch," Watson, 2, 12.
124. Ibid.

they might end in certainty, and at the same time, in *The Advancement of Learning*, suggested that some absolute laws of nature will be found at a future time that will reveal the essence of nature, the form of existence.[125] Dryden, like many of his contemporaries, is often closer to the medieval scholastics in his logical schemes than he is to the empirical thinkers of the next century. He often makes skepticism signify courtesy and good-natured humility of manner, as in his remarks on Plutarch, rather than a thoroughgoing distrust of mental fabrications.

125. Francis Bacon, *The Advancement of Learning*, Book II, in *Selected Writings of Francis Bacon*, ed. Hugh G. Dick (New York, 1955), p. 356.

The Heroic Plays and Dryden's Poetry

Astraea Redux, Annus Mirabilis, and the heroic plays are united by a common scheme of values.[1] In all these works Dryden indicates that man in the state of nature does not necessarily lead the nasty, brutish life Hobbes assigns to him. Instead, man has two tendencies, one to generosity and courage, one to revenge and insolent pride. According to Dryden, it is possible to create social harmony and justice on earth if the former tendency prevails and the latter is brought under restraint. Society, for Dryden, is not the antithesis of the state of nature; it does not replace natural impulses with servile observance of laws. Rather, it is the cultivation and bringing to fruition of the generous impulses of man in the natural state.

The will to revenge in heroic drama is often curbed because of a sense of personal obligation or of consideration for the common good. In *Astraea Redux,* similarly, Charles overlooks his grievances and forgives the rebels on his return to England, and in *Annus Mirabilis,* the English learn that they must use their newly acquired naval supremacy not to seek revenge and gain, but to unite and supply all nations through peaceful trade. What Schilling calls Dryden's conservatism is

1. Several critics have noticed, but only in passing, a connection between Dryden's narrative poems and his heroic plays. Speaking of *Absalom and Achitophel,* Schilling states that Dryden's "false politician and ideal king resemble characters in the heroic plays who show a standard set of qualities" (p. 12). George R. Noyes also makes this point about Dryden's heroic plays and his other poetry in "Dryden as Dramatist," *Selected Dramas of John Dryden* (Chicago, 1910), p. xxvii.

often an overriding concern for the common good.[2] The poet maintains that individual nations as well as individual citizens should curb their tendencies to insolent pride and to revenge and should seek the profit of all.

In all these works, too, Dryden shows a transformation from a state of anarchy to the restoration of lawful government. The former state is one of war and predatory hunting; men use brute force to prevail over one another instead of using persuasion; use of arms rather than arts is cultivated, and there is no room for freedom of conscience. When justice is restored in the heroic plays, in *Astraea Redux* and in *Annus Mirabilis*, it is brought back by means of self-restraint, sufferance, prudence, and calm persuasion. In the heroic plays the protagonist, such as Montezuma or Aureng-Zebe, may be reduced to bondage or may be faced with a loss of everything he loves. Still, he chooses this disaster rather than disobey moral and civil laws. Likewise in *Astraea Redux* Charles endures his exile patiently and learns the art of government during his travels instead of brooding on revenge. In *Annus Mirabilis*, also, the English (especially Charles and Albemarl) endure their trials in patience. In all these poems the apparent calamities are actually tests of strength; they are purgative rather than punitive disasters, because they force the heroic character or nation to choose virtue above selfish gain. When justice is restored, arts rather than arms are cultivated, freedom of conscience replaces coercion, and the common profit is sought instead of selfish gain.

The characterization in the historical poems *Astraea Redux* and *Annus Mirabilis* is parallel to that in the heroic plays. The

2. Schilling, *Dryden and the Conservative Myth*. This critic views Dryden as the kind of conservative who would place severe, external impediments upon individual energy; he seems to ignore Dryden's frequent remarks in favor of those who assert freedom of conscience and other basic liberties in the face of tyranny. Dryden's concern for the common good as well as for individual conscience makes him take a middle road in politics.

character of Charles in the first poem is as conceptualized an image of human nature as that of Montezuma in *The Indian Queen*. Both are Promethean figures, heroes who suffer in bondage as a result of historical circumstances beyond their control. But Charles in exile and Montezuma in voluntary chains are free in an inward way; they learn the value of moderation from seeing the limits of individual freedom within society, and they recognize the presence of a higher power than the human will in the shaping of history. Their bondage and suffering, therefore, constitute a learning experience. When Charles brings his "future rule" into "Method" during his exile, he purchases his kingdom anew: "His right indears it much, his purchase more" (86).[3] Similarly, Montezuma earns the right to the Mexican crown not merely by birth but by growing from a rebellious mercenary of the Peruvian king to a patient sufferer under tyrannical government. Such heroic "images" exemplify the uses of adversity in preparing a man to govern in society, in preparing him to accept both internal, moral law and external law.

All the heroic plays are about the restoration of justice within a secular and historical frame of reference, but *The Indian Emperour, Tyrannic Love,* and *The Conquest of Granada* are particularly concerned with the spread of Christianity in historical and geographical terms. Taken together, these three plays suggest a sort of inexorable expansion of Christianity at the expense of primitive religion, Roman paganism, and Islam. Similarly, Charles, at the end of *Astraea Redux,* is about to inaugurate a messianic age for England: "Our Nation with united Int'rest blest/ Not now content to poise, shall sway the rest" (296–97). This messianic role for England is even more clearly designated in *Annus Mirabilis,* where London receives foreign ambassadors as Christ did the Magi in Bethlehem:

3. *Works,* California edition, *1,* 21–31.

Now, like a Maiden Queen, she will behold,
From her high Turrets, hourly Sutors come:
The East with Incense, and the West with Gold,
Will stand, like Suppliants, to receive her doom.
(st. 297, ll. 1185–88)

England will thus unite the world and make of it one city where "all may be suppli'd." Economic prosperity, a more equal distribution of foodstuffs and other goods, is the type of redemption which Dryden forecasts in his nondramatic poetry; England is to be the savior of the world by implementing in the secular sphere the Christian redemption.[4]

The redemptive scheme which underlies nearly all of Dryden's early works is the following: First, brute force or, at best, the will of a single tyrant prevails; justice has left the realm. Next, the tyrants and ambitious rebels hasten their own and each others' ruin by their "impious wit." The rebels in *Astraea Redux*, the Dutch in *Annus Mirabilis*, Lyndaraxa in *The Conquest*, and Nourmahal in *Aureng-Zebe* alike are foiled by their own wiles. The Dutch ships, for instance, are too large and the fleets too crowded to fight effectively, and Lyndaraxa, by her unscrupulous pursuit of a crown, brings on her own assassination as well as the downfall of her country. Meanwhile the sympathetic, normative characters are waiting on the sidelines, learning to be patient in adversity. The redemptive scheme in these works, therefore, is essentially a historical process moving

4. In the commentary to *Astraea Redux* (California edition, *1*, 211–19), the editors do not give a sufficient explanation of Dryden's use of Christian Revelation. They reduce Dryden's metaphysical scheme to a simple contrast between black and white, evil and good; they assume that everything Christ-like belongs to Charles and the Restoration, everything wicked to the Rebellion and Interregnum. And yet, Dryden shows that Charles must undergo a learning process during his exile; thus, some good does come out of his having to earn his kingdom and to study the art of government as it is practiced in other nations. Dryden, moreover, shows that all of England—not just the Puritan segment—must be transformed through commerce and peaceful arts into a nation fit for international dominion.

from a lawless or anarchic state of affairs to right government. The restoration of government is achieved by way of moderation on the part of the virtuous. Unlike Milton, who could advocate the violent overthrow of a tyranny, Dryden suggests that a tyranny breeds rebellion in the least virtuous citizens, and so it is overthrown without the participation of the virtuous.

Astraea Redux

Like the heroic plays, *Astraea Redux* is a highly schematized poem, an intricately designed inquisition into the cause and the manner of Charles' restoration. Dryden suggests that history is governed by a higher power when he attributes Charles' restoration to heaven: "Heav'n would no bargain for its blessings drive/ But what we could not pay for, freely give" (137–38). Heaven seems to work here by what Alan Roper calls "special providence."[5] These two lines correspond to the prophecy scenes in the heroic plays, in which Dryden indicates that heaven has already determined the fall of a given kingdom. Shortly thereafter, in an apparent attempt to leave room for free will, Dryden indicates that heaven has been stormed by supplications, and the free gift has actually been ravished:

> Yet as he knew his blessings worth, take care
> That we should know it by repeated pray'r;
> Which storm'd the skies and ravish'd *Charles* from thence
> As Heav'n it self is took by violence.
>
> (141–44)

5. Alan Roper points out that Dryden's notion of providence is not that of a distant God acting through second causes, but "a direct and miraculous intervention of the first cause in mundane affairs" (*Dryden's Poetic Kingdoms* [London, 1965], p. 61). Not only is God always interfering in history just as he did in *Genesis*, but the original Fall is always recurring, too. Roper asserts that in the prologue to *The Unhappy Favourite* we see that "Metaphysically, man can fall but once; politically, he can fall as often as rebellion breaks the just bonds between subject and ruler" (p. 107).

Just as heaven in the heroic plays determines historical change such as the fall of Granada or of the Indian Empire, yet still allows men's virtuous or vicious actions to unfold the event, so heaven in *Astraea Redux* allows human prayers to storm and ravish Charles "from thence," that the gift of his restoration might be conferred on a deserving nation. The area of freedom appears to be internal; historical occurrences are on the largest scale controlled by providence, and the virtuous man cannot prevent the rise or fall of his own nation. He can, however, participate in the process of change by prayer and cautious actions. The prayers of the English and the prudence of General Monck lead up to the deliverance: " 'Twas hence at length just Vengeance thought it fit / To speed their ruine by their impious wit" (199–200).

Four temporal stages leading up to the restoration of Charles are made into four verse paragraphs in *Astraea Redux*. The first paragraph deals with time past, the Civil War. By a series of allusions, Dryden equates the English rebellion with other rebellions—the Giants against Jove (37–38), Otho against Galba (67–70), the Hebrews against David (79–82), and the League against Henry IV (97–104). These equations imply that lawlessness or rebellion is the same in every age and country; the rebellion against Charles I was no more warranted than that of the Giants against Jove. As in the heroic plays, then, he suggests that a violent overthrow of government is, without exception, damnable.

All the civil unrest depicted in the first verse paragraph would seem to point to man's fallen nature, to Adam's sin. The second verse paragraph opens with a flashback to the Golden Age when men lived in "supine felicity," and the tenth line alludes to Adam:

> Such is not *Charles* his too too active age,
> Which govern'd by the wild distemper'd rage

Of some black Star infecting all the Skies,
Made him at his own cost like *Adam* wise.

(111–14)

The design in this poem is "below ground," like those of the
heroic plays; thus, the connection between Adam and all the
lawlessness of the first verse paragraph is made explicit only
later in the poem.

The third verse paragraph and the fourth begin with the
word "now"; in the former "now" refers to time present, to
the arrival of Charles, but in the latter it refers to the beginning of a new age: "And now times whiter Series is begun/
Which in soft Centuries shall smoothly run" (292–93).

The intricacy of the design of *Astraea Redux* can be fully
appreciated only when one realizes that Dryden interweaves
two kinds of time in this poem: chronological time and psychological time.[6] In the four paragraphs the nation as a whole
moves during a twenty-year span from rebellion to restoration,
while the speaker shifts in mood from a deep pessimism at
Cromwell's death to an incandescent joy at the prospect of a
new Golden Age. At the start of the poem, the speaker expects
a renewal of civil turmoil; it is a "sullen Intervall of Warre,"
and everyone lies in expectation of the "Thunder," for "An
horrid Stillness first invades the ear." This "dreadful Quiet"
leads the speaker to think of the past rebellion and to exclaim
bitterly: "What King, what Crown from Treasons reach is
free,/ If *Jove* and *Heaven* can violated be?" His mood alters
with the change in Charles' fortunes in the second paragraph.
Charles seems to have been recalled, "For those loud stormes
that did against him rore/ Have cast his shipwrack'd Vessel on
the shore" (123–24). The speaker, still far from the prospect
of international unity which he envisions in the last paragraph,

6. Lowry Nelson, Jr. suggests that one of the "peculiar achievements" of
Baroque poetry is the "contemporaneity" of different time-planes, the "para-
dox of time seen under the aspect of eternity." *(Baroque Lyric Poetry* [New
Haven, 1961], p. 26).

seems belligerent: "Tremble ye Nations who secure before/ Laught at those Armes that 'gainst our selves we bore" (115–16).

With the actual return of Charles, the speaker's mood swiftly climbs to optimism about the future. In the second paragraph, he had looked back wistfully at a "lazy" epoch which was "lost in sleep and ease," the first Golden Age. Now he looks forward to a similar age, but one in which "Armes and Arts" will be cultivated, in which navigation and trade will unite the world. England, as mistress of the seas, reigns over "times whiter Series" just as Saturn did over the Golden Age: "And as Old Time his Off-spring swallow'd down/ Our Ocean in its depths all Seas shall drown" (302–03). The speaker's mood reaches a climax in the last four lines. In contrast to the "general Peace" of the opening line of *Astraea Redux,* a peace that was merely an interval between wars, the speaker now envisions a solid and fruitful peace:

> Oh Happy Age! Oh times like those alone
> By Fate reserv'd for Great *Augustus* Throne!
> When the joint growth of Armes and Arts foreshew
> The World a Monarch, and that Monarch *You.*

The mood which Dryden tries to create by the end of this poem is akin to that of Handel's *Royal Fireworks Suite:* one senses the magnificence and grandeur of the new age as well as its order and stability.

The interweaving of chronological or external time and the psychological time of the speaker is only one part of the scheme of *Astraea Redux.* Dryden further enhances his design by using the image of water to unite the poem. Water is at first merely what makes England "a World divided from the rest," but it is finally a means of redemption for England, for after the tempests and the storms at sea, the mariner Charles arrives by water to England and will shortly send trade ships to navigate to the farthest corners of the world. Water, then, is at once the sea of fortune upon which Charles is tossed, the cause of England's separation from the Continent, the source of England's joy when Charles returns, and the means of uniting England to the entire world by trade.

The entire Civil War is a tempest at sea, with Charles the mariner of the ship of state. In the opening lines England awaits a new storm: the "gales" which have disturbed it are the rabble, for "The Rabble now such Freedom did enjoy,/ As Winds at Sea that use it to destroy" (43–44). The Civil War is a "wild distemper'd rage" caused by "some black Star infecting all the Skies" (112–13). Charles is a cautious mariner, though "tossed by Fate and hurried up and down" (51); his antithesis is the "Ambitious Swede" who is tossed "like restless Billowes" not by fate but by his own passions. Charles' skill as a mariner corresponds to his growth in learning the art of government: he spends his time listening to "choise Remarques" and bringing "Method" to his idea of ruling because "those that 'gainst stiff gales laveering go" must be "resolv'd and skilful too." Charles' shipwrecked vessel finally arrives on shore (123–24); this image of newfound stability corresponds to that of a riveted throne in line 104: "Till Fortunes fruitless spight had made it known/ Her blowes not shook but riveted his Throne." Charles' enemies are related to the tempests of fortune by imagery: the rebels "durst with horses hoofs that beat the ground/ And Martial brass bely the thunders sound" (197–98), and, when they are removed from authority, they must spend their "Fogue" on trivial things.

The water imagery becomes even more complex as the poem progresses. Just as Charles' Declaration of Breda is an expression of goodwill and forgiveness which pacified the supporters of the Civil War, so Charles' sacrifice to "all the Sea-Gods" and the "Tempests of the Main" upon his reaching the shore is a pacifying gesture to these deities.[7] These become

7. Charles arrives on shore twice in *Astraea Redux*, once when he is shipwrecked on a strand and another time in triumph on the English shore. The first landing seems to represent a change in his fortunes, probably the arrival of General Monck on the scene, and the second his actual return from exile.

so well disposed, in fact, that they impede his progress; the sea is "smooth and clear," while the "winds that never Moderation knew/ Afraid to blow too much, too faintly blew" (242–43). This image of the winds and tide may be related to the well-disposed crowds that also impede Charles, "Preventing still your steps, and making hast/ To meet you often where so e're you past" (282–83).

The tempests and the English people are not merely becalmed when Charles returns; Dryden suggests that they have been transformed. The tempests have become trade winds, and the rebellious English are now enterprising merchants:

> So winds that tempests brew
> When through Arabian Groves they take their flight
> Made wanton with rich Odours, lose their spight.
> (269–71)

The same passions that brought civil discord have been transmuted: the clouds are "Dispell'd to farthest corners of the sky" just as the English tradesmen will navigate to the ends of the world: "Abroad your Empire shall no Limits know,/ But like the Sea in boundless Circles flow" (298–99). The beginning of this transformation occurs when the land actually comes out to the sea to greet Charles:

> It is no longer Motion cheats your view,
> As you meet it, the Land approacheth you.
> The Land returns, and in the white it wears
> The marks of penitence and sorrow bears.
> (252–55)

The image of the land clothed in white and advancing into the sea suggests baptism by immersion. Dryden in fact makes use of many theological words suggesting the Redemption after line 255. Charles, like Christ, enters his kingdom endowed with "Heav'nly Parentage and earthly too"; he shows "mildness" and "a forgiving mind." He has a goodness that is "above the Laws" and makes "softer" the "rigid letter" of those commands. The mention of "Generous Wine" in this context may have a sacramental overtone. Thus, the transformation of England from a war-torn island to the center of world trade and world government can be traced in the water imagery. The conclusions of both *Astraea Redux* and *Annus Mirabilis* suggest that British ships will guarantee freedom of trade on the high seas.

The image of water has, further, a Platonic meaning in *Astraea Redux*. Water mirrors an image of reality, and Charles, who is the "Sun," seems to be moving in the water when actually he is in the skies:

> As Souls reach Heav'n while yet in Bodies pent,
> So did he live above his Banishment.
> That Sun which we beheld with cous'ned eyes
> Within the water, mov'd along the skies.
>
> (59–62)

Similarly, the return of right government to England is mirrored as the mounting by Charles, York, and Gloucester of their separate ships. The *Naseby,* a name suggesting rebellious England, is "lost in Charles his name/ (Like some unequal Bride in nobler sheets)." The implication of betrothal or sexual union is even clearer when the *London* meets her "freight" in York and the *Swift-sure* "groans beneath Great Gloc'sters weight" (230–37). Earlier in the poem fate kept England from "*Charles* his Bed/ Whom Our first Flames and Virgin Love did wed." Thus, the betrothed pair, Charles and England, have been separated by rebels who, like the magician Busirane in *The Faerie Queene,* made the lovers' hearts "the May-game of malicious arts" (211–12). This extended allusion to the world of romance is so subtly woven into the design that it might go unobserved. Once perceived, however, it makes of the reunion between Charles and England a sort of epithalamion: the three ships coming gently into harbor are three brides "lost

. . . in nobler sheets." The fruitfulness of this union is fore-shadowed in the last paragraph, where England's mastery of the seas is shown to be the result of her marriage with Charles.

The water imagery in *Astraea Redux* unites, therefore, such apparently divergent elements as the past Civil War, England's future trade and shipping, and the return of Charles to his throne. Even fate is at first portrayed as a malevolent star that causes a tempest at sea (113), and later shown as a benevolent star that is a harbinger of Charles' glory (287–91). All of the "Miracles" of the poem occur at sea; in the first paragraph heaven "did Miracles create" to assuage an international temp-est even though it "seem'd regardless of our Fate," and, when Charles is sailing home to England, the words "indulgence," "bless'd" and "Miracles" describe the voyage, implying that heaven is watchful.

The elaborate design into which Dryden fits the events sur-rounding Charles' restoration to power removes it from the sphere of journalism. Rather than compose a mere verse chronicle, Dryden interweaves the historical events of his age with the internal time of the narrator, who moves from pessi-mism to hopeful joy within the confines of the poem. The sus-tained image of an adventure at sea is one aspect of the design which unifies the poem. Dryden also makes use of two tech-niques of the epic writer: he begins in media res, and makes use of flashbacks in the two first verse paragraphs, in both cases after line 20; the various allusions to heaven, miracles, and fate imply that a supernatural world is involved in these events. General Monck, for example, seems an agent of that other world:

> 'Twas MONCK whom Providence design'd to loose
> Those real bonds false freedom did impose.
> The blessed Saints that watch'd this turning Scene
> Did from their Stars with joyful wonder leane.
>
> (151–54)

Monck, like John the Baptist who was sent to prepare the way for Christ, is sent from heaven to prepare for the "Great Monarch" who is all mercy and forgiveness.

An entirely different view of the poem may be gained by looking at still another aspect, the movement from arms to arts. In the opening part of the poem, England seems entirely concerned with arms, and even the world is only at an interval of war; by the end of the work, however, a time has come for "the joint growth of Armes and Arts." Between these two points, Dryden alludes to several kinds of arts. Charles spends his exile "viewing Monarchs secret Arts of sway," so that "To bus'ness ripened by digestive thought/ His future rule is into Method brought" (89–90). In the second verse paragraph, Monck's activities are compared and contrasted with a series of arts and processes. For example, in lines 157–58, his civil leadership is likened to the craft of an artist sketching a face and changing it from a tearful to a smiling physiognomy. Shortly thereafter he is compared to "a patient Angler" and his manner of curing England to that of "Wise Leeches." His art is contrasted to the artifice of the chemist who makes false gold that "shuns the Mint." The next two comparisons blur art and nature. First, his activity in England is likened to that of the brain, muscles and nerves in bringing the body to motion: "Through viewless Conduits Spirits to dispense,/ The Springs of Motion from the Seat of Sense" (168–69). Second, his task is compared to the digestive process; he is the stomach embracing and then crushing its food when he makes use of "wise delay" in order to bring about Charles' return at an opportune moment. Because Monck's task is at once to wear a "vizard," or practice statecraft, and to passively provide a smooth period of transition, it is both an artistic and a natural process. Charles' restoration is consequently a natural and an artistic event; his return is compared simultaneously to a skillful painting and to a spring thaw:

Yet as wise Artists mix their colours so
That by degrees they from each other go,
Black steals unheeded from the neighb'ring white
Without offending the well cous'ned sight:
So on us stole our blessed change; while we
Th'effect did feel but scarce the manner see.
Frosts that constrain the ground, and birth deny
To flow'rs, that in its womb expecting lye,
Do seldom their usurping Pow'r withdraw,
But raging floods pursue their hasty thaw:
Our thaw was mild, the cold not chas'd away
But lost in kindly heat of lengthned day.

(125–36)

Not only does Charles learn the art of government in exile and Monck practice that art at home, but, after the restoration, all of England will devote itself to the "joint growth of Armes and Arts," with the effect that navigation and commerce will unite the entire world.

In *Astraea Redux,* therefore, Dryden is not so much recounting the historical event of Charles' restoration to England's throne, but using that event as the foundation on which to erect a monumental piece of architecture, a varied and comprehensive design like that of the heroic plays. *Astraea Redux* and *The Indian Queen* are essentially about the restoration of a rightful ruler; both the poem and the heroic play focus on a transition from a lawless, predatory state of war within the society to a return of good government. In both works, too, the rebels or usurpers destroy themselves: Zempoalla brings on Traxalla's death and commits suicide, while the rebels in *Astraea Redux* are brought to "ruine by their impious wit." The two works show the normative characters as learning the art of government by means of prudence, suffering and a willingness to follow both moral and civil law.

Annus Mirabilis

Although *Annus Mirabilis* has been described by one critic as "a piece of inspired journalism," Samuel Johnson's description is more accurate—one of the "most elaborate works" written by Dryden.[8] Earl Miner, in *Dryden's Poetry*, comes to grips with this complex and "radically historical" work and reveals a unity of language and of theme in a poem which, to many critics, consists of two unrelated subjects, the naval war and the London fire.[9] The unity of *Annus Mirabilis* can also be found in its mythical aspect, and it is in this aspect that the poem is closely related to the heroic plays and to *Astraea Redux*. Dryden describes the naval war as a predatory hunt, with England as the hunter; in the second part of the poem, the hunter becomes the hunted and heaven is predator. Only when heaven has subdued England can she be trusted with the mastery of economic life in Europe.

By imaging the naval war as a series of hunts, Dryden implies that the battles of 1666 are part of a larger scheme, that they are related to the state of war in fallen nature. At the start of the poem might is right. England's justification for entering a war with Holland is that she is powerful enough to wrest the supremacy of the seas from her wealthy rival: "What peace can be where both to one pretend?/ (But they more diligent, and we more strong) (st. 6, ll. 21–22). England

8. Edward N. Hooker calls this poem a "piece of inspired journalism" in which Dryden "appeals ingeniously to the self-interest of the citizens." He thus robs the poem of its metaphysical implications, reducing it to a politically expedient piece of verse. ("The Purpose of Dryden's *Annus Mirabilis*," *HLQ*, *10* [1946], 67). Alan Roper finds some "incoherence" in this work. Samuel Johnson, on the contrary, calls *Annus Mirabilis* one of Dryden's "greatest attempts," but finds that Dryden is always wandering away from his subject to "deduce consequences and make comparisons" ("Dryden," in *Lives*, pp. 184, 238). These very deductions and comparisons, however, are meant to imply a large metaphysical context for the events of the poem.

9. (Bloomington, 1967).

subdues Holland only to be cast down in turn by the London fire; heaven sends a winged predator against England so that she can be purged and transformed from a shepherdess to a queen. By her victory over Holland, England emerges the mistress of the seas, but by her suffering under the hand of heaven, she is made fit to fulfill her task well. Far from simply recounting the events of 1666, Dryden has drawn a clear moral from them; he schematizes these contemporary events just as he schematizes the events of the conquest of Mexico and of the conquest of Granada.

Exactly as Montezuma and Aureng-Zebe are reduced to bondage in the heroic plays and made fit to rule by means of suffering, so England is bowed down by her calamity in the last part of *Annus Mirabilis* and afterwards rises as a new nation, no longer eager for battle and rapine, but desirous of peace, free trade, and improved navigation. Holland, like Boabdelin or Maximin, has been a willful tyrant, but England will bring good government to the seas and make of the world "one City" where "all may be suppli'd" (st. 163, ll. 651–52).

Dryden makes two groups of statements in *Annus Mirabilis,* one about trade and navigation and the other about predotory hunting. The first group is found in stanzas 1–7, 139–67, and 293–304; in other words, Dryden arranges his remarks about trade and navigation symmetrically, so that they occur at the beginning, middle, and end. The design of his poem might have been too geometrical if he had not continued the subject of the war with Holland after the middle section on trade. After that section, however, the nature of the war with Holland changes; once the English get the upper hand, they become as tyrannical as the Dutch had been; they burn and destroy Dutch ships without risk to themselves (st. 202–10) just as the Dutch had tried to hold the "riches of the world" without jeopardy. The rapacity of "Our greedy Sea-men" leads directly to the London fire; thus, Dryden shows a cause and effect relationship between the later part of the conflict and the heaven-sent disaster:

> Swell'd with our late successes on the Foe,
>   Which *France* and *Holland* wanted power to cross:
> We urge an unseen Fate to lay us low,
>   And feed their envious eyes with *English* loss.
>
>   (st. 210, ll. 837–40)

When Dryden returns to the subject of trade and navigation at the end of *Annus Mirabilis,* it is to show that the fire was not merely punitive but also a means of purification and transformation for England. The messianic role of the British in bringing peace and a wide distribution of wealth through world trade is one which this nation is fit to play only after suffering such a calamity.

Dryden takes as a first principle in this poem that trade ought to be free. It should circulate like blood, he argues, so that the world's wealth can be distributed as widely as possible. Since the Dutch have had mastery of the seas, however, "Trade, which like bloud should circularly flow,/ Stop'd in their Channels, found its freedom lost" (5–6). By their tyranny the Dutch have created a state of war, a lawless, predatory world in which wealth belongs to the strongest. Therefore, the English must make Holland stoop just as Carthage stooped to Rome, "less wealthy, but more strong" (19). Like the tyrants of heroic drama, Holland is characterized as intolerably proud, domineering, and greedy, while at the same time a prey to base fears. Though the Dutch think that the "Heav'ns had kindly heat" for them alone, they fearfully court the king of England; they remain "Crouching at home" while they are bullies at sea. Dryden thus shows that England's war with Holland is both just and expedient ("For they would grow too powerful were it long"), for the Dutch, in tyrannically cornering the world market, have acted contrary to the common profit of mankind.

In the middle section of *Annus Mirabilis* (sts. 139–67), Dryden takes a historical point of view on trade and navigation. He compares the king's overseeing of the war to God's supervision of "each days labour" at Creation (sts. 140–41) and thus suggests that a new Creation is under way. Once before, in stanza 18, line 71, Dryden asserted that a "round of greater years" had begun with the accession of the "new-born King." As in *Astraea Redux,* where "times whiter Series" begins with Charles' restoration, the poet implies that in England the Redemption has been implemented in a secular way and right government has finally replaced lawless preying. Now right government must be extended to the world, and the war with Holland is the first step in this direction.

In this section of *Annus Mirabilis,* Dryden describes that "round of greater years" mentioned in stanza 18 as a period when "Instructed ships shall sail to quick Commerce" and "we upon our Globes last verge shall go" (sts. 163–64, ll. 649–53). The world will be brought together by improved navigation and poverty will be eliminated by improved trade. England's Royal Society will praise the "wise Creator" and behold the "rule of beings" in God's mind, drawing from that vision practical benefits for mankind: "And then, like Limbecks, rich Idea's draw,/ To fit the levell'd use of humane kind" (st. 166, ll. 663–64).[10] The second Creation is essentially the establishment by human endeavor of an economic and political paradise on earth. It is, Dryden suggests, the political and social implementation of Christian law.

Since navigation is an art which is vital to the "round of greater years," Dryden gives a short history of that art in stanzas 155–67. The origin of shipping, he shows, lies in some

10. Dryden seems to allude to Bacon in his "Apostrophe to the Royal Society." In his *Novum Organum* Bacon suggests that scientists should work for "experiments of light" and later on for "experiments of fruit." In the *Advancement of Learning,* Bacon uses the image of the lark soaring in flight for the former type of experiment, and the image of the hawk plunging after its prey for the latter.

man's careful observation of the anatomy of a fish. Art, he declares, is the construction of "mighty things" from raw materials and principles derived from nature: "By viewing Nature, Natures Hand-maid, Art,/ Makes mighty things from small beginnings grow" (st. 155, ll. 617–18). The rudder was modeled on a fish's tail and the prow on its head.

Thus, many nations developed a "sharp-keel'd" boat on the model of a fish. The next improvement in the art was the addition of a sail; then improved shipping brought about the beginning of "Commerce":

> Adde but a Sail, and *Saturn* so appear'd,
>   When, from lost Empire, he to Exile went,
> And with the Golden age to *Tyber* steer'd,
>   Where Coin & first Commerce he did invent.
>   (st. 158, ll. 629–32)

Dryden makes a pun on the word "golden" when he connects the Golden Age to the beginning of trade, but at the same time he is giving a divine originator—Saturn—to commerce and suggesting that commerce is associated with the felicity of the Golden Age.

The rest of the history of navigation includes the discovery of the compass and other instruments useful to shipmen. The skilled English, Dryden claims, will find just those instruments that "poor man-kinds benighted wit" sought "in vain" for so long (st. 161). Dryden even predicts that once the art of shipping is perfectly mastered, then the English will understand the ebbs of tides as "Arts Elements," and the entire world will be "one City." A still greater pursuit of knowledge will at that time be possible: "Then, we upon our Globes last verge shall go,/ And view the Ocean leaning on the sky." After exploring the world to its limits, man will view his "rolling Neighbours" and look upon the "Lunar world" securely (st. 164, ll. 653–56).

In the middle section of *Annus Mirabilis,* therefore, Dryden takes us from the early days of navigation, when men observed the fish, to a vision of a glorious future, where improved navigation and trade will bring about peace and wide distribution of wealth, and where this in turn will spur men on to greater discoveries and scientific advances. As in *Astraea Redux* and in the heroic plays, he shows the possibility of a stable and peaceful world, where lawless behavior is kept in check by good government; in such a new world, the avenues open to individual energies are the arts and sciences.

In the closing section of *Annus Mirabilis*, Dryden takes an apocalyptical view of navigation. Before the fire, London was a "rude and low" shepherdess, but afterwards she arises a "Maiden Queen" who knows all the "Arts of Modern pride." This "more than natural change" (st. 283) has a divine cause; Charles seems to realize this because after the fire he thanks God on "his redeemed ground." The city is indeed undergoing a regeneration; it is compared to the phoenix rising from its ashes, and, in this way, it is connected with Christ, for whom the phoenix is often a symbol. London, moreover, receives "Incense" and "Gold" from suitors of the East and West just as the Christ-Child did in Bethlehem. And, lest there be any doubt about the messianic role of London, and so of England, God has given that capital a charter like the one given to the Christian Church in the New Testament:

> And seems to have renew'd her Charters date,
> Which Heav'n will to the death of time allow.
>
> (st. 294, ll. 1175–76)

Just as Christ declares in Matthew 28:20 that his church will last "until the consummation of the world," so London's charter will last to the "death of time," for it is "More great than humane, now" (st. 295). The Thames, which formerly harbored warships, will now send ships to the "Spicy shore" and "vindicate" this trade without a fleet (st. 301). England's hospitality to merchants will be such that foreigners will come to London and "depart no more." A constant trade wind will

blow British ships to "Eastern wealth" so that, as at the end of
Astraea Redux, the British empire shall be without limits:
"But like the Sea in boundless Circles flow."

The second group of statements in *Annus Mirabilis* is about
war and predatory hunting. Both the naval war between England and Holland and the London fire are imaged as a series
of predatory hunts. This lawless state of nature stands in sharp
contrast to the scene of flourishing arts and commerce depicted
in the middle and last parts of *Annus Mirabilis.*

The naval war is described as a fight for a prize undertaken
by several kinds of animals. Between stanzas 24 and 31, a naval
engagement in which seven English ships attack the entire
Dutch fleet is compared to a hunt for "Castors" or "perfumed
prey" and to a hunt for the love of a married woman. Like
"Birds of prey" that gather fruit on "precipices" (st. 11), the
English attack a fleet that is flanked with rocks and armed
with cannon. The Dutch try to protect their wealth just as the
husband "fain would keep" his wife from the adulterer; they
are in the position of the dull tyrant Boabdelin trying to keep
Almahide out of the reach of Almanzor. The English win the
battle but lose the prey because of "Heavens inclemency."
This incident illustrates part of Dryden's scheme of values in
this work; the Dutch are greedy and fearful, hence they avoid
risks and move about in crowded fleets composed of large,
bulky vessels; the English, on the other hand, are hardy and
daring and, like a vigorous, young predator, stalk their prey
without care of danger.

In stanzas 54 to 82, Dryden clearly characterizes the English
as a vigorous but small creature attacking a slow and bulky
one.[11] They become the rhinoceros that defies the elephant

11. Ralph Davis, in the article "England and the Mediterranean, 1570–1670,"
in *Essays in the Economic and Social History of Tudor and Stuart England,*
ed. F. J. Fisher (Cambridge, 1961), pp. 117–37, remarks that English ships at
that time were built "with an eye to speed, manoeverability and defence, sac-
rificing cheapness of operation so that in ordinary commercial conditions it

(st. 59). The Dutch are portrayed as the whale that has swallowed a swordfish and cannot, for all its bulk, defend itself effectively: "The combat only seem'd a Civil War,/ Till through their bowels we our passage wrought" (st. 79, ll. 313–16). Even when the battered fleets are resting from conflict, they are compared to a pair of animals: the English are small but fearless swans "Whose creasts, advancing, do the waves divide," but the Dutch are "weary oxen," or "vast bulks which little souls but ill supply" (sts. 66–70).

From the image of a small animal attacking a bulky one, Dryden modulates to the image of a large pack of base aggressors forcing a single, noble animal to retreat. The "dastard Crow" is "safe in numbers" when it attacks the noble falcon; even so, it attacks only when that bird has been "maim'd" in a hunt. Similarly, a group of Lybian huntsmen dare to attack the lion because of their large number; the noble predator retreats with "loud disdain" (st. 96). By means of these two hunting metaphors, Dryden manages to praise the English even in their moment of defeat.

The "Birds of prey" to which Dryden alluded in stanza 11 reappear occasionally throughout the work; in stanzas 85–87 England is compared to a falcon, and in stanzas 107–11 Rupert is likened to an eagle which, after "beating widely on the wing for prey," comes home to find its young ones missing. Rupert goes out, like the eagle "Stung with her love," to rescue Albemarl's ship which is already surrounded by the Dutch, "greedy Hinds" closing in on the "harvest." The English welcome their rescuer like a thirsty Martlet flying toward

---

was impossible to compete (except in the carriage of high-value goods) with Dutch flyboats or Hanseatic hulks" (p. 127). At the other extreme, the great hulks of the Hanseatic were not defensible, and they became impractical for the dangerous waters of the Mediterranean. Thus British ships took over much of the trade; England became, by the middle of the seventeenth century, the economic center for the Western European world. Mediterranean countries became "complementary to the English economy" (p. 137).

the rain, but the Dutch crouch in fear like dogs or "Hinds" in a tempest: "Now look like those, when rowling thunders roar,/ And sheets of Lightning blast the standing field" (st. 112, ll. 447–48). In stanzas 131–32, the English are compared to a dog lying exhausted near a hare, but this dog is a hunter, not part of a pack of "greedy Hinds."

A sharp break occurs in the poem with stanza 139, as we have shown, for the repair of the ships becomes an occasion for a discussion of shipping and trade. Even here, however, Dryden compares England to a series of creatures: he connects the workmen repairing the ships with "labouring bees" (sts. 144–45) and alludes to falconry when he says that the king "imps" the "Navies molted wings" (st. 143). He calls the ship *London* a phoenix (st. 151) and a "Sea-wasp flying on the waves" (st. 153). The winged creatures in this section all seem related to the theme of creation and regeneration; even the falcon is mentioned in connection with healing.

Dryden continues to mention winged creatures when the war with Holland is renewed, comparing the Dutch to a "false Spider" that would like to catch a "strugling Fly" in its web (st. 180); like the spider, the Dutch are "Designing, subtil, diligent and close," but for all their wiles, they bring about their own downfall, as do the rebels in heroic drama and the enemies of Charles in *Astraea Redux*. The Dutch are finally entangled in their own webs: "Yet all those arts their vanity did cross,/And, by their pride, their prudence did betray" (st. 169, ll. 675–76). When the Dutch are beaten, Dryden makes another allusion to winged creatures, calling them "Larks," and explaining that they must avoid the "Hobbies flight," that is, the domain of the conquering English falcon.

After the war's end, England becomes in turn a greedy predator, and Dryden describes her with the same animal metaphors he had used for Holland. Whereas the Dutch were spiders in stanza 180, the English are spiders that "lie asleep with prizes in their nets" in stanza 202. The Dutch were represented as the whale that swallowed a swordfish in stanza 79; now the English are "huge Leviathans" that give no chase but "swallow in the frie" in stanza 203. The Dutch were "greedy Hinds" in stanza 112; the English had become "greedy Seamen" in stanza 208. The English, moreover, now match the Dutch in impiety: the Dutch had been likened to "fall'n Angels" and "Fiends" in stanzas 114 and 137, and the English are compared to sacrilegious priests, "who with their gods make bold,/Take what they like, and sacrifice the rest," in stanza 208.

The English, therefore, call down the fire of London by their greed and rapacity: "We urge an unseen Fate to lay us low" (st. 210). His countrymen are "Swell'd" with their successes, Dryden points out, so that God, the controller of the elements, brings down by means of fire the nation he had raised by water: "Who as by one he did our Nation raise,/So now he with another pulls us down" (st. 211, ll. 843–44). Thus, Dryden makes the events of 1666 highly instructive by revealing that the London Fire was a just punishment. In the *Essay of Dramatic Poesy*, which was previously discussed, Eugenius and Lisideius show that the chief part of instruction lies in the fable, in which the "laws of justice" are illustrated—that is, heaven allots to each man his due.

The London fire is described in predatory imagery which is parallel to that of the naval war. The image of the bird of prey which can be found throughout the description of that war is enlarged here; the fire is portrayed as a huge bird of prey with God as its falconer. At the start of the disaster, the "infant monster" feeds in silence, but later, "with devouring strong,/Walk'd boldly upright with exalted head" (st. 218). Later still, the fire stretches out its wings (st. 233), and its young ones extend their necks from side to side and feed (st. 234). The fire's predatory hunt after the wealth of London is compared to a sexual hunt, just as the English attack on the Dutch fleet in stanza 28 was compared to the hunt of a young bachelor after the affection of a married woman. The winds are "crafty Courtezans" that hold back the lover or fire to increase his ardor: "And now, no longer letted of his prey,/He leaps up at it with inrag'd desire" (st. 222, ll. 885–86). Dryden also links this section with the middle part of *Annus Mirabilis* by a new reference to bees. In stanzas 144–45, he describes the division of labor among bees that are building a hive, but, in stanza 228, he describes the panic of the bees when their "well-stor'd Hive" is invaded by "night-robbers." Another image of predatory behavior is that of invading armies; the fire is compared to armies dividing "for prey" as they enter a town; the flames seek out the wealthy houses in "Squadron" formation and even march against the "Imperial Palace" (st. 235). A few Londoners take some booty at the risk of being burned, like the birds of prey that gather fruit on precipices in stanza 11. The "Hydra-like" and bird-like predator reduces the Londoners to such a state of helplessness that they are "like herded beasts" (st. 258); their state of exhaustion, in fact, resembles that of the "fearful Hare" lying before the dog in stanza 131.

So completely has the hunter become the hunted, that England is powerless against the predatory fire. When the king finds that he cannot stop the flames by blowing up houses, he turns to prayer and begs heaven not to reduce England to such a state that "foreign foes" may invade the land. As a consequence of that prayer, an angel prevents the fire from reaching the "Naval Magazins." Moreover, the direct hand of heaven in sending and stopping this fire is illustrated when God, portrayed as a falconer, puts a gigantic hood over the flames which are "full with feeding" yet still striving "to their quarry":

281

An hollow Chrystal Pyramid he takes,
   In firmamental waters dipt above;
Of it a brode Extinguisher he makes,
   And hoods the flames that to their quarry strove.

The vanquish'd fires withdraw from every place,
   Or full with feeding, sink into a sleep:
                           282
Each household Genius again his face,
   And, from the hearths, the little Lares creep.
                                   (1121–28)

The flames, then, must be hooded to prevent them from wreaking more havoc, from feeding on new "quarry."

Interwoven with this image of God as falconer is that of God as alchemist.[12] In the passage just cited, the words "hollow chrystal Pyramid" and "brode Extinguisher" bring to mind the laboratory of the alchemist. The theme of transmuting base metal of gold becomes important at the end of the poem, when predatory hunting has come to an end and the golden age of commercial competition has arrived.

Dryden calls the fire a "Chymick flame" and asserts that he sees "a City of more precious mold" arise, paved with silver and "all divine with Gold." He suggests that the new London is also the new Jerusalem that is meant to be the capital of the apocalyptic kingdom of peace. Earlier in the poem, the English among the Dutch were compared to the Hebrews among the Egyptians: "Thus *Israel* safe from the *Egyptian's* pride,/By flaming pillars, and by clouds did go" (st. 92, ll. 367–68). Albemarl's ship, which was compared to the Ark of the Covenant in stanza 94, was rescued by Prince Rupert on the third day of its distress (st. 105). Dryden also reminds the reader of the destruction of Jerusalem in the days of Cyrus (st. 290), and he connects the present destruction of London with the Last Judgment: "Great as the worlds which at the death of time/Must fall, and rise a nobler frame by fire" (st. 212).

Dryden draws parallels between England and the chosen

12. Bruce A. Rosenberg, *"Annus Mirabilis* Distilled," *PMLA,* 79 (1964), 254–58. See also James Kinsley, "The 'Three Glorious Victories' in *Annus Mirabilis,*" *RES,* n.s. 7 (1956), 30–37).

people, on the one hand, and between England and the Messiah, on the other. The Dutch general sails to his revenge like a "trodden Serpent" in stanza 123, and the harrowing of hell is implied in the description of the battered Dutch ships: "Their open'd sides receive a gloomy light,/Dreadful as day let in to shades below" (st. 129). The Dutch acknowledge the superior might of the English "as when Fiends did Miracles avow" (st. 137). Through these allusions to biblical history, Dryden makes the war with Holland an epitome of the entire scheme of salvation, from Moses to Christ. While the war resembles the struggles of the Hebrews against their enemies and of Christ against Satan, the fire suggests an apocalyptical vision of the new world rising from its ashes like a phoenix.

In *Annus Mirabilis* the events of a single year in English history are described as having a clear moral and providential design. Such events may seem to be brought about by chance, he suggests, but they are actually part of a larger pattern. In two long interpolations on fate (sts. 32–39, 197–202), Dryden considers how nations, as well as men, can only be instruments in the designs of heaven.[13] England's defeat of Spain in the sixteenth century seemed an unmitigated good at the time, but that victory led to the rise of France and Holland and even led to "Rebellion" within her own boundaries:

> *England,* which first, by leading them [Belgians] astray,
>   Hatch'd up Rebellion to destroy her King.
>
> 199
>
> Our Fathers bent their baneful industry
>   To check a Monarchy that slowly grew:

13. This idea of free will is the traditional one which Erasmus upheld against Luther's innovations in the *Diatribe seu collatio de libero arbitrio.* Erasmus explains that there are three stages of a good act: knowing, willing, and doing. In knowing and doing, we are effective only because of God's grace; in the intermediate stage, we merely choose to "cooperate" with His grace. This is also the notion of free will which the early Christian church advanced against Pelagius, who exaggerated man's power to do good, according to them, and against Manes and his Manichees, who went to the other extreme.

> But did not *France* or *Holland's* fate foresee,
> Whose rising pow'r to swift Dominion flew.
>
> (791–96)

It is impossible, Dryden implies here, to plan or control history, since heaven is so directly involved in the rise and fall of kingdoms: "In fortunes Empire blindly thus we go,/And wander after pathless destiny" (st. 200).

In *Annus Mirabilis*, then, as in *Astraea Redux* and in the heroic plays, Dryden takes a large political event and makes of it a universal pattern. In all cases he begins with a state of lawlessness, of predatory hunting, or of war, and works up slowly to a restoration of right government. In *Annus Mirabilis* he is concerned with international law and government, and so portrays Holland as a tyrant of the seas and England as the nation designated by heaven to control the seas and make of the world "one City," in which "some may gain, and all may be suppli'd" (st. 163). England is in the position here of the young, vigorous heroes such as Montezuma, Cortez, Almanzor, and Porphyrius: the nation must be prepared for its future role by a test of strength and of endurance. The test of strength occurs during the naval war; but the test of endurance, which is comparable to the bondage suffered by Montezuma in *The Indian Queen* or by Aureng-Zebe, occurs during the fire, for then England is brought low in order that the rude shepherdess may arise again a "Maiden Queen." In all the heroic plays, likewise, the heroes must learn patience and fortitude in order to merit the reward which finally comes to them.

Conclusion

In all of his heroic plays, as well as in his early narrative poems *Astraea Redux* and *Annus Mirabilis*, Dryden addresses himself to the political-moral dilemmas of his time and suggests that these can be resolved by moderation on the part of king and subject at the national level, and on the part of the British empire-builders at the international level. The king can show moderation by not trying to force the conscience of his subject and by distinguishing civil law from his arbitrary private will. The subject, on the other hand, can show moderation by engaging in merely passive resistance to unjust laws—that is, by not overturning the civil structure for the sake of private conscience. At the international level, the empire-builders can show moderation by not becoming greedy and proud in the manner of Holland, and by making "one City of the Universe."

This scheme of values is only implicit in the heroic plays and early narrative poems, but it is clearly formulated in one of Dryden's late poems "To my Honour'd Kinsman, John Driden." In the following lines, taken from the end of the poem, Dryden indicates that a balance must be maintained between the privilege of the king and the prerogative of the people:

> A Patriot, both the King and Country serves;
> Prerogative, and Privilege preserves:
> Of Each, our Laws the certain Limit show;
> One must not ebb, nor t'other overflow:
> Betwixt the Prince and Parliament we stand;
> The Barriers of the State on either Hand:
> May neither overflow, for then they drown the Land.
> When both are full, they feed our bless'd Abode;
> Like those, that water'd once, the Paradise of God.
>
> Some Overpoise of Sway, by Turns they share;
> In Peace the People, and the Prince in War:

Consuls of mod'rate Pow'r in Calms were made;
When the *Gauls* came, one sole Dictator sway'd.

   Patriots, in Peace, assert the Peoples Right;
With noble Stubbornness resisting Might:
No Lawless Mandates from the Court receive,
Nor lend by Force; but in a Body give.
Such was your gen'rous Grandsire; free to grant
In Parliaments, that weigh'd their Prince's Want:
But so tenacious of the Common Cause,
As not to lend the King against his Laws.
And, in a lothsom Dungeon doom'd to lie,
In Bonds retain'd his Birthright Liberty,
And sham'd Oppression, till it set him free.

                             (171–94)

In this passage Dryden suggests that the patriot must support the "Overpoise of Sway" of the king at a time of war, but he must be jealous of the people's rights in time of peace. If the king demands anything contrary to his country's laws, then the patriot must resist passively in the manner of John Driden's grandsire. It is appropriate that this grandsire retains his "Birthright Liberty" in a prison cell, much as Aureng-Zebe, rather than carry arms, accepts bondage in order to retain the "birthright of my mind," thus shaming his oppressor without dethroning his king. The point that Dryden is making is that constitutional government is best; both king and parliament must stay within the limits marked by "our Laws." The image of the flood in lines 174–79 applies to tyranny as well as to rebellion; Dryden suggests here, as in the heroic plays, that the undermining of constitutional government unleashes destructive natural forces.

   In "To my Honour'd Kinsman" Dryden also shows the necessity for moderation at the international level, much as he did in *Annus Mirabilis* and *The Indian Emperour*. In lines 144–45, he suggests that a "secure" international peace is

needed so that "securely we may trade." War may be needed
to bring about eventual peace, but it should not be pur-
sued to the point of domination over the enemy, for "Vic-
tors are by Victories undone"; England is "uncertain of Success" in war, but an umpire of the peace at the end of hostilities (164–70). Thus, even on the international scene, men
should be guided by a concern for the common good. England
must maintain free trade and secure a state of peace in Europe,
not so that she can prey on her neighbors but so that, eventually, a more prosperous and unified world may come to be.

Dryden supports a norm of tolerance with regard to political
factions and religious belief; he favors freedom of conscience
to the extent that the civil order is safeguarded. He would not
have freedom of conscience enlarged to the point that it would
encompass armed rebellion against established authority. In
his preface to *The Hind and the Panther,* he is indignant at the
revocation of the Edict of Nantes, even though he is no longer
a Protestant himself; similarly in *Tyrannic Love* he expresses,
by means of Porphyrius, his revulsion at Maximin's attempt
to rule the consciences of his subjects. In all of the works analyzed, Dryden suggests that private conviction must in some
way be balanced against the common good. Dryden's so-called
conservatism, then, is not merely based on a fear of individual
energy, a suspicion that anarchy lurks behind every private
conscience, but on the somewhat traditional view that the individual, while entitled to pursue private goals, should, in
Chaucer's words, busily "werche and wysse / To commune profit" *(Parlement of Foules,* ll. 74–75).

List of Works Consulted

Aden, John M., "Dryden and the Imagination: the First Phase," *PMLA*, 74 (March, 1959), 28–40.

Allen, J. W., "Sir Robert Filmer," *Social and Political Ideas of Some Great Thinkers of the Sixteenth and Seventeenth Centuries*, ed. F. J. C. Hearnshaw (London, 1928), pp. 27–46.

Alssid, Michael W., "The Perfect Conquest: A Study of Theme, Structure and Character in Dryden's *The Indian Emperour*, *SP*, 59 (1962), 539–59.

———, "The Design of Dryden's *Aureng-Zebe*," *JEGP*, 64 (1965), 452–69.

Aristophanes, *The Frogs*, in *The Complete Plays*, ed. Moses Hadas, New York, 1962.

Aristotle, *Poetics*, in *The Basic Works of Aristotle*, ed. Richard McKeon, New York, 1941.

Aubrey, John, *Brief Lives*, ed. Andrew Clark, Oxford, 1898.

Bacon, Francis, *The Advancement of Learning*, in *Selected Writings of Francis Bacon*, with an introduction and notes by Hugh G. Dick, New York, 1955.

———, *The New Organon and Related Writings*, ed. Fulton H. Anderson, Indianapolis and New York, 1960.

Ball, Albert, "Charles II: Dryden's Christian Hero," *MP*, 59 (1961), 25–33.

Brevold, Louis I., "Dryden, Hobbes, and the Royal Society," *MP*, 25 (1928), 417–38.

———, *The Intellectual Milieu of John Dryden*, Ann Arbor, Mich., 1934.

———, "The Tendency toward Platonism in Neo-Classical Esthetics," *ELH*, 1 (Sept., 1934), 91–119.

Brower, Reuben Arthur, "Dryden's Epic Manner and Virgil," *PMLA*, *55* (1940), 119–38.

Bundy, Murray W., " 'Invention' and 'Imagination' in the Renaissance," *JEGP*, *29 (Oct.*, 1930), 535–45.

Butt, John, *The Augustan Age*, London, 1965.

Chase, Lewis Nathaniel, *The English Heroic Play*, New York, 1965; first published, 1903.

Child, C. G., "The Rise of the Heroic Play," *MLN*, *19* (1904), 166–73.

Clark, William S., "Dryden's Relations with Howard and Orrery," *MLN*, *42* (1927), 16–20.

———, "The Platonic Element in the Restoration Heroic Play," *PMLA*, *45* (1930) 623–24.

———, "The Sources of the Restoration Heroic Play," RES, *4* (Jan., 1928), 49–63.

Davis, Ralph, "England and the Mediterranean, 1570–1670," in *Essays in the Economic and Social History of Tudor and Stuart England*, ed. F. J. Fisher, Cambridge, 1961.

Deane, Cecil V., *Dramatic Theory and the Rhymed Heroic Play*, London, 1931.

Dobrée, Bonamy, Introduction, *Five Heroic Plays*, London, 1960.

———, *Restoration Tragedy 1660–1720*, Oxford, 1929.

Dryden, John, *John Dryden (Three Plays)*, ed. George Saintsbury, New York, n.d.

———, *The Poems and Fables of John Dryden*, ed. James Kinsley, London, 1962.

———, *The Works of John Dryden*, ed. Sir Walter Scott and George Saintsbury, Edinburgh, 1882–93.

———, *The Works of John Dryden*, University of California Edition, Vol. 1 ed. Edward Niles Hooker and H. T. Swedenberg, Jr., Vol. 8 ed. John Harrington Smith, Dougald MacMillan, and Vinton A. Dearing, Vol. 9 ed. John Loftis and Vinton A. Dearing, Berkeley and Los Angeles, 1961–66.

Eliot, T. S., *Homage to John Dryden*, London, 1924.

———, *John Dryden, the Poet, the Dramatist, the Critic, Three Essays*, New York, 1932.

Filmer, Sir Robert, *Patriarcha and Other Political Works of Sir Robert Filmer*, ed. Peter Laslett, Oxford, 1949.

Fujimura, Thomas H., "The Appeal of Dryden's Heroic Plays," *PMLA*, *75*, (1960), 37–45.

Gagen, Jean, "Love and Honor in Dryden's Heroic Plays," *PMLA*, *77* (1962), 208–20.

Harbage, Alfred, *Cavalier Drama*, New York, 1936.

Hartsock, M. E., "Dryden's Plays: A Study in Ideas," in *Seventeenth Century Studies*, ed. R. Shafer, 2d ser., Princeton, 1933, pp. 71–176.

Hathaway, Baxter, "John Dryden and the Function of Tragedy," *PMLA*, *58* (1943), 665–73.

Hill, H. W., La Calprenède's Romances and Restoration Drama," *University of Nevada Studies*, 2d ser., 1910; 3d ser., 1911.

Hobbes, Thomas, *Leviathan*, ed. Michael Oakeshott, Oxford, 1957.

Holzhausen, P., "Dryden's heroisches Drama," *E. Studien*, *13*, *15*, *16* (1889–91).

Hooker, Edward N., "The Purpose of Dryden's *Annus Mirabilis*," *HLQ*, *10* (1946), 49–67.

Horace, *The Art of Poetry*, in *The Poems of Horace*, trans. A. Hamilton Bryce, London, 1907.

Horsman, E. A., "Dryden's French Borrowings," *RES*, n.s. *1*, 1950.

Jefferson, D. W., "The Significance of Dryden's Heroic Plays," in *Restoration Drama: Modern Essays in Criticism*, ed. John Loftis, New York, 1966, pp. 161–79.

Johnson, Samuel, *Lives of the English Poets*, 2 vols. New York, 1946; reprinted from the edition of 1925.

King, Bruce, "Dryden, Tillotson, and *Tyrannic Love*," *RES*, n.s. *16*, no. 64 (1965), 364–77.

Kinsley, James, "The 'Three Glorious Victories' in *Annus Mirabilis*," *RES*, n.s. 7 (1956), 30–37.

Kirsch, Arthur C., "Dryden, Corneille, and the Heroic Play," *MP*, *59* (1962), 248–64.

———, *Dryden's Heroic Drama*, Princeton, 1965.

———, "The Significance of Dryden's Aureng-Zebe," *ELH*, *29* (1962), 160–74.

LeConte, E. S., "*Samson Agonistes* and *Aureng-Zebe*," *Etudes anglaises*, *2* (1958), 18–22.

Leech, Clifford, "Restoration Tragedy: A Reconsideration," *Durham University Journal*, *42* (1950), 106–15; reprinted in *Restoration Drama: Modern Essays in Criticism*, ed. John Loftis (New York, 1966), pp. 144–60.

Locke, John, *Two Treatises of Government*, ed. Peter Laslett, Cambridge, 1960.

Lucretius, *The Nature of the Universe*, trans. Ronald Latham, Aylesbury, 1955.

Lynch, Kathleen, "Conventions of Platonic Drama in the Heroic Plays of Orrery and Dryden," *PMLA*, *44* (1929), 456–71.

———, *The Social Mode of Restoration Comedy*, New York, 1926.

MacMillan, Dougald, "The Sources of Dryden's *The Indian Emperour*," *HLQ*, *13* (1950), 355–70.

Mann, W., *Dryden's heroische Tragödien als Ausdruck höfischer Borockkultur in England*, Wurtemberg, 1932.

Mills, L. J., "The Friendship Theme in Orrery's Plays," *PMLA*, *53* (1938), 795–806.

Milton, John, *The Works of John Milton*, Columbia University Edition, New York, 1931–38; with three supplements and Index, 2 vols. New York, 1940.

————, *Complete Prose Works*, Yale University Edition, 4 vols. New Haven, 1953–62.

Miner, Earl, *Dryden's Poetry*, Bloomington, 1967.

Mintz, Samuel I., *The Hunting of Leviathan*, Cambridge, 1962.

Moore, Robert Etheridge, *Henry Purcell and the Restoration Theatre*, Cambridge, Mass., 1961.

Morton, Richard, "By No Strong Passion Swayed: A Note on John Dryden's *Aureng-Zebe*," *English Studies in Africa, 1* (1958), 59–68.

Nelson, Lowry, *Baroque Lyric Poetry*, New Haven, 1961.

Nettleton, George H., "Dryden and the Heroic Drama," in *English Drama of the Restoration and the Eighteenth Century* (New York, 1914), pp. 53–70.

Nicoll, Allardyce, "Origin and Types of the Heroic Tragedy," *Anglia, 44* (1920), 325–36.

————, *Restoration Drama 1660–1700*, vol. 1 of *A History of English Drama 1660–1900*, 4th ed., Cambridge, 1961.

Osborn, Scott C., "Heroical Love in Dryden's Heroic Drama," *PMLA, 73* (1958), 480–90.

Parsons, A. E., "The English Heroic Play," *MLR, 33* (1938), 1–14.

Pendlebury, Bevis J., *Dryden's Heroic Plays: A Study of the Origins*, London, 1923.

Perkins, Merle L., "Dryden's *The Indian Emperour* and Voltaire's *Alzire*," *CL, 9* (1957), 229–37.

Poston, Mervyn L., "The Origin of the English Heroic Play," *MLR, 16* (1921), 18–22.

Price, Martin, *To the Palace of Wisdom: Studies in Order and Energy from Dryden to Blake*, New York, 1964.

Priestley, J. B., *The Art of the Dramatist*, London, 1957.

Prior, Moody E., "Joseph Glanvill, Witchcraft, and Seventeenth-Century Science," *MP, 30 (1932–33)*, 167–93.

————, *The Language of Tragedy*, New York, 1947.

Roper, Alan, *Dryden's Poetic Kingdoms*, London, 1965.

Rosenberg, Bruce A., *"Annus Mirabilis* Distilled," *PMLA, 79* (1964), 254–58.

Russell, Trusten W., *Voltaire, Dryden and Heroic Tragedy*, New York, 1946.

Schilling, Bernard N., *Dryden and the Conservative Myth*, New Haven, 1961.

Scott, Sir Walter, *The Life of John Dryden*, the 1834 edition with notes by John Gibson Lockhart, ed. Bernard Kreissman, Lincoln, Neb., 1963.

Shaw, George Bernard, "Mr. Shaw on Mr. Shaw," *New York Times* (June 12, 1927); reprinted in *Shaw on Theatre*, ed. E. J. West, New York, 1958.

Sherwood, Margaret, *Dryden's Dramatic Theory and Practice*, New York, 1966; first published, 1898.

Sidney, Sir Philip, *The Prose Works of Sir Philip Sidney*, ed. Albert Feuillerat, 4 vols. Cambridge, 1962.

Singer, Charles, *A Short History of Scientific Ideas to 1900*, Oxford, 1960.

Spingarn, J. E., *Critical Essays of the Seventeenth Century*, 3 vols. Oxford, 1908–09.

Teeter, Louis, "The Dramatic Use of Hobbes' Political Ideas," *ELH, 3* (1936), 140–69.

Thorpe, Clarence De Witt, "The Psychological Approach in Dryden," in *The Aesthetic Theory of Thomas Hobbes* (Ann Arbor, Mich., 1940), pp. 189–220.

Tupper, J. W., "The Relation of the Heroic Play to the Romances of Beaumont and Fletcher," *PMLA, 20* (1905), 584–621.

Ure, Peter and N. D. Shergold, "Dryden and Calderon: A New Spanish Source for *The Indian Emperour,*" *MLN, 61* (1966), 369–83.

Waith, Eugene M., *The Herculean Hero in Marlowe, Chapman, Shakespeare and Dryden,* New York, 1962.

Ward, Charles E., "Massinger and Dryden," *ELH, 3* (1935), 263–66.

Warrender, Howard, *The Political Philosophy of Hobbes; His Theory of Obligation,* Oxford, 1957.

Winterbottom, John A., "The Development of the Hero in Dryden's Tragedies," *JEGP,* 52 (1953), 161–73.

———, "The Place of Hobbesian Ideas in Dryden's Tragedies," *JEGP,* 57 (1958), 665–83.

———, "Stoicism in Dryden's Tragedies," *JEGP, 61* (1962), 868–83.

Zebouni, Selma Assir, *Dryden: A Study in Heroic Characterization,* Baton Rouge, La., 1965.

Index